DR. ADOLF KATZENELLENBOGEN (1901-1965) was
Professor of the History of Art and Chairman of the
Department of Fine Arts at the Johns Hopkins University.

He received his Dr. jur. degree from the University
of Giessen and his Ph.D. degree from the University of
Hamburg. Before coming to Johns Hopkins, he belonged
to the faculty of Vassar College. In 1963 he was visiting
professor at the University of Freiburg, Germany.

His publications include *The Sculptural Programs of
Chartres Cathedral; Allegories of the Virtues and Vices
in Mediæval Art; The Central Tympanum of Vézelay;*
and *The Sarcophagus of S. Ambrogio.*

Adolf Katzenellenbogen

THE SCULPTURAL PROGRAMS

OF Chartres Cathedral

CHRIST ❋ MARY ❋ ECCLESIA

NEW YORK The Norton Library

W · W · NORTON & COMPANY · INC ·

Books That Live
The Norton imprint on a book means that in the publisher's
estimation it is a book not for a single season but for the years.
W. W. Norton & Company, Inc.

ISBN 0 393 00233 0

PRINTED IN THE UNITED STATES OF AMERICA

6 7 8 9 0

Introduction

City of Chartres, enriched not only by numerous burghers,
Likewise also enriched by its clergy so mighty, so splendid,
And by its beautiful church, for none can be found in the whole world;
None that would equal its structure, its size and decor in my judgment.
Countless the signs and the favors of grace by which the Blessed Virgin
Shows that the Mother of Christ has a special love for this one church,
Granting a minor place, as it were, to all other churches,
Deeming it right to be frequently called the Lady of Chartres.
This is also the place where every one worships the tunic
Worn on the day of the birth of the Lamb, by the Virgin as garment.
He is the one who not only carried the sins of the world but
Also purified the world from original sin by His pure blood.
He sanctified as a very pure throne the Virgin who gladly
Is being honored as Mother, while still remaining a Virgin.[1]

WITH THESE VERSES Guillaume le Breton, historian and court poet of the
early thirteenth century, praised the close relation between the Virgin Mary
and the cathedral dedicated to her. Various ties seemed to him proof and

guarantee of this relation. They might be called in part intangible, like the Virgin's predilection for the church and her acceptance of the title "Lady of Chartres," in part tangible, namely numerous miracles ascribed to her, and a visible token: the cathedral owned as its most precious relic the Virgin's tunic, according to tradition a gift of Emperor Charles the Bald. Twice the salvation of Chartres and its cathedral was ascribed to the miraculous effect of this relic, first in 911 when the Normans attacked the city, and again in 1119, while the city was in similar danger because the Count of Chartres sided with the English against King Louis VI.[2]

The conviction that Mary, the Lady of Chartres, was intimately linked with the cathedral did not diminish in the later middle ages. On the contrary, a statue of the Virgin and Child in the crypt of the cathedral apparently gave rise to a legend chronicled late in the fourteenth century. As early as pre-Christian times, so the story goes, the statue of a virgin holding a child, with the prophetic inscription, *"Virgini pariturae,"* was worshiped by pagans in a cave at Chartres because they believed in the coming of a savior born by a virgin.[3] A local ruler had ordered that the statue be made, and he gave to the virgin and her son the city with its surrounding region. It was obviously the aim of this legend to establish the priority of the Cathedral of Chartres and of its cult of the Virgin over all other churches, by claiming a pre-Christian origin for the statue in the crypt and for the devotion it aroused.

The Cathedral of Chartres strongly bound to the Virgin Mary, as Guillaume le Breton describes it, is also intimately linked to the bishop of Chartres, as a twelfth-century document defines it. The New Testament had likened Christ to the Bridegroom, the Church to His Bride. It became customary, therefore, to apply the same metaphor to a bishop and his own see. This allegorical concept could hardly have been spun out more poetically and lovingly than in the letter written by the Chapter of Chartres to greet John of Salisbury after his election as bishop in 1176: "It has brought joy to the heavenly court, we believe, that the Church of the blessed Virgin, conceiving through the Holy Spirit, has brought forth a shepherd beloved by God and mankind. With the voice of every one acclaiming, the Church of Chartres asks, therefore, for the one she desires, and incessantly longs for the one she loves and has elected. Languishing in her desire for the bridegroom she asks: 'Let him kiss me with the kiss of his mouth' " (Cant. 1:2).[4] In this passage the Church of Chartres is identified with the cathedral, "the Church of the blessed Virgin," and is seen ideally as the loving mother and bride who, in analogy to Mary, brings forth the bishop as her child and bridegroom.

Finally, the cathedral—so closely tied to the Virgin and so strongly joined to its bishop—owed its existence to the contributions of human society for whose religious needs it was to provide a magnificent place. Like other cathedrals it was built and decorated with the help of men and women of many social strata, reaching from the burghers of Chartres to members of the royal house of France. Their contributions are revealed by contemporary testimonies of very different natures. On the one hand, Robert of Torigni, abbot of Mont-Saint-Michel, wrote in a glowing report of epic grandeur that in 1145 men and women, noble and common people, associated to dedicate themselves with all their physical resources and spiritual strength, in a spontaneous wave of religious enthusiasm, to the task of transporting in hand-drawn carts material for the building of the towers.[5] The degree to which actual happenings were exalted and idealized in this report cannot be ascertained. One should also remember that stories of this kind were by no means limited to Chartres, but were linked to the building of other churches too.[6] There exist, on the other hand, documents about generous gifts for the cathedral. From coats of arms and donor emblems in the stained-glass windows, furthermore, we know for certain that the windows were given by kings and queens, by nobles, clerics, corporations of artisans and merchants alike.

Whatever the contributions for the embellishment of the cathedral, whatever the reasons motivating the donors, these gifts express visibly the devotion enjoyed by the Lady of Chartres. Her image shines in many of its stained-glass windows. From whatever side the churchgoer enters the cathedral, whether from the west, the north, or the south, he sees the Virgin Mary carved in stone as the Mother of Christ, as the Queen enthroned with Him in heaven, as the Intercessor for mankind on the day of the Last Judgment. Represented in four of the nine tympana decorating the west façade and the transept wings, she is second in importance only to Christ who appears in every tympanum.

The sculptural decoration of the cathedral was not the work of one generation. The west façade—or Royal Portal, as it was already called in the thirteenth century—had been decorated between about 1145 and 1155. Originally attached to Bishop Fulbert's cathedral of the eleventh century, the building preceding the present one, it survived the disastrous fire of 1194 and was retained as façade for the new church started immediately afterwards. The sculptures of the transept wings and their porches were carved between about 1205 and 1235.

This means that several workshops, separated by two generations, steeped in different traditions and possessed of different artistic aims, contributed to the total sculptural decoration as we see it today. It also means that theological advisers separated by the same span of time and by corresponding changes in the historical situation suggested to the leading masters the programs of representation.

Research of French, German, and American scholars has elucidated many problems posed by the sculptures of Chartres. To name only the most important studies: Abbé Bulteau has thoroughly (but not always convincingly) identified the subject matter and given literary sources for its understanding.[7] In his monumental works on the iconography of French art in the twelfth and thirteenth centuries Emile Mâle has defined the meaning of the Chartres

Mâle —

sculptures within the evolution of ideas carved in stone. The great French scholar has also devoted a monograph to the Cathedral of Chartres.[8] Wilhelm Vöge's book *Die Anfänge des monumentalen Stiles im Mittelalter* and his article "Die Bahnbrecher des Naturstudiums um 1200" still retain fundamental value in their incisive stylistic analysis, the beautiful definitions of expressive content, and the attribution of the sculptures to various masters.[9] Other studies have dealt with the particular problems of the genesis and the artistic sources of the different sculptural cycles.[10]

Any new attempt to discuss the Chartres sculptures will show its great indebtedness to earlier research. It is the purpose of this study to investigate a number of basic questions not yet, or not yet fully, answered. They concern above all the main ideas governing the iconography of the various programs, their connection with specific historical and ideological situations, and the relation of cycles carved at different times.

To state these questions briefly: What is the skeletal frame, so to speak, which sustains and gives structure to the multiple parts of the programs? What are its literary sources? Could the liturgy have contributed its share? To what extent are certain facets of church history, current theological, philosophical, and political concepts reflected in the choice of subject matter? Did the planners of the transept wings take into consideration what had been represented before on the Royal Portal?

In spite of the tremendous variety of subject matter, in spite of the interval between the two main phases of sculptural decoration, certain figures and ideas of central importance stand out distinctly within the iconographic programs: Christ—Mary—Ecclesia as the Bride of Christ, as His Body, and as the Community of Saints—and the eucharistic concept uniting the Church with Christ. Some of these ideas are made clearly visible on the Royal Portal. Others appear here in an incipient stage, to be widened and sharpened on the transept façades and their porches. Still others are the exclusive property of the later cycles.

school of Chartres —

To what extent do the programs mirror the historical and ideological situation of their time? It should be kept in mind that the plan for the Royal Portal was conceived in those years when the School of Chartres was flourishing at its height and counted some of the foremost thinkers among its teachers.[11] William of Conches was attached to the school for some years. Gilbert de la Porrée had been its chancellor until 1141 when he was succeeded by Thierry of Chartres, brother of the famous Bernard and teacher of John of Salisbury and Clarenbaldus of Arras. The bishop of Chartres, Geoffroy II de Lèves, close friend of St. Bernard, was then apostolic legate of Aquitaine, and in this capacity he was instrumental in suppressing schism and heresy. Heated controversies on questions of theology and church politics caused strong unrest.

Albigeois?.

The sculptures of the transept wings were created in an era when the University of Paris, center of renascent Aristotelianism, was assuming the importance held by cathedral schools in the preceding century. Heresies threatened anew the dogmas of the Church, and it may have seemed appropriate to reaffirm visibly some basic beliefs at the entrances to the cathedral.

Inextricably linked with the iconographic programs are the forms in which these programs were made visible. Formal problems that have been thoroughly discussed and debated in the past (the genesis of the Royal Portal and of the transept wings, the attribution of the sculptures to different workshops and masters) shall be taken up only as far as they have direct bearing on the main points of this study. There remain, on the other hand, some questions about the interrelation of form and meaning. They shall be more fully examined.

The Royal Portal was decorated a few years after the architecture and sculpture of the Abbey Church of Saint-Denis had revolutionized medieval art and ushered in the Gothic style. In what way was the meaning of the iconographic program affected by the new sculptural style, the new clarity of total configuration and individual forms, the new consonance among the parts of sculptural decoration, the new lucidity in the hierarchical gradation governing the attitudes of figures, their mutual relation, and the definition of space? How did the sculptors of the transept wings strive for new solutions to artistic problems solved only a few years before on other church façades? Did they adopt some formal principles of representation from the Royal Portal, thereby enhancing the coherence of iconographic programs conceived in different times?

FOR THEIR GENEROUS HELP I am greatly indebted to Professor Erwin Panofsky and Professor Ernst H. Kantorowicz of the Institute for Advanced Study in Princeton. My sincere thanks are due also to M. le Chanoine Yves Delaporte of Chartres who was most kind in putting at my disposal his excerpts from liturgical manuscripts that once belonged to the Bibliothèque de la Ville at Chartres, but were destroyed in the disastrous fire of 1944. Repeatedly I received excellent suggestions from Professor Harry Bober and Mrs. Linda Nochlin.

Furthermore, I would like to thank the Institute for Advanced Study for giving me membership in the year 1953 and, thereby, the opportunity to work *procul negotiis*, to the American Philosophical Society for a grant from the Penrose Fund, and to Vassar College for a faculty fellowship and a grant from the Salmon Fund. Finally I want to express my gratitude to the Bollingen Foundation whose generous grant made the publication of this study possible.

Contents

PART ONE   The Sculptures of the

Royal Portal

CHAPTER I

Relation to Earlier

Church Façades

THE SCULPTURAL DECORATION on the façade of Saint-Denis apparently created what later Gothic planners considered to be a norm of basic validity.[1] It meant a decisive change in the relation of sculpture and architecture. On the one hand, sculpture was made more independent of the wall. On the other hand, it began to conform and contribute to the strict discipline of the architectural design. The result of these new stylistic aims was a screen of reliefs and statues—these no longer exist at Saint-Denis—hiding the mass of the wall, enhancing the main architectural lines and the vertical energies they express. This general layout was readily adopted but clarified and sharpened by the planners of the Royal Portal at Chartres (figs. 1–3).

The masters of Saint-Denis and Chartres, while creating a new stylistic vocabulary and new compositional types, also harmonized contrasting principles of Romanesque art.

The sculptural decoration of church façades in Burgundy and the Languedoc was restricted to the areas around the doorways where it counteracted by its densely woven patterns of composition the simple architectural design (fig. 4). On Norman church façades, on the other hand, the basic clarity of architectural design was stressed by mere architectural articulation without the use of sculpture accentuating the doorways (fig. 5).

The masters of Saint-Denis and Chartres resolved these diametrically opposed principles into an essentially new harmony. Like their Norman predecessors they aimed at a clear articulation of the façade (now no longer conceived of as an agglomeration of massive wall units). Unlike the Norman architects they used in the lower part of the façade sculpture as an equivalent for architectural forms, an equivalent charged with meaning, a screen rather than a system closely tied to the wall surface. Like the masters of Burgundy and the Languedoc they relied on sculpture to give emphasis to the portals, but it was an emphasis through consonance, not contrast, with the architectural design. The new function of the sculpture in articulating the architectural structure at the same time gave a new clarity to the structure of the iconographic program.

The masters of Saint-Denis and Chartres also harmonized differences in the importance accorded to tympana and archivolts in various regions during the preceding decades. Sculptors of Burgundy and the Languedoc had stressed the tympana by figure reliefs at the expense of archivolts (figs. 4, 37). Doorways were either cut into the walls or not too deeply splayed so that the tympana as sections of the wall plane were given preference. This made it possible to show to the churchgoer large and impressive figure compositions with strong central accents.[2] In contrast, the doorways of churches in western France were deeply splayed (fig. 6). Consequently, the archivolts expressing the thickness of the wall were emphasized by ornamental and figure decoration while tympana usually were omitted. Thereby the subject matter was spread without strong central accents over the curved bands of the archivolts.[3] The façade of Saint-Denis and the Royal Portal received splayed portals; yet, as if harmonizing earlier divergent tendencies, the planners emphasized by figure reliefs both the tympana and the archivolts, thus combining and fully utilizing large centralized and peripheral bandlike compositions.

Finally, they synthesized different relationships between jamb statues, tympana, and ornamented wall areas. On the west façade of the cathedral at Ferrara, for instance, the jamb figures of the Prophets appear related to the tympanum, since they were placed diagonally to it, but because of their small size they became lost within the ornamental richness of the splayed jambs (fig. 7). At Saint-Gilles, on the other hand, a balance in size was established between the main tympanum and the statues of the four Apostles which flank the central doorway and are framed at top and bottom only by ornamented areas. These statues are close to the tympanum but also kept apart from it since they were placed at right angles to it (fig. 8).[4]

As at Saint-Gilles, but in contrast to Ferrara, the tympana and jamb figures of Saint-Denis and Chartres were given about the same emphasis. In contrast to Saint-Gilles, but in harmony with Ferrara, the jamb figures were more closely tied to the tympanum by their diagonal placing, and richly ornamented columns were used, although now restricted to subsidiary areas underneath and between the large statues. In this way the jamb statues lead to the tympanum and equal it in importance.

The master responsible for the layout of the Royal Portal went one step further than the planner of Saint-Denis in unifying the sculptural decoration of the three portals. Both lateral tympana are sculptured, while at Saint-Denis one had contained a mosaic. Made larger in size, they are less strongly subordinated to the main tympanum. To further this idea they were placed on the same level as the central tympanum. With the three portals more closely drawn together between the flanking towers, the jamb figures screen the whole façade rather than the sections next to each entrance. Figured capital friezes became the equivalent of definite horizontal bands tying the three portals together.

When the sculptures were put into place, some considerable readjustments had to be made on both lateral portals. Here the lintels were shortened and the archivolts trimmed at the bottom. The tympana were narrowed, and the baldachin once crowning the Virgin and Child in the right tympanum was sacrificed.[5] These changes have given rise to the theory that the Royal Portal was originally erected in a place farther back and, some time later, shifted to its present position.[6] The excavations undertaken in 1938 by Etienne Fels have disproved this theory.[7] They indicate that the façade was never moved forward. The readjustments, however, are far too drastic to be explained by original miscalculations about the dimensions of the present site. It seems likely, therefore, that the façade was at first planned for a location somewhat behind the area between the towers and wider than the present site, and that the sculptures were carved but never put up there because of a sudden change in plan. With the present site given preference for the façade, the sculptures were then put into place where they are now. This made considerable readjustments necessary because of the somewhat narrower site. In other words: the Royal Portal was never moved forward but it was originally devised for another location with different dimensions.[8]

The sculptures evidently were put into place in a hurry. One of the columns once supporting the baldachin was only in part removed (fig. 9). The lintels over the same doorway were cut shorter than necessary and then shifted somewhat to the right, with a gap left at the other end. The two figures cut in half were not completely chiseled off. These small shortcomings, however, hardly mar the beauty of the whole at it was conceived: a system of sculptural decoration in which iconography and form have the same structural clarity.

The three tympana and their lintels represent the fundamentals of the

Christological dogma (fig. 2). On the right-hand side, the Incarnation is shown by a number of scenes: Annunciation, Visitation, Nativity and Annunciation to the Shepherds in the lower lintel, Presentation of Christ in the upper lintel, the whole crowned by the group of Mary and Child among Angels swinging their censers. On the left-hand side, the Ascension of Christ is represented, and in the center His Second Coming at the end of the days.

Tripartite systems of similar scope had been created during the preceding decades on other church façades in France. A dominating tympanum in the south porch of Saint-Pierre in Moissac was flanked by two lateral walls decorated with reliefs.[9] In the narthex of La Madeleine at Vézelay and on the façade of Saint-Gilles a large tympanum has its place in each case between two smaller ones.[10] The Incarnation cycle on the right wall at Moissac had no corresponding Christological counterpart, but was dramatically contrasted with the Parable of Lazarus and Dives illustrating Avarice, and with the Punishment of Luxury. This juxtaposition results in a highly original combination of conflicting concepts. At Vézelay scenes from the beginning of Christ's life on earth (right tympanum) were balanced by His last self-revelations on earth (left tympanum), by events that were new as subject matter for a tympanum but play only a minor role within the Christological dogma. At Saint-Gilles only a few events from Christ's life were carved in the lateral tympana: the Adoration of the Magi (with the Angel warning Joseph) and the Crucifixion. There was no desire to develop one tympanum into a comprehensive Incarnation cycle.

The planners of Chartres were concerned neither with narrative complexity of any original kind as is to be found in the cycles of Moissac and Vézelay, nor with the narrative simplicity of the Saint-Gilles tympana, but with the clearest possible representation of salient dogmatic truths. What gives the iconography of the Chartres tympana its distinct character is a new lucidity, a new explicitness. It makes definite ideas immediately intelligible. The importance of Christ within the whole program could not have been more clearly revealed. In the same frontal pose and with the same gesture of blessing He is shown in the center of each tympanum.

CHAPTER II   The Tympana and

Capital Friezes

I   THE SUBJECT MATTER of the Incar-
nation cycle at Chartres is but a link in a long tradition (figs. 9, 10). And yet,
never before or afterwards were the various scenes so organized compositionally that they divulge a comprehensive ideographic system. In contrast
to the earlier cycles at Vézelay and Moissac, the tympanum and its lintels show
a radical change of aims; they show a definite shift from dynamic narratives
to a static and diagrammatic system, from a complex lack of clarity to an all-
inclusive clarity, from a highly emotional tension to a strongly intellectual
tenor.

At Vézelay the right-hand tympanum and its lintel (*ca.* 1125; fig. 11)
are similar in subject matter to the Incarnation cycles at Chartres. Both
tympana glorify the Infant Jesus, but at Vézelay the glorification is clothed
in a dramatic narrative radiating a strong emotional effect, the Adoration of
the Magi. At Chartres Virgin and Child are isolated from a transitory scene.
They are worshiped by Angels and not by earthly Magi. This simplifies the
composition and sharpens the meaning. Instead of three worshipers augmented

7

by attendants and irregularly placed, only two figures flank the central group symmetrically. At Vézelay the Magi bring their different gifts that embody a multiplicity of meaning. They honor Christ the King with gold, Christ the God with frankincense, and Christ the mortal being with myrrh.[1] At Chartres the Angels hold only censers in their hands.

Likewise, on the lower level the newborn Child is not as in Vézelay tightly locked in a crowded composition vibrating with activity, since it combines both the Nativity and the scene of the Annunciation to the Shepherds. At Chartres He is removed from all transitory commotion. Descriptive accidentals that had enriched the narrative quality of the Vézelay scenes do not exist, such as the house of Zacharias or the midwife in the Nativity. Only essentials are important.

At Vézelay no formal relation had been intended between the Nativity and the Virgin and Child of the Adoration. The two scenes remain separate narratives. In Chartres a definite central axis ties the group in the tympanum to the Nativity. Thereby a meaningful relation between the Child enthroned on His mother's lap and the Child lying on the manger is established and becomes immediately apparent. This axial relation is furthermore strengthened by the Child on the altar in the Presentation and accentuated by figures framing the center and turned toward Him.

Like the composition the individual forms have gained a new clarity contributing to the clarity of the whole. Their design has lost all the elements of distortion which at Vézelay had heightened the emotional intensity. Figures are no longer elongated and contorted. No longer are their poses tense, their contours complicated, their drapery rhythm agitated. The proportions at Chartres are more natural and more easily understandable, the contours self-contained, the poses for the most part static, the gestures restrained. Movements are controlled by compositional balance. The drapery does not electrify but rather clarifies the volume of the body. Even the few objects still remaining are given a mathematical purity of shape. The manger of the Child is transformed into an altar-like table with a very precise sacramental meaning.

In the Incarnation cycle of Moissac (*ca.* 1125; fig. 12) the emphasis had been—as in Vézelay—on emotional restlessness and passionate figure relations, not on structural clarity of form and meaning. The whole cycle was conceived and designed as part of a dramatic contrast between good and evil. The varying importance accorded its parts was determined less by dogmatic significance than by its co-ordination with the accents in the story of sinfulness. Annunciation and Visitation were given the largest size. As examples of charity and purity they are opposed to the frightening Punishment of Avarice and Luxury. The Nativity, the core of the Incarnation, is missing. The Adoration of the Magi glorifies the Child, but because of its intermediary position and size is not made the climax of the whole cycle.

Much closer to the Chartres scenes in subject matter and anticipating their design are the lintel reliefs of the Abbey Church at La Charité-sur-Loire (*ca.* 1140; figs. 13, 14).[2] There as in Chartres the motif of an altar-like table or altar appears in both Nativity and Presentation, but the two events are shown above different doorways. This excludes the tight and meaningful organization achieved at Chartres through superposition of the two lintels elucidating the implicit sense of the manger as altar in the Nativity. Furthermore, in neither of the two tympana at La Charité is Christ definitely related to the Child on the lintel, so that the clarity of individual forms conflicts with the restlessness of the whole composition. In the Presentation scene at La Charité the Child is made part of a dramatic scene. He is shown at the moment when the Virgin raises Him above the altar and hands Him over to Simeon. At Chartres the Child stands calmly on the altar, facing the beholder. By His statuesque pose a transitory moment has been made permanent as part of a whole ideographic system.

Cycles of a later date indicate a tendency away from conceptual clarity towards narrative enrichment. On the north portal at Bourges the group of Mary and Child is enlarged into the Adoration of the Magi, and the Nativity is omitted.[3] In the right tympanum of Notre-Dame in Paris (*ca.* 1165; fig. 15) the group is likewise widened by other figures and is no longer axially related to the Nativity in the lintel.

Only at Chartres was a clear system sought and realized by its planners (figs. 9, 10). The backbone of this system, so to speak, is the central axis containing on three levels the Virgin and the Child. The components of the central axis are explicit as embodiments of ideas. Isolated from any specific time the group in the tympanum is conceptualized iconographically and formally through its strict frontality and immobility. The same idea of permanence pervades the lower parts of the central axis.

The central axis is enhanced by the insistence on pure rectangular shapes: bed and mensa in the lower lintel, altar in the upper lintel, throne and (originally) canopy in the tympanum. Although from the formal point of view this axis appears simple, its meaning is comprehensive. It makes clearly visible the essence of Christ and Mary within the context of the Incarnation.

The Child, whether enthroned on His mother's lap, whether lying or standing on an altar, contains in one person both Godhead and manhood. Yet the idea of the hypostatic union of the two natures is made visible by variations in emphasis. In the Child enthroned and related to the Angels of the tympanum and the adjoining archivolt, the Godhead of Him who is God and man is emphasized. In the Child on the altar His manhood is stressed.[4]

Medieval artists had mastered the difficult but apparently challenging task of showing to the beholder the Godhead and manhood of Christ in a variety of ways. On the sarcophagus in Sant'Ambrogio in Milan, for example, this idea is presented by figure scene and symbols. One narrow side of the lid shows in the center the Infant in the manger. The other side contains in the center the monogram of Christ amid Alpha and Omega, the symbols of eternity.[5] Often Christ in majesty is placed above the newborn Babe or above the Child held in His mother's arms.[6] The single figure of the ascending Christ in the central tympanum at Vézelay implies the same idea in yet another way (fig. 16). In the lower part of the figure—still remaining in the realm of the Apostles—the position of the legs is twisted, the drapery folds are agitated. The upper part of the figure appears in regular frontality and the drapery pattern is calmer, while the head reaches into an area beyond the clouds and the semi-circle containing Christ's body and the Apostles: "The head is in heaven, the body on earth."[7]

At Chartres the idea of Godhead and manhood is demonstrated with utmost clarity and stillness without strong differentiation between superposed figures or between parts of a single figure. The Child enthroned is not enclosed by a mandorla, an emanation of light and the strongest revelation of His Godhead.[8] On each level He is related to His mother. It is not Christ in heavenly majesty who dominates the Child on earth, but the Child enthroned and worshiped by Angels is shown above the Child of the Nativity and Presentation. If the beholder looks at the central axis in its temporal sequence, his eye is led upwards from the manifestations of manhood by the Godhead incarnate to the manifestation of Godhead by Christ the man.

At the same time the central axis honors on three levels the Virgin Mary together with her Son. She complements, so to speak, His essence. Because of the two natures of Christ she is shown as the Mother of Christ as God and man.

The worship of the Virgin Mary, strongly fostered by St. Bernard and the Cistercian Order, had taken firm roots in Chartres long before the time of St. Bernard. A sermon of Bishop Fulbert (died 1028) had stressed the importance of celebrating the day of her Nativity.[9] It praised all her virtues and stated emphatically that she is always willing to help not only the just ones but also repentant sinners. This sermon proved to be exemplary. Henceforth it was included in all lectionaries of France. Bishop Geoffroy de Lèves must have been equally devoted to the Virgin Mary. When Gualterus of Cluny wrote a book about the miracles of the Virgin, he gave special credit to Geoffroy for telling them to him.[10]

Many churches in France were dedicated to the Virgin Mary, but her role within the whole sculptural decoration of these buildings was a modest one. Greater importance was given to her within the Incarnation cycle on the façades of other churches, although they were not dedicated to her (La Madeleine in Vézelay, Saint-Pierre in Moissac). But is was on the right-hand portal of Chartres Cathedral, the Notre-Dame par excellence, that her close relation to the Child is revealed along the central axis and her importance as instrument of Christ's Incarnation is made evident.

The individual components of the cycle have a long ancestry. On Palestinian ampullae of the sixth century the Virgin and Child are shown in strict frontality either between worshiping Magi and Shepherds (fig. 17) or between adoring Angels.[11] Sixth-century mosaicists adapted the same type to different purposes. On the northern nave wall in Sant' Apollinare Nuovo at Ravenna the group is approached by a long procession of female Martyrs headed by the Magi, but separated from these worshipers by flanking Angels.[12] This composition stresses the direction towards the altar. In the apse mosaic of the basilica at Parenzo the group is framed by Angels and Saints, and dominates the church by its central position.[13]

Throughout the middle ages this type of Mary and Christ remained common. In sculptures, frescoes, and miniatures it continued to play an important role either within the context of the Adoration of the Magi, or flanked by Angels, or completely isolated.[14]

The principle of giving the group a symbolically large size and placing it above a scene with smaller figures may be traced back to the sixth century. An ivory of the sixth century indicates the two natures of Christ in this way (fig. 18). Among the worshiping Magi, Mary and the Child are placed above the smaller, and thus subordinated, Nativity.[15] The type of the Child in the manger with Mary resting underneath on a bed also was well established (fig. 19).[16] And yet, in spite of the use made of traditional types of representation, the Chartres tympanum and its lintels are unique in their total configuration and structural clarity.

The dogmas represented also had been valid for many centuries. The union of the divine and human natures in Christ had been reaffirmed strongly in the fourth century as the outcome of the Arian controversy. The belief in Mary as the Theotokos had become a dogma with the defeat suffered by Nestorius in the Council of Ephesus.

These dogmas were reiterated in theological writings, especially when challenged time and again by heretics. They found their way into homilies that later on became part of the canonical office. These sermons complement selected readings from the Bible. In a clear and simple manner they point out the dogmatic significance of biblical events. Read as part of the office, they reminded the clergy every year of the true significance of the events that were celebrated. One might say generally, therefore, that the tympanum and its lintels make dogmas of the Church visible; but one might add specifically that the meaning of the reliefs corresponds to homilies used in the office, homilies in which certain dogmatic concepts are concentrated and related to the very events represented in the tympanum and the lintels. These sermons, therefore, may provide a more specific key for an understanding of the meaning than the dogmas at large.

In a homily of the Venerable Bede, read on Christmas day, the Godhead and manhood of Christ are repeatedly and with great insistence recalled to the cleric's mind: "The same man Jesus Christ was full of grace. By a singular gift it was given to Him before all other mortals that as soon as He was conceived in the Virgin's womb and began to become man, He would also be the true God." The faithful are then admonished to keep the two natures of Christ in mind: "It is, therefore, necessary that we who remember today the human birth of our Savior with annual devotion lovingly embrace forever His divine and human nature, not just annually but continuously."[17] The tympanum and the lower lintel fulfill admirably the function of reminding the clergy and the churchgoers every day of Christ's Godhead and manhood.

The same idea is reiterated in a homily of Bede used on the day of Mary's Purification when Christ was presented in the temple: "Always remembering our salvation, the Lord deemed it worthy not only to become man for our own sake, while being God, but also poor, while being rich so as to make us participants of His richness and divinity by virtue of His poverty and manhood."[18]

The close relation of Mary and the Child so clearly shown on all three levels of the central axis is stressed in the same lessons. According to the Christmas homily of Bede, the glorious Virgin should be confessed as the mother not only of Christ the man but also of God.[19] According to the sermon of Bede for the day of the Purification, this feast is dedicated primarily to the humility of the Lord, but at the same time also to His mother.[20]

I I   THE sacramental importance of the Incarnation is not touched upon in the story of Christ's birth as Luke tells it, but it is explained by Christ Himself to His apostles in the Gospel according to John: "I am," says Christ, "the living bread which came down from heaven: if any man eat of this bread, he shall live for ever: and the bread that I will give for the life of the world is my flesh" (John 6:51).

The simile of the living bread was incorporated in a homily of St. Gregory used for the office on Christmas: "He is also for good reasons born in Bethlehem, for Bethlehem means House of Bread. He is namely the one who says: 'I am the living bread which came down from heaven.' Therefore the place where the Lord is born has been called before the House of Bread because it should indeed happen that He would appear there in the flesh, who refreshes the minds of the elect with inner abundance."[21] Then the sermon relates the eucharistic idea to the ox and ass, symbols of the faithful (once flanking the Child on the Chartres lintel, they are now missing): "The new-born babe lies in the manger to refresh all the faithful, namely the holy animals, with the grain of His flesh."[22]

The representational type of the Child on an altar-shaped manger has a long tradition in art. Its roots may be found in both literary exegesis and liturgical practice. Theologians had drawn a parallel between altar and manger.[23] In Santa Maria Maggiore at Rome the pope celebrated Mass during Christmas night in a subterranean oratory "at the manger."[24] The new iconographic element at Chartres is, therefore, not the motif of the newborn Infant on the altar as such, but His relation to the group in the tympanum, and the insistence on the eucharistic idea. This idea is strengthened by the Child of the Presentation. It is reiterated by some key scenes within the capital friezes (fig. 21). Here, near the tympanum, the Last Supper and the Supper at Emmaus are shown. In the Entombment Christ's body is laid down as if on an altar.

From the days of the early Church Fathers the eucharistic reality of Christ's body was one of the most important questions for theologians. They realized that after the Resurrection the body of Christ had changed in its nature although not in its substance. Again and again they sought, therefore, to determine what body, what flesh of Christ is present in the Eucharist given every day throughout the world. Was it His suffering body in its earthly existence, His real flesh sacrificed just once on the cross? Or was it His body no longer suffering, His spiritual flesh existing forever in heaven?[25]

In the ninth century, Paschasius Radbertus met determined opposition when he favored the first alternative. In a treatise commissioned by Charles the Bald, Ratramnus of Corbie reaffirmed the belief that the body of Christ who ascended into heaven and is sitting at the right side of the Father is the true substance of the Eucharist.[26] This reaffirmation was reflected immediately in art. In the first Bible of Charles the Bald, Christ enthroned in majesty among the four Symbols of the Evangelists holds the host of the Eucharist in His right hand.[27]

The belief that the substance of the Eucharist is linked to the body no longer suffering—the spiritual flesh of Christ—continued to be prevalent until the end of the eleventh century and thereafter remained strong for some more decades to come. Consequently, the eucharistic reality was made visible during the first half of the twelfth century in French tympana and frescoes by the superposition of Christ in heaven over the Last Supper (fig. 22).[28] Here the glorified body of the Lord dominates the Institution of the Eucharist and provides a visible answer to the question: Did the Lord during the Last Supper give to the disciples His mortal or His immortal body?[29]

Towards the middle of the century, however, the eucharistic reality was represented in entirely new ways. On the tympanum of Condrieu, for instance, the figure of Christ in the Last Supper is no longer placed underneath Christ in heaven, but underneath Christ crucified (fig. 23.)[30] At Chartres the Child Himself lies on the mensa below the Godhead incarnate. In these reliefs, therefore, the body of Christ in its earthly existence, His *corpus verum*, dominates the Institution of the Eucharist—or at Chartres, the Child on an altar-like table. Yet the reliefs differ in the degree of ideographic abstraction. At Condrieu two biblical scenes are arranged according to a new theological interpretation. The central axis of the Chartres cycle reveals this interpretation directly within the context of Christ's Incarnation.

Just at that time a basic shift in the concept of the eucharistic reality had taken place, as Henri de Lubac shows in a brilliant study.[31] It was the *corpus verum,* His real flesh, that was now considered to be the true substance of the Eucharist. At the end of the eleventh century some theologians had begun to assert that the host had the same essence as the flesh Christ had assumed from the Virgin Mary.[32] Some decades later this idea was stressed even more strongly. William of St. Thierry went so far as to speak of the material flesh of Christ, whether it is sacrificed on the cross or on the altar.[33] It is also significant that he changed the emphasis in his interpretation of the heavenly bread. Instead of stressing that the living bread came down from heaven, he said that God brought forth the bread from the earth (Ps. 103:14 [104:14]) when He brought forth from the field of the earthly body the mystery of the heavenly bread.[34]

Seen in the light of this shift in the concept of the eucharistic reality, the Child on the mensa, the *corpus verum,* the heavenly bread, is represented as the true substance of the Eucharist underneath the Child as the Godhead incarnate.

One might add as a marginal note that Joseph is shown on the lintel as the protector of the heavenly bread. This is to be deduced not merely from his nearness to the mensa and his tender gesture of protection. According to St. Bernard, Joseph received the guardianship of the heavenly bread for himself and for the whole world.[35]

The eucharistic concept apparent in the Nativity is intensified in the scene of the Presentation of Christ. The sacramental meaning of the scene is again obvious. By His very position the Child becomes identified with the host to be sacrificed on the altar.[36]

The same scene had been carved only a few years before in a very similar style on the right lintel at La Charité-sur-Loire (fig. 14). But a significant difference of representation and concept distinguishes the two scenes. At La Charité the Virgin raises the Child above the altar. Does the scene symbolize a dramatic moment in the celebration of the Mass: the elevation of the host which, to our knowledge, was not practiced before about 1200? At Chartres the scene has lost its climactic character. Calmly standing on the altar, the Child symbolizes a permanent idea, the idea that His true body is forever the reality of the Eucharist. The concept of the *corpus verum* in the Eucharist is complemented by the idea that through the Eucharist the members of the Church are joined to Christ. In contrast to the Incarnation cycles of Moissac, Vézelay, and La Charité, this idea pervades the Chartres lintels more clearly. In the lower lintel it is expressed symbolically by the Holy Animals. They stand for the faithful refreshed by Christ's flesh.[37] What is more important, the idea of the Church also enters the scene of the Presentation.

The central group of Simeon, Mary, and the Child is enlarged by other figures approaching the altar in solemn processions. From a formal point of view the length of the lintel made the rather unusual addition of these figures necessary. But they are more than space fillers. They prefigure the Church to come. According to a sermon of Fulgentius of Ruspe (copied in a twelfth-century lectionary which once belonged to the library of the Chartres Chapter), the Virgin and her kinsfolk prefigure the Church out of Jews who believed in the apostles. They came from Nazareth to Jerusalem into the temple of the Lord, "since the primitive Church of the first disciples, rejected by the Jews, brought the stewardship of His redemption to the knowledge of the Gentiles."[38]

By virtue of its particular structure, the deeper significance, the doctrinal meaning of the Incarnation cycle, is made clear. Only the essentials of the various events are given. The objects reveal their symbolic significance. The central axis has an ideographic function. This lucidity in itself might well indicate the influence of a great intellectual center. The effect of the School of Chartres may be seen, however, in yet another way and more directly.

III   AS THE second person of the Trinity, the Child enthroned as Godhead incarnate is also Wisdom incarnate.[39] In the Christmas homily of Bede He is called "the Wisdom of the Lord who assumed flesh in which He could be seen."[40] The identification of Christ the Logos with the Wisdom of the Lord is rooted in concepts of St. Paul, which are, in turn, based on Platonic ideas.[41] This identification was expounded in the writings of the early Church Fathers. Later on it was typologically related to Solomon to whom the Lord had given wisdom. According to Guibert of Nogent, for instance, Christ, the Wisdom of God, was prefigured by Solomon. Like the Jewish king Wisdom built a throne, when He prepared a seat for Himself in the Virgin.[42]

The traditional type of the *Sedes Sapientiae* gains at Chartres a more specific and profound meaning, because the Wisdom incarnate is related to human wisdom as exemplified by its instruments, that is, the seven Liberal Arts and their representatives, in the archivolts.

Personifications of the liberal arts had illustrated scientific treatises.[43] As far as we can judge from literary sources, their cycle had served as wall decoration in a palace of Charlemagne, thus proclaiming the role played by the emperor in the revival of learning.[44] On mosaics of church floors groups of the Arts were complemented by cycles of the Virtues, of the twelve Months and the Signs of the Zodiac (or of Seasons), and of the Rivers of Paradise, thereby forming part of comprehensive "fundamental" schemes of moral and scientific knowledge.[45] In the description Baudri of Bourgueil gave—about 1100—of the bedchamber of Adela, countess of Chartres, in verses that according to the poet himself are poetic fiction (of a very erudite kind), statues of Philosophy and of the seven Liberal Arts carry the baldachin over the bed. They guarantee to its owner, one might like to surmise, the right understanding of the religious, mythological, and historical scenes displayed on wall tapestries, and of the images of Sky and Earth shown on ceiling and floor.[46]

In contrast to these different kinds of representation, at Chartres the personifications of secular learning were for the first time, as far as I know, considered important enough to frame a theological cycle. While in the tympanum and its lintels theological concepts are made understandable to the intellect through the ideographic clarity of their representation, in the archivolts are shown the intellectual means that prepare the wisdom seeker for such an understanding. Underneath each of the Liberal Arts is represented an author who by his thoughts and writings had primarily contributed to the substance of that art. That the seven branches of secular learning and seven authors of the past, mostly pagan, were given a place on a church façade is, indeed, a tangible example of the protohumanism pervading the School of Chartres.

The meaningful configuration of Divine Wisdom and human wisdom has its immediate roots in the writings of the Chartres School. Its deeper roots, however, reach down to much earlier concepts, pre-Christian and Christian. Many great thinkers had been concerned with the profound question as to whether the philosopher, the lover of wisdom, can understand the truth of the Divine through his own intellectual endeavors and what fruit he might reap for himself through these efforts.[47] Some writers were satisfied with classifying the various branches of learning, and describing their content and methods for the practical purpose of their use in schools.

Grammar had been taught by the Sophists, who were engaged also in logical and rhetorical studies. In addition, they were concerned with the mathematical sciences considered by Plato as essential steps for philosophy. In the first century B. C., Varro was probably the first one to establish the formal system of the seven liberal arts (to which he added medicine and architecture).[48] In his allegorical-scientific treatise *De nuptiis Philologiae et Mercurii,* written between 410 and 439 A. D., Martianus Capella personified the seven arts and, with an obvious delight in erudite allegorical adornment, gave an elaborate and graphic description of their appearance and attributes. His work, one of the most popular textbooks in the schools of the middle ages, contributed a large share to the formation of the cycle of the Liberal Arts at Chartres. It provided ingredients that could be translated into visible forms. As in the book, the arts are personified and hold some of the attributes there described. But what the learned book cannot explain is the configuration of human wisdom and Divine Wisdom.

The main literary sources for the relation between the two kinds of wisdom seem to be embedded and concentrated in the writings of Boethius. Boethius both defined the connection between human wisdom and Divine Wisdom and classified succinctly the means available to human wisdom.

Combining and condensing as in a burning glass the manifold rays of earlier philosophical notions, Boethius gave the intellectual powers of the faithful direction and hope. He described the endeavor of human wisdom to progress towards an understanding of Divine Wisdom and indicated the means necessary to achieve this aim. "Philosophy," he said, "is in some way the love, the search, the friendship for Wisdom, not of that wisdom that is engaged in some arts and in some artful science and knowledge, but of that Wisdom that is not dependent on anything else, being the living Mind and the only primary Reason of things. But this love for Wisdom on the part of the understanding soul means illumination by that pure Wisdom and in some way a return to itself and a recall. Therefore, it seems that the search for Wisdom is the search for the Divine and the love for that pure Mind."[49]

Divine Wisdom is here defined as the illuminating source and the goal of human wisdom. It can bestow on the seeker of wisdom its own likeness and bring him back to the purity of its own nature. "From it springs the truth of search and thinking and the holy and pure chastity of action."[50] This means that philosophy leads both to the right kind of intellectual endeavor and to moral perfection.

In order to become truly wise, man should know the seven liberal arts. He should be experienced in the three sciences that concern the right exposition: grammar, dialectic and rhetoric. He must use the sciences that deal with nature and are branches of mathematics, "the fourfold path," the Quadrivium, as Boethius terms them: arithmetic, music, geometry, and astronomy.[51]

The peripheral place of the Liberal Arts in relation to the central position of Christ, the Divine Wisdom, on the Royal Portal corresponds to these concepts of Boethius. Their place implies that human wisdom is dependent on Divine Wisdom and directed towards it.

The enlightenment of human wisdom by Divine Wisdom was for Boethius not just a general theory but personal experience. He saw in his own mind nothing but a spark of fire illuminated by the Light Divine.[52]

Boethius also linked the wisdom seekers of the pagan past with the liberal arts. He considered those who, under the leadership of Pythagoras, were strong in the purer reason of mind, to have provided valid proof for the effectiveness of the Quadrivium.[53] This concept, too, lies at the very base of the close link between the arts and the pagan authors on the Royal Portal.

The definitions of Boethius might be taken, therefore, as the main sources for the configuration of Divine Wisdom and human wisdom at Chartres, all the more so since the flowering of protohumanism at Chartres was, to no small degree, due to the fertilizing effect of Boethius' thoughts. In other words, as the writings of the School of Chartres during the second quarter of the twelfth century were based largely on the works of Boethius—Gilbert de la Porrée, William of Conches, Thierry of Chartres, and Clarenbaldus of Arras wrote commentaries on his writings—so the system of human wisdom and Divine Wisdom on the Royal Portal is likewise rooted in concepts of Boethius.

Authors of the twelfth century reformulated and explained Boethius' definition of philosophy, his notions of human and Divine Wisdom. They were men of very different attitudes, some more mystical, others more rationally inclined. And yet, the programmatic statements of Boethius appealed to them. His thoughts served the cause of those who saw in philosophy primarily a means of achieving moral perfection and thereby regaining true likeness to God. Boethius' concepts were equally fruitful for those who regarded philosophy before all as a preparatory step towards understanding God.

More mystically inclined, Hugh of St. Victor emphasized the liberal arts as a way by which man can attain greater perfection. Through them the image of God can be restored in him: "The more we conform to it, the more we know. Then begins to shine in us again what was always in His Reason, for what is transitory in us, exists without change in Him."[54]

More rationally inclined, William of Conches regarded the liberal arts as steps that lead man on his way towards an understanding of God. He explained the proper sequence of these studies. At first a threefold instruction in the art of eloquence is necessary. Grammar teaches how to write and to read in the right manner, dialectic teaches how to prove what must be proved, rhetoric teaches how to adorn words and sentences. Instruction in the Trivium provides the weapons for the study of philosophy. This study should be pursued in the following order: at first the Quadrivium (arithmetic, music, geometry, and astronomy) and after that, the Holy Scriptures. Thus knowledge of the created leads to an understanding of the Creator. William of Conches gave a clear structure to the body of the liberal arts by specifically defining their function within the hierarchical system of studies. The Trivium deals with definitions. It has propaedeutic importance. The Quadrivium has as its object the properties of things. As the lower part of philosophy it is subordinated to theology, the higher part of philosophy.[55]

Gilbert de la Porrée, praised by John of Salisbury as a master in the sciences (which he made subservient to theology), was concerned especially with the particular methods and rules applying to each art so that any confusion could be avoided.[56]

Just at the time when the program of the Royal Portal was conceived Thierry of Chartres had finished his great enterprise of compiling texts in his *Heptateuchon,* the handbook of the seven liberal arts. In the prologue to his work he stated its accomplishment and purpose. He had brought together in his book and married as it were the Trivium and the Quadrivium so that the noble tribe of philosophers might increase. "Philosophy," he said, with far greater diagrammatic precision than William of Conches, "has two principal instruments, the mind and its expression. The mind is enlightened by the Quadrivium. Its expression, elegant, reasonable, ornate, is provided by the

Trivium. Thus it is manifest that the *Heptateuchon* is the proper and only instrument of all philosophy."[57]

One may assume that Thierry suggested the representation of the liberal arts on the Royal Portal. In the first place, he was chancellor of the School of Chartres. Furthermore, he was called "a most zealous investigator of the Arts."[58] There are specific reasons to substantiate this assumption. William of Conches confessed that human wisdom could not grasp the essence of God directly, but only indirectly by understanding His creation.[59] Thierry, on the other hand, went further. He used the Quadrivium for an explanation of theological truths.

While William of Conches restricted the Quadrivium to the understanding of natural phenomena, Thierry sought to clarify for the intellect the mystery of the Creator and the creation through direct proofs provided by "the four kinds of reasoning," especially arithmetic and geometry.[60] He was, as far as I know, the first author in the twelfth century to use extensive mathematical reasoning of a Neo-Pythagorean kind for the exposition of theological doctrines. He explained the difference between the Creator and the creation by contrasting the One that stands for the eternity, divinity, and omnipotence of God, with the various changeable numbers that proceed from the One and signify created things.[61] He used the square as a symbol for the creation of the Son by the One. As the number two or the number four multiplied by itself constitutes a square, so does the number one multiplied by itself form the first square. Since the One is the substance of the Father and creates by itself the Equal One, the first square denotes the creation of the Son and therefore the Son Himself. Its equal sides illustrate, in analogy to the sides of the equilateral triangle, the equality of the Son with the Father.[62]

Furthermore, Thierry had great confidence in the powers of human wisdom. William of Conches felt uneasy that in his discussion of God he might have overstepped the narrow boundaries of his knowledge.[63] In Thierry's writings no such confession of his own limitations, no such expression of scruples appears.

Both he and William of Conches defined the possession of wisdom in its higher degree according to Plato's *Timaeus* in the translation of Chalcidius. The power of comprehending ideas in their truth belongs to God, but is given also to a few men. William of Conches left it at that. Thierry went further. In an apparent fusion of a rhetorical phrase and genuine admiration he exalted these few: "Those who are able to understand things in their purity should be considered like gods among all other men."[64]

Thierry's belief in the liberal arts and their heightened use, combined with his trust in the possible achievements of human wisdom, could well have caused the decision to let the instruments of human wisdom frame Divine Wisdom in the tympanum.

"As for us," he declared in the prologue to the *Heptateuchon*, "we have arranged in one volume with care and in order not our own inventions, but those of the principal teachers of the arts."[65] Since these teachers belong, for the most part, to pagan antiquity, Thierry's words are a clear affirmation of his belief in the validity of classical writings. This trust is reflected visibly in the archivolts where seven great masters of the past are represented.

Thierry was famous for the sharpness of his tongue "that cuts like a sword."[66] The definitions in the prologue to the *Heptateuchon* are certainly succinct and of diagrammatic precision. One might add as a footnote, there-fore, that the clarity and precision of his thought and expression had found their equivalent in the diagrammatically lucid configuration of human wisdom and Divine Wisdom.

The arrangement of the Liberal Arts in the archivolts is somewhat irregular, owing to their uneven number. Six Arts and their masters are contained in the outer archivolt. Music and her representative are placed at the bottom of the inner archivolt to the right, balanced by two Signs of the Zodiac, Gemini and Pisces, on the other side. The two Signs pose a particular problem for which no definite solution may be offered. They could not have fitted into the zodiacal cycle in the archivolts of the left portal (fig. 25). This weakens the theory that they were transplanted from their legitimate places. If, on the other hand, they were planned from the beginning for their present places, what special meaning could they have? And why would an incomplete zodiacal cycle have been laid out for the left portal?[67]

The sequence of the Liberal Arts corresponds roughly to a circle. Grammar forms the starting point at the lower right. The series continues clockwise at the lower left with Dialectic, then it follows the rise and fall of the archivolt with Rhetoric, Geometry, Arithmetic, Astronomy, and ends with Music.

The sequence of the Quadrivium differs from the order adopted by Thierry in his *Heptateuchon* (arithmetic, music, geometry, astronomy). At first glance, one might be tempted, therefore, to say either that the sequence of the sculptured cycle is the result of some confusion, or that the wish to give Music more attributes than the other figures made it necessary to place her where the archivolt is more deeply hollowed out and could contain a more elaborate representation. However, the sequence as it was put into place corresponds exactly to the order established by Martianus Capella.

The actual arrangement might even serve a special purpose. It places Geometry and Arithmetic, not Arithmetic and Music, at the very top of the archivolt. Thierry had used these two mathematical disciplines to define the creation of the Son and His equality with the Father.

For the most part the thinkers exemplifying the liberal arts have been identified according to Thierry's *Heptateuchon*. The principal authors whose works he had chosen for the Handbook were Priscian for grammar, Aristotle for dialectic, Cicero for rhetoric, Boethius for arithmetic, and Ptolemy for astronomy. Geometry is probably not represented on the portal by any of the various writers whose treatises Thierry had selected, but by the author on whose concepts these treatises are based, namely Euclid. Music is most likely accompanied by Pythagoras, for she displays those instruments that, according to tradition, enabled the Greek philosopher to develop his theory of intervals, "A certain Gaudentius writing about music says that Pythagoras invented the principles of this discipline from the sound of bells and the percussive extension of chords."[68]

In the archivolts five of the Liberal Arts practice their particular methods, some of them using instruments: Grammar is teaching two boys, Rhetoric is speaking, Geometry is tracing figures on a tablet, Astronomy is contemplating the sky, and Music is playing instruments. The attribute of Arithmetic no longer exists. Only Dialectic is characterized by symbols of good and evil, a flower and a dragon-like creature with the head of a dog.[69]

The authors, on the other hand, are meditating or writing. Thus the actual task of each art is still indicated on the ideal level of personifications, while the authors are shown as they conceive or write down their ideas. They can still be termed a secularized version of Evangelists, not only because they resemble in their attitudes the traditional representations of the four saints, but also because they share with them inspiration by Wisdom. "Wisdom," John of Salisbury wrote, "is a fountain from which emanate rivers irrigating the whole earth. They do not solely fill the garden of delights of the Holy Scriptures but also reach the Gentiles."[70]

The choice of the seven authors and their role within the whole cycle reflect the particular kind of protohumanism of the Chartres School. On the one hand, their writings are indispensable for human wisdom. On the other hand, their place close to the religious cycle makes it obvious that their works will serve the purpose of understanding Christ, the Wisdom of the Lord.

Seen within the frame of secular knowledge, a particular aspect of the lintel scenes becomes clear. While the secular cycle concerns man as he seeks to understand the Wisdom of the Lord through intellectual endeavors, in the biblical scenes the Incarnation of God's Wisdom is revealed to a few chosen ones, not because of their intellectual endeavors but through simple acts of grace.

The Angel Gabriel reveals to Mary that she will conceive the Son of man through the Holy Ghost. According to theological interpretation, Mary did not express any doubts by saying: "How do I know this?" Instead she replied prudently: "How shall this be, seeing I know not a man (Luke 1:34)?" because it is not easy for a human being to understand a mystery hidden in God from the beginning.[71]

That Christ had been conceived was revealed to Elisabeth and she was filled with the Holy Ghost when the babe was leaping in her womb and, exulting in a mysterious way, felt the grace before she did.

To the Shepherds the birth was revealed by the Angel, and the Holy Ghost revealed to Simeon that he should not see death before he had seen the Lord's Christ.

Thus a synopsis of the tympanum, its lintels and archivolts shows Christ, the Divine Wisdom incarnate, the source and object of human wisdom. It shows knowledge infused by grace alone, and knowledge to be acquired by man, but inevitably dependent on enlightenment by God.

IV   SOME of the concepts represented in tympanum and lintels—the two natures of Christ and the Eucharist—had a special actuality at the time the iconographic program was conceived. The Church felt endangered by the heated antirational, antidogmatic simplicity of faith shown by various heretical movements.

Antiheretical decisions made by the Church during those years may be reflected in the emphasis given certain ideas in the iconographic program. Seen within the whole history of heresies, the heretical movements in France during the first half of the twelfth century seem to be of little importance compared with those of Arius and Nestorius, which had rocked the dogmas of the Church in their very foundations. And yet, seen through the eyes of their contemporaries, men like Peter of Bruys and Henry of Lausanne were regarded as most dangerous. The militant treatise of Peter the Venerable against the Petrobrusians, the letters of high clergymen show this fierce concern.[72]

The fight against heresies apparently influenced the choice of specific representations on some church façades. The relief with the unusual Story of Theophilus, at Souillac, was most likely meant for the heretics of the region as an encouraging example that even great sinners may find grace if they repent and ask Mary directly for mercy.[73] The particular iconography of the façade sculpture of Saint-Gilles may be explained as a strong protest against the tenets of Peter of Bruys who was burnt at Saint-Gilles, possibly as early as 1126.[74] He had denied the validity of the Mass. He hated crosses. As Peter the Venerable reports with deep indignation, the heretic set fire to a whole pile of crosses on Good Friday. Then he blasphemously roasted meat over the flames and ate it publicly.[75] On the façade of the church the Last Supper is prominently displayed on the central lintel. The sculptures of the lateral wings allude even more strongly to the heresy recently defeated. Not only is the Crucifixion represented in the right tympanum; more important, the Angels conquering dragons and devils underneath their feet (at the ends of the façade) exemplify the Fall of the Rebel Angels, the prototypes of all heretics.[76] It is equally significant that some of the small Angels decorating the embrasures of the Royal Portal likewise triumphantly tread dragons under their feet.[77]

In 1139 the second Lateran Council condemned those who denied the validity of the Eucharist (and who also advocated the destruction of altars on the ground that no real sacrifice could be performed on them).[78] As if illustrating a newly reaffirmed belief, the Child on mensa and altar, in conjunction with the relief of the Last Supper, reveals the truth of the sacrament with even greater insistence than the reliefs at Saint-Gilles and La Charité-sur-Loire.

The visible refutation of heretical concepts at the entrance to the church corresponds to the role of the See of Chartres within the history of the fight against heresies. Bishop Fulbert was an outspoken defender of orthodox tenets early in the eleventh century. In some treatise-like letters he defined the two natures of Christ, strongly condemned Nestorius, and gave a lengthy explanation of the Eucharist. His advice was sought for the ruthless suppression of heretics in Orléans.[79] Before and during the appearance of Peter of Bruys and Henry of Lausanne the bishops of Chartres became active again. In a forceful letter to Pope Paschal II, Bishop Ivo took the initiative. Asserting that he was the spokesman for a whole group of bishops, he urged the pope to entrust his legate in France, the archbishop of Lyon, with a thorough investigation of the ruinous state of the Church so that quick remedy could be applied.[80] When in 1145 Alberic, cardinal-bishop of Ostia and papal legate, went to Aquitaine to combat the heresy spread by Henry of Lausanne, he chose as helpers St. Bernard and Bishop Geoffroy.[81] The lively interest and the active contributions of two former bishops of Chartres and of Bishop Geoffroy to this seemingly never-ending struggle corresponds to the strong emphasis on orthodox tenets in the program of tympanum, lintels, and capitals.

To show pagan authors in a definite relation to Christian subject matter was also very timely. It meant nothing less than a rebuttal of those more practical-minded opponents of the traditional course of studies, who derided the extensive study of classical authors as a sheer waste of time and as harmful to Christian faith. These Cornificians, as they were called after Cornificius, the detractor of Vergil, appeared on the scene about 1130. They insisted that the study of grammar from pagan writings could be cut short without harm. They felt that the more this was studied, the more wisdom was lessened.

With all the bitterness of irony Thierry himself complained that Envy, falsely dressed up as Dialectic, had slandered him before Rumor and caused her to accuse falsely and revile him everywhere.[82] John of Salisbury tells us how Thierry and other teachers took a strong stand against these new ideas of education. At one point he reports regretfully that two of his teachers had to give up, but he also describes the defeat and dispersion of the Cornificians.[83] Quoting Quintilian he praises the value of grammar: "Those who deride this art as petty and thin, deserve even less toleration. For if Grammar does not lay beforehand a firm foundation for the orator, the whole structure will collapse."[84]

The representation of Grammar shows only too clearly the troubles of this discipline (fig. 24). She teaches two boys. (This may refer to her double function: to instruct in the right kinds of writing and of speaking).[85] The boys are strongly contrasted. One is shown semi-nude; the other wears a monk's cowl. This in itself implies a definite contrast of moral values. But more, the semi-nude boy, obviously not very eager to learn, is naughty and impetuous. He pulls the hair of his companion and prevents him from studying. The victim is unable to offer resistance. By their attitudes the boys embody conflicting concepts about the study of grammar. When John of Salisbury describes the teaching methods of Bernard of Chartres, he points out that thorough study requires loving care and humility. One cannot serve at the same time letters and carnal vices.[86] In the relief the boy in the cowl is intent on serving letters. The nakedness of the little aggressor alludes to the idea that he is serving vices. He represents the impetuosity of the stupid crowd, as John of Salisbury calls it.

V   IN CONTRAST to the Incarnation cycle, the two other tympana are simple in meaning. Neither the Ascension nor the Second Coming of Christ had caused the same elaborate theological discussions as the dogma of Christ's two natures and the sacrament of His body. Both tympana share with the Incarnation cycle the ideographic clarity which distinguishes them from earlier representations of the same kind.

The Ascension of Christ (fig. 25) had a strong iconographic and formal tradition in the Romanesque tympana of France, especially in Burgundy.[87] Yet in contrast to these immediate predecessors, the idea of the Ascension is made more explicit at Chartres. Already Christ is received by a cloud, and the four Angels predict His return more emphatically to the Apostles than on other tympana.

The Ascension is framed by the Signs of the Zodiac and the Occupations of the Months.[88] Burgundian archivolts had shown such cycles: at Vézelay in conjunction with Christ ascending to heaven (fig. 16), at Autun in conjunction with the Last Judgment.[89] On the Royal Portal a balance is achieved between the cycle of the Year and the cycle of the Liberal Arts. While on the right side the figures demonstrate Christ as the ruler and the ultimate object of secular learning, the figures on the left side show Him as lord of heaven and earth, and of time with its various activities. We are reminded of biblical concepts: "And he changeth the times and the seasons," said Daniel; ". . . he giveth wisdom unto the wise, and knowledge to them that know understanding" (Dan. 2:21).

A further balance exists between the two cycles. At either side special activities are illustrated as they are dominated by the Liberal Arts or the Signs of the Zodiac. The writers of Antiquity represent intellectual work. The figures on the left portal are concerned with menial work or other everyday activities.

The central tympanum—emphasized formally by place and size, iconographically by Christ in majesty—is with its lintel and archivolts more unified in concept (figs. 26, 27). While the Incarnation cycle comprises a variety of figure scenes and is framed by a subsidiary series of figures, while the Ascension tympanum is dedicated with its lintels to a single event, yet is enclosed by a variegated cycle, the Second Coming of Christ combines tympanum, lintel, and archivolts in one grandiose scene.

His return in glory is witnessed by the Angels and the twenty-four Elders, as it had been represented before in illuminated manuscripts of the Beatus Apocalypse and in the tympanum of Saint-Pierre in Moissac.[90] But unlike these earlier representations, the representation here makes evident the purpose of His return, to judge the quick and the dead. On the lintel the twelve Apostles are added. Christ had promised that they would be His helpers on the day of Judgment (Matt. 19:28). They are arranged in four groups of three. This implies that they had preached the Trinity to the four corners of the earth.[91] The two standing figures framing the Apostles are most likely Elijah and Enoch, who will return to earth just before the end of the world to convert all mankind.[92] This would mean a further strengthening of the eschatological idea.

The tympanum thus harmonizes into one comprehensive concept the idea of the Second Coming of Christ, as it was represented in Moissac, with that of the Last Judgment. At Chartres the idea of the Last Judgment is represented, but not its actual drama that had been rendered before in Autun, Beaulieu, and, in a more restrained manner, in Saint-Denis. As in the Incarnation cycle, here too the idea distills narratives until only essentials remain. Christ enthroned in majesty is not actually shown as king wearing a crown (as at Moissac), but the idea of His kingship is made clear by the crown held by two Angels in the archivolts.

VI   THE relief friezes of the capitals (figs. 2, 20, 21) are in subject matter and emphasis related to the tympana. Mainly devoted to the life of Christ, they also show a number of scenes from the early life of the Virgin.[93] Bishop Fulbert had voiced strong regrets that the stories of Mary's birth and infancy could not be recited in the church on the day of her Nativity, since the Fathers had considered them to be apocryphal.[94] A century later the veneration of the Virgin had grown so strong that the cycle of her early life was given a place on the Royal Portal and thus accorded the same right as the evangelical stories of Christ's life.

The relief friezes are subordinated in importance to the tympana not only by their place; they are subordinated also in form, because their figures are of small size, and in meaning, because they are restricted to the lives of Christ or Mary on earth. The function of the friezes in the two spheres of form and meaning is the same. Formally, they tie the three portals together like horizontal bands. Iconographically, they link the selected subject matter of the three tympana. The friezes accompany and complement the tympana as historical notes in a margin might accompany a dogmatic text. They do not run in a single direction from one end of the façade to the other, but spread from the center towards either side. This establishes a specific connection between the subject matter of the lateral tympana and that of the capital cycles. Scenes from the early life of Christ lead to the tympanum of the Ascension; scenes of His public activity and Passion lead to the Incarnation cycle.

The left-hand frieze begins with the story of Mary's birth and youth. Then follow scenes from the childhood of Christ. Annunciation, Visitation, and Nativity are not omitted, although this means a duplication. The completeness and continuity of the historical frieze is thereby preserved. But more important, the three key scenes are given prominence on the buttress between central and left portals. Placed near the Ascension of Christ, Annunciation and Nativity (fig. 20) reaffirm that He who is taken up to heaven is the one who descended to earth.

The friezes on the right-hand side show more scenes from the youth and public life of Christ, then His Passion and the events that follow it. The Crucifixion is omitted so that the Last Supper becomes the most important scene (fig. 21).[95] It corresponds in place exactly to the Incarnation scenes on the other side. Near the lintel of Christ's Incarnation, it reaffirms that He who is born will give His body in the sacrament of the Mass. Thus the significance of the events represented on the lateral tympana and lintels is stressed anew by key scenes within the sequence of Christ's life.

CHAPTER III   The Jamb Statues:

Regnum and *Sacerdotium*

I   IN THE DECO-
ration of the jambs of the Royal Portal at Chartres the new solution of Saint-
Denis was adopted. They were lined with twenty-four statues, male and female,
crowned and uncrowned (figs. 2, 28–33). (Four no longer exist. They were
replaced by columns. One statue was transformed into an Angel holding a
sundial and put at the southwest corner of the cathedral.) Approximated in
shape and by the immobility of their pose to the columns to which they are
addorsed, they seem to be infused with the idea of inner stability.

The identity of these statues and those of Saint-Denis has kept scholars
puzzled for a long time. In his *Monumens de la monarchie françoise,* published
in 1729, Bernard de Montfaucon identified the Saint-Denis statues (since
destroyed) as the Merovingian kings and queens.[1] Abbé Lebeuf rejected this
theory in 1751 and suggested instead that the statues on the royal portals
should be regarded as personalities of the Old Testament. His opinion generally
prevailed,[2] until Ernst Kitzinger proposed that the biblical Kings at Saint-
Denis are the antecedents both of Christ and the Kings of France.[3] He has

not given any proof, but his interpretation seems to lead in the right direction.

It should be emphasized that not all the Saint-Denis figures had royal status. The right-hand portal—where in Montfaucon's time one statue was missing—was framed by male statues, all of them wearing ornamented hats (fig. 34). Since they form a distinctive group because of their unified appearance, and since Moses was among them (in the center of the left-hand jamb; fig. 34, upper center), they could possibly be a series of Patriarchs and early Leaders of the Jewish people.

The statues lining the central and left portals were of a different kind (figs. 35, 36). Of the fourteen figures still existing when the drawings were made, seven were Kings, two were female figures (one of them crowned, another one uncrowned), and three were male figures wearing shell caps. The other two statues, whose heads were missing may be identified as a woman and a man of royal status.[4] On these two portals, therefore, the emphasis is on royal personages interspersed with some nonroyal figures.

What could be the reason for honoring at the entrance to the abbey church the French rulers in the image of Old Testament personages? Before all, Saint-Denis had been chosen as burial church by kings of the Merovingian, Carolingian, and Capetian dynasties. Pepin the Short had been anointed king there by Pope Stephen II in 754. Charles the Bald had become lay abbot of the monastery, a title likewise assumed by later rulers, and the royal insignia customarily were deposited in the church. These facts alone could have prompted Suger to honor the rulers of France in front of the church, since he was closely attached and deeply devoted to the house of Capet.[5]

But why select for this purpose both royal and nonroyal personages of the Old Testament?

From Carolingian times the fervent hope was expressed in coronation rites that the Lord would bestow the virtues of Old Testament kings and of early leaders of the Jewish people on those who were regarded as their spiritual successors.[6] The *Ordo* for the coronation of Louis II, the Stammerer, performed by Hincmar of Reims in 877 at Compiègne, includes a prayer that, because of its reference to personages of the Old Testament, belongs to the class of paradigmatic prayers: "Almighty eternal God, Creator and Ruler of heaven and earth, Establisher and Disposer of angels and men, who hast made Abraham, thy servant, triumph over his enemies, who hast given Moses and Joshua, the leaders of thy people, multiple victory, who hast raised the humble David, thy child, to the height of the kingdom . . . and hast enriched Solomon with the ineffable gift of wisdom and peace, look down, we ask, on our humble prayers and adorn through manifold benediction of honor this thy servant with the virtues with which thou hast adorned the afore-mentioned faithful!"[7] The same prayer apparently was spoken during the coronation of King Philip I of France in 1059.[8]

A coronation *Ordo* written about 980 in Saint-Vaast at Arras, the so-called *Fulrad Ordo,* contains a different prayer, but retains the references to the Old Testament. It was in all likelihood used for the coronation of Louis VI in 1108. In this prayer the king is visualized as being strengthened by the faith of Abraham, equipped with the clemency of Moses, fortified with the strength of Joshua, exalted by the humility of David, and adorned with the wisdom of Solomon.[9]

After the coronation the high hopes uttered in the prayer seemed fulfilled and the rulers were addressed in letters and eulogizing poems with an even wider range of Old Testament names, those not only of the kings and leaders but also of the patriarchs. Pepin the Short was called by Pope Stephen II a new Moses and a shining David.[10] (The epithet of a new Moses goes back to the time of Constantine the Great. The *Vita Constantini* ascribed to Eusebius had praised the emperor as a new and greater Moses. By referring to the man chosen by God as leader of His people, the author obviously wanted to enhance the authority of the first Christian emperor.)[11] Charles the Bald was compared by Ratramnus of Corbie to the two foremost Jewish kings, David and Solomon, and in addition, to Hezekiah and Josiah.[12] The names of Abraham, Isaac, Jacob, Joseph, Moses, and Joshua, together with those of David and Solomon, were showered time and again on Carolingian rulers by their court poets.[13]

This custom continued unbroken after the end of the Carolingian dynasty. Cardinal Hyacinth praised Louis VII because "from the time that he was anointed as king, he had followed the humility of David, the wisdom of Solomon and the patience of Job."[14] The epitaph of the king in Saint-Denis calls him "humble king, peaceful king, David and Solomon."[15] The exploits of the great Jewish leaders were seen in direct relation to events of contemporary history. When Louis VII took the cross, Peter the Venerable, abbot of Cluny, wrote to him: "The old times are renewed in our own age and the miracles of the old people are revived in the days of the new grace. From Egypt broke forth Moses and he destroyed the kings of the Ammorhites with the peoples subjected to them. Joshua, his successor prostrated, on God's command, the kings of Canaan with their countless peoples, and after the impious had been destroyed, he divided that country by lot among the people of God. Starting out from the utmost ends of the West, yes indeed from the sunset itself, the Christian king threatens the Orient and, armed with the cross of Christ, he attacks the nefarious people of the Arabs or Persians who had tried to subjugate anew the Holy Land."[16]

This long tradition of paradigmatic prayers, as they were spoken during coronation rites, and of similar references to the Old Testament, as they were used in poems and letters, is rooted in Jewish prayers and prayers of the Early Christian Church. These oldest prayers had once provided inspiration for the representation of Abraham, Isaac, Noah, Moses, Job, Daniel, Jonah, and others in catacomb frescoes and on sarcophagi, where they visibly exemplify, and thus promise, salvation from suffering and death. The comparison of

French rulers with patriarchs, early leaders, and kings of the Jewish people might also have influenced the choice and meaning of the statues on the façade of Saint-Denis.

At this point one might, therefore, draw two conclusions: first, that here the kings of France are honored in the image of Patriarchs and early Leaders of the Jews (right portal), and in the image of Jewish Kings (central and left portals); second, that the whole series of statues may be read in a temporal sequence from right to left, from the era of the patriarchs to the time of the kings.

The group of Kings certainly includes David (the first in the series of Kings, that is, the third statue to the right of the central portal; fig. 35, lower right) and Solomon (the statue next to the right side of the central portal; fig. 35, lower left). The other Kings could have been chosen from those successors of Solomon whom the Old Testament calls good and pious.

That rulers are honored here in the image of Old Testament personalities is but a link in a long chain of representations relating the living to ideal prototypes of the past by virtue of various ideological associations, all of them meant to enhance the prestige of the living.

In sculptured images and on coins Roman emperors were assimilated to individual gods—primarily to Jupiter, but also to Mercury and Hercules, the demi-god—by being endowed with their particular attributes.[17] A portrait bust glorifies Commodus as he wears the skin of the Nemean lion and proudly wields a club in imitation of Hercules. Yet more, the emperor appeared in public impersonating Hercules, thus boldly claiming the powers of this demi-god for himself.[18]

The Joshua Roll illustrating the conquest of Palestine by the hero of the Old Testament could well have been intended as a visible example for the endeavors of Emperor Constantine VII Porphyrogenitus to reconquer the Holy Land.[19] The Old Testament personalities on the façade of Saint-Denis might provide yet a different part in the whole chain. Rather than being important simply as an accumulation of single figures, they possess a collective significance. Rather than individually prefiguring specific rulers of France, they refer as a group to the idea of kingship as such.

The art of the fifteenth and sixteenth centuries represented secular and spiritual leaders, on the one hand, in the guise of saints within the context of religious ideas, on the other hand, in the guise of classical gods within the framework of political ideas. Roger van der Weyden, for instance, lent the youthful Magus in the Adoration of the Magi the features of Charles the Bold.[20] In Botticelli's Adoration of the Magi, commissioned in 1475, Cosimo de' Medici and his two sons were identified with the Magi.[21] Exalted above the level merely of devout onlookers, they were drawn as worshipers into the core of the holy event. The primary members of the ruling family in Florence thus proclaimed in the image of rulers their vassalage towards Christ. Cardinal

Albrecht of Brandenburg assumed the guise of saints, a role colored by
humanist ideas. In Grünewald's famous painting of St. Erasmus and St.
Mauritius, St. Erasmus whose very name had humanist connotations is given
Albrecht's features. The personality of the archbishop is, thereby, absorbed
by the personality of the saint. "For an orthodox Catholic of the sixteenth
century this was a privileged method of approaching the Saint and securing
his blessing."[22] In the same vein Lucas Cranach painted Albrecht in the likeness
of St. Jerome working in his study.[23]

Reviving an idea of the kind that had represented Octavian as a sea god
on a Roman cameo, Bronzino portrayed Andrea Doria, admiral of the Genoese
and of Charles V, as Neptune.[24] The kings of France and their queens were
visibly glorified as Jupiter and Juno. Leonard Limousin represented Henry II
and Catherine de' Medici in this guise.[25] Henry IV and Mary de' Medici take
the place of the gods in the allegorical Marriage scene painted by Rubens so
that actual history, mythology, and allegory merge into a grandiose and
exuberant whole.[26]

In the art of Antiquity, of the Renaissance and the Baroque period,
individuals are represented in the guise of a god or a saint, whether they play
their parts boldly (Commodus, Andrea Doria, Henry II, Henry IV) or more
modestly within traditional Christian themes (Cosimo de' Medici, Cardinal
Albrecht). At Saint-Denis, to the contrary, individual rulers of France do not
seem to take on such a role. Rather, the personalities of the Old Testament
assume as a whole group an added collective role, that of prefiguring the idea
of the *regnum* in France.

What, one might ask now, is the relation of the female statues on the
façade of Saint-Denis to the queens of France? The queens were addressed on
solemn occasions with the same kind of reference to the past as their husbands.
When in 856 Judith, the daughter of Charles the Bald, was married to
Aethelwulf, king of the Anglo-Saxons, and was crowned, this formula was
spoken: "I espouse thee to one husband as a chaste and virtuous virgin to be
married, as were the holy women to their husbands: Sarah, Rebecca, Rachel,
Esther, Judith, Hannah, Naomi, with the blessing of the creator and sanctifier
of marriages, Jesus Christ our Lord, who lives and rules forever."[27] With
obvious allusions to the Queen of Sheba, Ivo of Chartres expressed the wish
that Queen Matilda of England might hear the wisdom of Solomon in the ends
of the earth.[28]

Like the kings of France their queens were anointed and crowned. They
had a limited but nevertheless legitimate share in the government. They acted
as regents for their sons if these became kings at a minor age. For about ten
years Louis VI dated documents according to the reign of his wife.[29] Kings
and queens assumed definite responsibilities towards the Church through their
coronation. The king made a solemn pledge to defend the Church and he
received a sceptre as symbol of this duty. Kings and queens alike were given

rings as tokens that they would avoid and destroy heresies.[30] It was not uncommon that in difficult situations popes enlisted the help of French queens.[31] On the façade of Saint-Denis a Queen stands between the first and the second Kings, identified as David and Solomon (fig. 35, third statue from the lower right). She is in all likelihood the Queen of Sheba since she was represented on later church façades. The uncrowned woman may be interpreted as one of the Old Testament heroines (fig. 35, upper left). Both figures could have been looked at as spiritual ancestors of the queens of France.

How may one finally explain the three statues of the central and left portals who wear shell caps. (figs. 35, 36)? Interspersed among the Kings they could hardly be patriarchs. They might, however, be either Priests or Prophets active during the era of the kings of Judah.

But why did the planner of the program, most likely Abbot Suger himself, suggest that some Priests or Prophets should be shown among the series of Kings? Could this prefigure the harmony of *regnum* and *sacerdotium?* At the time when in other parts of Europe the deep cleavage separated the temporal and spiritual powers in the great struggle about investiture, no such breach existed between kingship and priesthood in France.

Bishop Ivo of Chartres, in his time the greatest authority in matters of Church law and Church politics on French soil, took an intermediate position between the radical opponents in the investiture controversy. He upheld the right of the king to bestow temporal, but not spiritual, power on a newly elected bishop, to give him the wordly possession of the church, but not the insignia of his office. As a result of the efforts of Ivo, the struggle about investiture came *de facto* to an end in France more than twenty years before the Concordat of Worms brought a formal solution in Germany to the opposite claims of pope and emperor. In 1098 Pope Urban II acquiesced to Ivo's pleas and reasoning when—over the protest of his own legate, Hugh of Lyon—he consecrated the newly elected archbishop of Sens, although the archbishop had accepted investiture from King Philip I.[32] From then on the solution proposed by Ivo was recognized in principle as the right procedure. Although occasional frictions occurred between Church and State a close relation between the two powers existed henceforth in France. Ivo had been instrumental in achieving this.

Time and again he pointed out the necessity of harmony between kingship and priesthood. He gave a grim picture of disunity between the two powers and its disastrous effects on the Church in a letter to Berno, primate of Belgium: "We see kingship and priesthood divided, on which the state of God's tabernacle was firmly established as though on principal and very strong pillars, so that it would not be overthrown by the onslaught of violent attacks and storms. In such a cleavage, in such an onslaught the Mother Church cannot flourish and bear fruit, of whom it is said: 'One is my dove, my bride' " (Cant. 6:8, according to the *Vulgate*).[33] He takes the same view in a letter to Pope

Paschal II, which furthermore lauds the character of King Louis VI and praises his attitude towards the Church: "Since therefore the King of France, a man of simple nature, is devoted to the Church of God, and benevolent towards the apostolic See, we ask and counsel that no deception may draw you away, no persuasion separate you from his benevolence, for your fatherly love knows that, with kingship and priesthood in harmony, the world is well ruled and the Church flourishes and bears fruit. But if they disagree, not only small things cannot grow but also large things collapse miserably."[34]

In the same vein Abbot Suger had stressed the harmony of kingship and priesthood in a letter to Samson, archbishop of Reims: "That the glory of Christ's body, that is the Church of God, consists in the indissoluble unity of kingship and priesthood is perfectly clear, because he who provides for the other helps him. It is therefore evident to everyone who can discern that the temporal kingdom becomes stable through the Church of God, and the Church of God progresses through the temporal kingdom."[35] The equality and close association of kings and priests were emphasized by still another argument. A charter given by Louis VII to the Church of Paris in 1143 points out that, by the authority of the Old Testament, even now only kings and priests are consecrated through the unction with the holy oil, and therefore are linked together to rule the people of God.[36] Related ideas might well have been carved in stone on the façade of Saint-Denis: Old Testament statues meant to prefigure *regnum* and *sacerdotium* protect in mutual harmony the entrances to the church.

The question whether the prototypes of *sacerdotium* are priests or prophets of the Old Testament cannot be answered unequivocally. In general, Jewish priesthood was considered to prefigure Christian priesthood. Yet the prophets also were regarded as prototypes. This is not due to the fact that the bishops, the successors of the apostles, who in turn are the sons of the prophets, may be regarded as "grandchildren" of the prophets. During the struggle of investiture, writers saw in the prophets the prototypes of *sacerdotium*. Prophets had anointed kings and been their counselors.[37] To Honorius Augustodunensis prophets and priests were almost the same. In secular affairs the prophets were subordinated to the kings while the kings were subjected to them in religious matters. Honorius quotes as examples for the superiority of the prophets over the kings Isaiah and Hezekiah, Elijah and Ahab, Elisha and Joas, Jeremiah and Josiah.[38] Gerhoh of Reichersberg speaks of the fruitful co-operation between regal power and sacerdotal dignity in the kingdom of Christ, as if this harmony were shaped after the relation of David to Nathan, of Hezekiah to Isaiah, and of Josiah to Jeremiah.[39] Hugh of Fleury, close friend and admirer of Ivo of Chartres, believed that the priests in his own time held the power of the holy prophets.[40] At a later date this theory was specifically applied by Peter of Blois, when he wrote to John of Coutances, bishop of Winchester, that he was constituted among the sons of the prophets.[41]

On the façade of Saint-Denis the first statue, after the series of Patriarchs has come to an end, is a man wearing a shell cap (fig. 35, lower right). He precedes the first of the Kings, David, and therefore could be Samuel, rather than a priest. Samuel, "a true prophet of the Lord" (I Sam. 3:20), had anointed David. It seems therefore likely that the two other men wearing shell caps are also Prophets and not priests.

If this whole interpretation is accepted, the series of statues on the façade of the royal Abbey Church at Saint-Denis fulfills a threefold function. First, all the statues exemplify the history of the Old Testament from the era of the patriarchs through the time of the kings. Thereby they form the foundation for the three tympana. Second, most of the statues could be looked at as spiritual ancestors of the rulers of France. Third, the idea of harmony between temporal and spiritual powers received here, for the first time, a monument in stone. The statues reminded the beholder that once Christ had combined kingship and priesthood in His person, and that the concordance of the two powers had been beneficial in the era of the Old Testament, thus setting an example for all later times.

The stained-glass window with the Tree of Jesse, as Suger devised it for the chevet, comprises within the context of Christ's genealogy the same two classes of spiritual and royal leaders. Although not the oldest representation of a Tree of Jesse, it is the first one to show two Kings, David and Solomon, within the Tree framed by Prophets.[42] David and Solomon were not only the two most prominent royal ancestors of Christ. They were also the two most prominent spiritual ancestors of the French kings.

II   STATUES similar to those at Saint-Denis decorate the single portal at Notre-Dame in Etampes, and the three doorways of the Royal Portal at Chartres (figs. 2, 28–33).[43] Should this be considered a mere mechanical transfer of an iconographic program from a royal abbey church to two churches that were patronized by the royal house of France but less closely linked to it than Saint-Denis? The answer to be given is in the negative.

The statues of Chartres differ from those of Saint-Denis in some significant respects. First of all, the group of men wearing hats, most likely Patriarchs and Leaders preceding the kings, has disappeared, and with them a whole class of personages prefiguring the kings of France. Secondly, in addition to two statues with shell caps, four bareheaded statues of men make their appearance at Chartres. Both types of figures might represent Prophets (as they did later on the west façade of the cathedral at Amiens). The increase in the number of uncrowned statues, interpreted as Prophets, would mean a somewhat more even balance between the prototypes of *regnum* and *sacerdotium*. The original plan for the south portal of the cathedral at Etampes had envisaged a similar balance.[44] On later royal portals greater numerical superiority was once again given to Kings and Queens, although hardly ever to the same extent as in Saint-Denis.[45]

At Saint-Denis most of the statues were in all likelihood meant to bestow their virtues on the royal house of France, while the addition of a few Prophets indicates the exemplary harmony of *regnum* and *sacerdotium*. On the Royal Portal at Chartres the idea of honoring the *regnum* seems to have become less important, while the concept of the harmony between the two powers has grown stronger.

A church façade was in itself an ideal place for displaying this harmony, for it corresponds to the metaphor of the protective wall applied to both king and priest. On the one hand, Louis VI and his son were urged "to prove themselves as a most strong wall for the Church."[46] On the other hand, Bishop Geoffroy, for instance, was praised in his obituary because he was in his time "a strong column of the Church of God in sacerdotal dignity and for the honor of the kingdom" and because "he defended the Church vigorously against numerous perturbations, by setting himself up as a most powerful wall for it."[47] Through the Royal Portal, where the prototypes of spiritual and secular power were carved in stone, the bishops and kings entered the cathedral.

Twenty to twenty-five years after the decoration of the Royal Portal the exemplary co-operation between *regnum* and *sacerdotium* was directly, not figuratively as in the earlier period, represented on the right tympanum of the west façade of Notre-Dame in Paris (fig. 15). Here Louis VII gives a privilege to the Virgin Mary, the patron saint of the cathedral, and Maurice of Sully, bishop of Paris, accepts it, illustrating the harmony of king and priest in relation to the Church.

At Saint-Denis the idea of *regnum* and *sacerdotium* seems to have been represented for the first time. It was to remain a most important theme on French church exteriors for a century to come. One might briefly define its evolution as follows. On the façade of the royal Abbey Church at Saint-Denis the jamb statues honor primarily the *regnum*. On the façade of the Bishop's Church in Chartres (and in a more abbreviated manner on other churches) crowned and uncrowned figures are still intermingled, but tribute is paid more equitably to both *regnum* and *sacerdotium*. In the thirteenth century statues honoring the *regnum* are, for the first time, represented as a unified group of Kings in the gallery underneath the western rose window of Notre-Dame in Paris. At Amiens their homogeneous series forms the counterpart to the homogeneous series of Prophets on the front of the lower façade part. At Reims, where the kings of France were crowned, the idea of *regnum* is intensified. The Gallery of Kings is extended around the flanks of the cathedral. Ideal statues of Kings stand as protectors in the tabernacles of pier buttresses. With the Gallery of Kings thus becoming a norm, it was adopted in the thirteenth century for a wall section above the rose window of the Royal

Portal at Chartres, while statues of Bishops protect the sides of the church in the tabernacles crowning the buttresses. Thus the idea of the harmony between *regnum* and *sacerdotium* was formulated anew, more clearly and more directly.

The primary function of the statues on the Royal Portal within the whole theological program, however, is to form the foundation of the Old Testament for the scenes of the New Testament honoring Christ, and with Him, the Virgin Mary. Seen in relation to the tympana, the male statues, crowned and uncrowned, prefigure *regnum* and *sacerdotium* as they had been united in the person of Christ. The Queens on the façade of the cathedral dedicated to the Virgin Mary may well refer to her. This may be deduced from the program for the north portal of Bourges Cathedral. Only two statues of Old Testament Queens decorate its jambs and they are related to the Theotokos of the tympanum.[48] At Chartres the program of tympana, lintels, and capital friezes is in part devoted to the Virgin. On the lower part of the façade she receives a similar share within the context of the Old Testament.[49]

CHAPTER IV   Form and Meaning

I   THE ICONOGRAPHIC PROGRAM spun over the whole of the Royal
Portal gains its clarity not only from its ideological structure, but from its
formal organization as well.

There is, in the first place, a perfect relationship and consonance among
the three tympana. At Vézelay and Saint-Gilles the lateral tympana were not
only subordinated by their smaller size to the main tympanum, but also
separated from it by wide intervals. The meaning of the tympana, therefore,
could be grasped only in an additive manner. The tympana of the Royal Portal,
on the other hand, are more equal in size, more closely drawn together; they
are parts of a tightly organized and unified whole (fig. 2). In each, Christ
assumes the same frontal position and has the same gesture. His central
importance is stressed by framing figures turned towards Him: Angels in the
lateral tympana, the Symbols of Angel and Eagle in the center. This compositional device creates, on the one hand, an over-all formal unity. On the other
hand, it strengthens visibly the idea of an over-all iconographic unity.

Secondly, there exists—as at Saint-Denis—a balanced proportion between all the components of sculptural decoration, namely tympana, lintels, archivolts, and jamb statues, where in preceding decades tympana were stressed at the expense of the other parts (Burgundy, Languedoc), archivolts, were emphasized (western France) or archivolts were de-emphasized, while tympana and jamb statues were harmonized in size (Provence).

Thirdly, there is at Chartres—in contrast to Romanesque church façades —a perfect consonance between sculptural and architectural design. In order to arouse the churchgoer's emotion and to accentuate by dramatic means the entrance into the church, the planners of Vézelay had created tensions between sculpture and architecture (fig. 4). The reliefs were kept flat to the wall plane, but their dynamically asymmetrical compositions of agitated figures contrasted with the simple, compact architectural shapes. Other Romanesque sculptors had used the architectural design to break up iconographic and compositional unity and create tensions between separated parts. On the right-hand wall at Moissac, for instance, the twin arch splits the single scene of the Adoration of the Magi into halves (fig. 12). Architectural articulation thus creates a barrier between the Magi and the Child, to be overcome by the strength of their relation. Even at Saint-Gilles, where emotional restraint is the keynote of the sculptural decoration, the continuity of the Passion cycle conflicts with the sharp angular segmentation of the friezes on which it is represented (fig. 8).

At Chartres, on the contrary, the sculpture articulates and clarifies the architectural design (fig. 2). The shape of each tympanum is echoed by the group of Christ and framing figures that accentuate by the curves of their wings the apex of the tympanum. The oblong rectangular shape of the lintels is emphasized by the equidistant or almost regular lining up of figures and, in part, by series of arches, where at Vézelay, at Autun, and to a lesser degree at Saint-Gilles, figures press against each other and against the molding that separates lintel and tympanum. The upward curves of the archivolts are stressed by the superposition of figures and, on the lateral doorways, by their iconographic arrangement. On the left, the cycle of the Year is broken up into four parts. Each of them has to be read from bottom to top. On the right, the outer archivolt leads from the Trivium to the Quadrivium. At Vézelay, on the other hand, a deliberate restlessness was created by placing the figures in the eight irregularly sized compartments of the inner "archivolt" either tangentially or radially in relation to the circumference of the tympanum (fig. 16). Approximated in shape to columns, the large statues act as verticals while they screen the mass of the wall. The capital friezes articulate the two stories and tie the three parts of the façade together. Their continuity is enhanced by unbroken rows of crowning turrets which establish an even architectural rhythm above irregular figure compositions and create a vertical element lessening too definite a separation of the two stories.

At Chartres tympana, lintels, and archivolts are clearly defined, because each group of figures or sequence of figure groups is contained within a section of its own, yet is related to the whole—in contrast to the interpenetration of parts which characterizes the central tympanum of Vézelay or the intricate pattern achieved at Moissac by the crowding together and the partial interaction of the figures within the tympanum itself.

II   THE subordination of the lintels to the tympana and the peripheral relation of archivolts to both the tympana and lintels coincides with, and clarifies, the relative importance of the figures assigned to these sections. This hierarchy of values had existed before in Romanesque art, but at Chartres it is now more clearly intelligible. While the ascending Christ of Vézelay (fig. 16) or the supreme Judge of Autun, and even the smaller Apostles in both tympana, were separated by tremendous symbolic differences in size from ordinary mankind, the Christ in the central tympanum at Chartres is closer in size to the humble shepherds of the lower right lintel. Incomprehensible differences have given way to variations less overpowering in effect and more easily understandable.

The Moissac tympanum largely coincides in subject matter with the central tympanum of Chartres, but while at Moissac an immobile Christ is strikingly contrasted with the violently twisted Symbols of the Evangelists (fig. 37), the main tympanum at Chartres displays, like the lateral ones, a gradual and well-measured increase in the particularization of activities (figs. 9, 25, 26).

In each tympanum of the Royal Portal the oneness and immobility of Christ is accentuated by the movements of flanking figures, movements that are stabilized through exact symmetry of poses. By superposition He dominates the single groups of Apostles in various attitudes controlled by framing arches, or the multiplicity of Incarnation scenes controlled by greater stillness of attitudes. In the archivolts of the lateral tympana, finally, figures are engaged in a pronounced variety of secular activities.

This hierarchical gradation of attitudes coincides with a gradual increase in the degree of relatedness of figures to each other. In the center, Christ in divine majesty is enclosed by a mandorla and thereby completely isolated from the Apocalyptic Creatures. In the lateral tympana Christ incarnate and ascending to heaven is less strongly separated from the attending Angels by canopy or cloud band. The lintel figures do not, for the most part, interact with one another. Where they are combined into groups, their relation is one of restraint and hieratic solemnity (Visitation, central group of the Presentation). Where groups occur in the archivolts, however, the relation of the figures to each other is more active, more incidental, and therefore more natural (Grammar teaching, Vintage scene of September, Meal of December).

The hierarchical gradation of values is, finally, accompanied by a gradual decrease in the ideal quality of space in which figures exist. Christ in majesty is contained within a mandorla defining an ideal sphere. His throne does not stand on a horizontal plane. Its place is merely fixed but not defined.

In the lateral tympana, however, the throne of Mary stands on the same horizontal plane as the attending Angels, and the ascending Christ is on the same level as the Angels surrounding Him.

The lintel figures exist on stages whose setting, if there is any at all, is reduced to a minimum of objects with a maximum of symbolic significance (altar-like manger of the Nativity, altar of the Presentation). In the lintels of the right-hand portal the actual existence of the figures on a stage is made explicit by the position of their feet. The diagonal placing of the sheep, likewise, defines the place of the shepherds on the stage.[1]

In the archivolts of the lateral portals, finally, the space is in parts even more realistically described (figs. 9, 25). Specific elements of outdoor or indoor setting are given, such as the field of grain (July), the vat filled with vine grapes (September), or the tables at which figures sit (January, December). Some curved back planes even gain the reality of walls, when shelves with quills are attached to them ("cubicles" of Aristotle, Pythagoras, etc.). And yet, even where the reaper stands in the midst of the grainfield or people sit behind tables, no credible existence of the figures in a natural volume of space is intended, since the figures are emphasized by size and bulk at the expense of space that could contain them.

There is not, therefore, an a priori concept of an even degree of spatial definition. The gradual decrease in the ideal quality of space and the corresponding increase in reality corroborate the gradual decrease in importance: from Christ enthroned in heaven to Christ incarnate and ascending to heaven, to the lintel figures (not all of them holy), to the secular activities of mankind.

The jamb statues, an ideal community of those who had lived at different times, do not stand on horizontal pedestals that would constitute segments of a stage. They are dependent on the columns to which they are attached, and they exist in an ideal sphere in front of the walls.

As far as the attribution of the sculptures to different artists is concerned, a wide area of agreement (with some boundary lines fluctuating) is shared by art historians, thanks to the penetrating observations of Wilhelm Vöge.[2] To state the main attributions briefly: there are obvious differences between the more old-fashioned style of the statues on the outermost jambs and the modern style of the other statues. Of the more conservative sculptors a master possibly coming from Saint-Denis carved the two male statues on the outer jambs to the right (fig. 33), a sculptor active at Etampes the two figures at the extreme left of the façade (fig. 28). The two remaining female statues on the outer jambs may be ascribed to another artist. The Head Master of the workshop carved the large statues and the tympanum of the central portal (figs. 26, 30, 31) while sculptors of his workshop created under his close supervision the central lintel and the statues on the inner jambs of the lateral portals (figs. 29, 32). The right-hand tympanum and the left one with its upper lintel are the work of the "Master of the Angels" (figs. 9, 25). The two lintels of the right-hand portal were carved by two masters strongly conforming to the style of the Head Master.[3]

Stylistic differences between the jamb statues, strong though they may be, do not in themselves necessarily lead to the conclusion that the statues could not have been carved in one workshop at the same time. There exists, however, an outspoken, even disquieting contrast. While the outermost statues are standing above or on small figures which are for the most part unruly, the statues of the center stand on simple sloping pedestals. Does it seem likely that the Head Master who exerted such a strong control over the work of some members of his workshop made allowance for this striking discrepancy in his general plan for the façade? Does this not rather suggest that it is a break in the activity that accounts for the stylistic break?

It seems likely that the work was at first entrusted to an older workshop which comprised the masters of Saint-Denis and Etampes. This workshop carved, apart from the statues now at the outermost jambs, also the lower lintel of the left-hand tympanum. These sculptures might have been intended originally for the central portal together with the lintel originally containing twelve Apostles. It seems possible that the older workshop was soon replaced by the more progressive Head Master and his workshop, and that he used the sculptures left behind by his predecessors and assigned them their peripheral place, with the Apostles' lintel shortened by two figures.[4] It seems possible also that the Head Master, when using the "older" statues for the ends of the façade, sought to smooth out differences between them and the statues carved by members of his own workshop. This he achieved by giving the more "modern" statues of the lateral doorway the same kind of canopies that had been planned for the "older" statues. He even let two of the "modern" statues stand on little figures that, however, are very unobtrusive.

III   THE Head Master fully developed the boldest achievement of the sculptors active at Saint-Denis: the columnar statue, released from the plane of the wall and thereby imbued with a limited existence of its own, yet linked to the architecture by the column to which it is attached and whose shape it echoes. The essence of the columnar statue cannot be better described than by Erwin Panofsky's felicitous characterization: "The figures in Gothic statuary . . . give the impression of being crystallized around a central axis of their own. In Romanesque sculpture the figure is conceived in relation, not to an axis within it but to a surface behind it, a surface from which it protrudes much as a convex garnet or moonstone does from its setting."[5]

The Head Master of Chartres further enhanced both the columnar quality and the limited self-existence of the jamb statues. He gave them an ideal purity of forms, and at the same time, elements of human warmth.

The statues of the outermost jambs are still somewhat restless in design (figs. 28, 33). Their outlines bulge out slightly, thereby denying a complete consonance between figure and column. The static pose of the two male statues to the right—carved by the Saint-Denis master—conflicts with their dynamic, curvilinear, even whirlpool-like drapery lines. The two statues to the very left, works of the Etampes master, show other tensions: namely, between the richness of dense lines and the hardness of design and carving, between the feet flattened against the columns and the roundness of the shafts.

Although these statues are immobile in pose, an element of restlessness is added by the representation of their triumph over evil exemplified in the figures underneath their feet.

The statues carved either by the Head Master or by other sculptors under his close supervision, however, have lost all elements of tension (figs. 29–32). Their elongated forms, contained within vertical outlines, with the arms closely bound to the slender volume of the body, correspond to slightly flattened cylinders in perfect consonance with the columns behind them, and they are effectively contrasted with the small-scale, rhythmically moved decoration of the intermediary columns.[6] Their tectonic quality is enhanced by the verticality of multiple linear folds. The statues carved by the Head Master are purest in form. Among them the female figures show most clearly the keynote of the design, that is to say, verticality. Their long sleeves, the fall of their braids or the ends of their girdles enhance this vertical element and therefore the weightlessness of the figures.

The perfection of forms given these statues expresses a moral idea which does away with the necessity to represent evil underneath their feet. On the lateral portals canopies break the continuity of the columns and obscure them in part. The omission of the canopies on the central portal heightens the harmony of statues and columns.

On none of the other royal portals still existing is this harmony proclaimed with such clarity and purity. Only on the central portal at Chartres do the columns continue without interruption above the figure while the lower shafts extend the columnar shape downwards. On other façades this consonance is either minimized or altogether given up.[7]

The statues carved by the Head Master (and those on the left jamb of the right doorway, carved by a close collaborator) are unique also in other respects (figs. 30–32). They express the idea of upward direction not only by the vertical emphasis of design, not only by the particular kind of elongation— being attenuated only in the lower part of their bodies, the figures seem to rise weightlessly—but by other means which also are used to achieve this effect.

While the heads and hands of these ngures are on the same level, the length
of the bodies decreases somewhat towards the doorway. Furthermore, the feet
gradually assume a more and more slanting position so that the figures appear
increasingly weightless and suspended in an ideal manner. Thus the statues
not only lead to the entrance but direct the churchgoer's view upwards, away
from the actual ground on which the Royal Portal is built.[8]

The perfect control and severity of design is combined with elements of
incipient humanization. The statues were given a human warmth that did not
exist even in those less abstract Romanesque statues—like the Apostles at
Saint-Gilles—in spite of their natural bulk and their independence from
columns (fig. 38).

The statues at Chartres are immobile without being constrained, columnar
without being compressed, easily fitting into an ideal shape. They fulfill a strict
architectural function, but this does not mean complete abstractness and denial
of the body. By vertical drapery lines they were made part of the architectural
design. The curved drapery folds, on the other hand, define parts of the body.
There is a suggestion of breasts in the figures of the young Queens. The body is,
therefore, neither completely denied nor given autonomy. The result is a
harmony between tectonic and natural qualities. Still, the ideal elements
dominate. The figures do not stand by natural right and with their own natural
weight on the sloping pedestals.

The incipient humanization is likewise apparent in the heads. The three
heads of Kings from Saint-Denis (now in the Walters Art Gallery in Baltimore
and the Fogg Museum in Cambridge) and those of the older statues at Chartres
still have a masklike character (figs. 28, 33).[9] Their eyes, either enlarged and
strongly delineated for emphasis, or narrowed and hardly separated from the
eyelids, remain close to the surface of the head. They are blank in expression.
They show no spark of inner life. The eyes of the figures carved by the Head
Master are not incised on the very surface but form a more organic part of
the head, although they are emphasized and singled out by delineation. The
glances of these eyes are no longer inanimate. They vary in expression from
meditation, as in the Prophet next to the left side of the door, to positive
radiation, as shown by the young Queen on the same jamb.

This differentiation of types is also carried out in the carving of the whole
heads. By the fullness of its forms the head of the Queen typifies all the beauty
of youth. The bony shapes and the sharper lines of the Prophet's head show an
older, ascetic type, and the experiences of his life are engraved in the wrinkles
on his forehead.

It has been pointed out rightly that towards the middle of the twelfth
century a strong concern with psychological problems made itself felt rather
suddenly and that this new interest is reflected in the works of the Head Master
at Chartres.[10] A considerable number of treatises on the soul and its relation
to the body were written at that time. Hugh of St. Victor, for instance, still

considered the body to be an appendage of the soul.[11] William of Conches took a different view. The soul, he said, is more active from within man than from without and is, therefore, not something appended to the body.[12] It is the same concept of animation from within that shapes the statues carved by the Head Master.

In these same years other philosophical concepts, considered valid hitherto, underwent similar changes. To Gilbert de la Porrée individuals were different from each other not because of accidentals, as Platonists of an uncompromising kind still believed, but by virtue of properties in substance.[13] The work of the Head Master seems to reflect this concept. The jamb statues are differentiated not merely by variations in the shape of their heads or in the design of their hair and beards. He achieved his aim primarily by giving them singular inner attitudes, properties in substance.

This incipient concept of humanized forms is more fully realized in the figure of Christ in the central tympanum (fig. 27). Unlike the jamb statues, He is not restricted in pose and gestures. His attitude is less rigid than that of the judging Christ at Saint-Denis who echoes the cross behind Him. He differs strongly from the apocalyptic Christ of Moissac (fig. 37).[14] This figure, in spite of its calm pose and gestures, was infused with energy by the design of the drapery. A few simple folds across His breast contrast with the more agitated drapery rhythm in the lower part of His garment. The Head Master at Chartres was not concerned with such differentiation. Christ's drapery folds have throughout the same controlled rhythm. Evenly spaced and forming either parallel straight lines or concentric curves, the folds are bound to the clear shapes of the body. Thus a balance of line and volume is achieved. The folds fulfill a threefold function: they form a beautiful pattern, clarify shapes, and calmly emphasize by their direction the hands of Christ. Straight and curved lines alike lead from the lower hem of the garment to the hand that holds the book. Then they swing across the body to the blessing hand. His glance is differentiated from those of the jamb statues. The upper eyelids partly overlap the pupils thus shielding them to some extent and giving them the poise of inner concentration, as if He were conceiving ideas apart from the material world.

The large statues and smaller figures carved under the supervision of the Head Master (lintels of the right tympanum) show the marks of his style: clarified shapes, simple outlines, harmony between mathematically pure line and volume, restrained poses and gestures, differentiation of attitudes. The old Shepherd, for instance, understandingly receives the Angel's message, while his young companion exemplifies those who are simple in spirit. Even the movements of the Angels in the lateral tympana are perfectly balanced against each other.

In the archivolts of the lateral tympana with their secular subject matter, the attitudes of the figures are more varied and specific, and their natural bulk, at least in the lower parts is emphasized.

I V   OF THE three tympana, the Incarnation cycle shows by its relation to the secular cycle of the Liberal Arts and pagan writers strong iconographic links with ideas rooted in Antiquity. The reliefs of the two lintels too are close to Roman art (fig. 10). The shapes of the figures and their self-sufficient existence on a stage that creates a definite although limited layer of space give them an element of natural human dignity. Their facial expressions, their tender gestures infuse them with inner life. The calm and balanced composition lends the scenes an ideal stillness and serenity.

But there exist more than general analogies between the two epochs of art separated by many centuries. The master of the Presentation actually borrowed motifs and compositional devices from antique relief sculpture and adapted them to a new content. It is significant that the models were not chosen at random for formal reasons only. They are similar in meaning to the theme the artist wanted to represent. Formal changes are kept at a minimum so that the essence of the models is preserved to a large degree.

The Child on the altar resembles in His garment and statuesque pose the statue of a deity, which stands on a high pedestal behind an altar, as in the Hadrianic relief medallion on the Arch of Constantine (fig. 39). The altar of the Presentation is similar in shape and articulation to Roman altars.

The use of classical motifs was, of course, wide-spread in medieval art. At Vézelay, for instance, the figure of the Spinario was quoted in the inner "archivolt," but the sculptor had radically transformed him by tightening the pose, sharpening the contours, disregarding the natural structure, and complicating the design through the addition of restless drapery.[15] Absorbed by the dynamic style of the Burgundian sculptor, the quotation has completely lost its original form. At Chartres, on the other hand, a quotation from Antiquity has not been changed basically in its form.

The procession of figures holding doves and other gifts is iconographically and compositionally, in its evenly measured rhythm and the spatial separation of the figures, close to, and most likely derived from, sacrificial processions on Roman reliefs (fig. 40).[16] The medieval sculptor has given his figures stockier proportions and emphasized their heads by large size. In order to show Simeon's eagerness to receive the Child, the sculptor has lent the drapery lines of Simeon's mantle a strong directional force. But in spite of these changes, the dignity of natural forms, the controlled attitude of the figures remains intact, and the composition as a whole retains its similarity to the type of antique processions. On the central lintel at Vézelay the motif of a Roman sacrifice was used. Although here the iconography did not have to be changed, a complete transformation of form and expression made the scene entirely different from any antique model (figs. 41, 42). The Presentation scene of La Charité-sur-Loire, although similar in style to the Chartres relief, is in its dramatic action and even in the shape of the altar farther removed from the art of Antiquity (fig. 14). It was at Chartres that Roman art was quoted in such a way that the scene retains a quasi-antique harmony and serene stillness.

In contrast to the master of the Presentation, the sculptor of the lower lintel represents scenes for which no antecedents had existed in the pagan art of Rome (fig. 10). Yet the four scenes share with the Presentation the stillness of composition and the calm attitudes of the figures. The sculptor gives the figures slender proportions and a beautiful purity of line and volume. The forms of Mary Annunciate, the oval shape of her head, could not have been derived from Roman art. The Angel Gabriel, on the other hand, reflects the influence of antique sculpture in his pose, his form-defining drapery folds, and the type of head. Nevertheless, the two figures, different as they are in derivation, are in perfect harmony with each other.

In their use of antique models the masters of Chartres, therefore, differ basically from the sculptors active at Vézelay. There only a very few antique motifs had been used and inserted as minor details into a thoroughly un-antique whole. They were radically changed into a style separated from antique art by an insurmountable gap. In the Chartres lintels elements derived from the antique are more prominent within the context of the whole. Such elements, moreover, were easily combined with others, not derived from Antiquity, because these very elements were no longer separated by any unbridgeable gap from classical art.

As the School of Chartres stressed the value of antique learning and made it subservient to theological ends, as the iconographic program immortalized the authors of the great past as helpers to an understanding of theological truths, so did the masters of the lintels take individual motifs or compositional devices from the art of Antiquity, wherever these motifs fitted and strengthened their own style.[17]

V   HOW may one briefly define, then, the place of the Royal Portal within the history of forms and ideas? In contrast to the tympana of Vézelay and Autun, where new types of representation seem freely invented almost to the last detail by a boundless imagination, iconographic antecedents may be found for many motifs of the Chartres tympana and lintels. It is all the more wonderful that, with ingredients which are not the first of their kind, something essentially new was created because the formal principle becomes one of perfect clarity of individual shapes and total composition in consonance with the iconographic principle of perfect lucidity. By structural configuration and emphasis, ideas both old and new are sharply revealed. The old concept of Christ's Godhead and manhood, the idea of Wisdom incarnate, complemented by Mary as Theotokos and *Sedes Sapientiae,* are presented with utmost clarity.

Statues of the Old Testament, traditionally regarded as the foundation of the New Testament, assume most likely—as in Saint-Denis—a new added meaning. They proclaim the harmony of *regnum* and *sacerdotium,* and thus prefigure the ideal relation between the two great powers of Christian society. Moreover, entirely new concepts enter the program: the eucharistic reality of Christ's *corpus verum* and the importance accorded intellectual endeavors.

As far as we can judge from extant monuments, the Christological cycle of the Royal Portal is in its comprehensive and grandiose scope and its ideo-graphic clarity more closely akin to the program of mosaics in Santa Maria Maggiore in Rome, from which it is separated by more than seven centuries, than to the cycles of Vézelay or Moissac created not more than two or three decades earlier than the Royal Portal.[18] As in the Early Christian church the relation of the Old Testament to the New is broadly stated, although not by means of progression and figure scenes but rather by subordination and single figures of the Old Testament. In Santa Maria Maggiore the throne of the *Hetoimasia* forms the keystone of the triumphal arch above the scenes of Christ's Incarnation and His manifestations to the Jews and Gentiles. At Chartres analogous ideas are represented in the right-hand tympanum, and yet not by a mere symbol of power but by the Child as Godhead incarnate enthroned above the Nativity and the Presentation.

Looking ahead in time one might venture to say that the Incarnation cycle at Chartres is an antecedent, remote, modest, and embryonic, to be sure, of Raphael's frescoes in the Camera della Segnatura.[19] Here the truth of the eucharistic reality and the value of secular learning are represented once more. It is hardly necessary to mention the essential changes in forms and ideas that have taken place and the balance achieved between secular philosophy and Christian theology in the Camera, whereas at Chartres the philosophers were given only a peripheral place in relation to religious truth.

The clarity with which actual forms and their arrangement make the ideas represented understandable for the intellect may well show the effect of a great intellectual center of art. The jamb statues and the consonance between them reveal the idea of inherent columnar strength and mutual harmony. The addition of the twelve Apostles to the Second Coming of Christ stresses the idea of the Last Judgment. The central axis of the Incarnation cycle makes visible the union of the two natures in the person of Christ and the reality of the Eucharist. The gradual decrease in the ideal quality of the attitudes of the figures, in their relation to one another, and in the definition of space expresses the idea of the hierarchy of values.

The particular protohumanism of the School of Chartres also pervades the iconography. Classical erudition and ancient philosophers are given a monument in stone. The power of reason is strongly and definitely stated in the Liberal Arts but not accorded autonomy. Reason remains dependent and centered on Divine Wisdom. Seen within the context of the whole iconographic program it has limited importance only. The main emphasis is placed on theological truths which are made clear to the mind at the expense of narrative exuberance and emotional intensity.

The protohumanism might account for the incipient humanization of the forms conceived and realized by the artists. Even the figures most strongly stylized, as the jamb statues, begin to be infused with human warmth. Yet in contrast to the humanist art of later centuries, the figures decorating various parts of the façade differ in degree of natural qualities, and none of them is represented as an autonomous rational being.

Proportions clarify the design of the figures; in contrast to the art of the Renaissance, however, their normative quality is not evolved from the natural forms of the human body but rather the forms of the human body are fitted into an ideographic quasi-columnar shape.[20]

The relation of figures to space begins to be more easily understandable, but only in a graded manner, according to a definite hierarchy of values. It is never carried to the point where man's environment is completely rationalized. With varying degrees of humanization the figures form an integral part of the cathedral as a whole and remain subordinated to it.

Like the sculptures of Saint-Denis those of the Royal Portal were created in those years which were eminently fruitful for the emergence of new forms and concepts. Romanesque sculpture had spent its force. In Burgundy the tympanum of Saint-Lazare in Autun shows the characteristics of a late phase. An unresolved tension exists between the heightened emotionalism of the narrative and the rigid patterning of the brittle design.[21] The same kind of freezing process took its course in the Languedoc. The figure of St. Peter at Moissac is a final grandiose exaggeration of the style that had shaped the Isaiah of Souillac.[22] No further step was possible in the same direction.

Yet in Late Romanesque art some tendencies indicating new directions came to the fore. When Master Gilabertus carved his Apostles for the Chapter House of Saint-Etienne in Toulouse he broke away from the dramatically charged and restless style of Souillac, Moissac, and his own workshop. In Lombardy Master Niccolo allowed his figures to project more and more from the jambs (fig. 7).

It was left to the Saint-Denis masters to free jamb statues from their direct contact with the plane of the wall, and to the Head Master of Chartres to lend them inner animation.

The statues of the central doorway of the Royal Portal still form part of a whole ideal system. They share with each other the quasi-columnar shape and the idea it implies. And yet they possess a limited self-existence, some natural qualities, and above all, specific inner attitudes. This gives them intrinsic values that are their very own. The incipient emphasis on individual characteristics, on animation from within, constitutes a definite shift. This does not seem to be just an isolated and merely formal phenomenon.

It corresponds to new psychological concepts and to new philosophical ideas.

It should also not be forgotten that the incipient humanization of sculptured figures took place at the very time when the concept of the eucharistic reality underwent a decisive change: from the concept of Christ removed from earth and no longer suffering to that of Christ born on earth so as to suffer death for mankind.

PART TWO The Sculptures of the

Transept Wings

CHAPTER I Genesis of the Sculp-

tural Cycles

Proving through word and through deed to be the Lady of Chartres,
Mary, the Mother of God, desired to rebuild the church in
Much more praiseworthy form, especially for her own sake,
Claiming the church as her own. A miraculous accident happened
Through the fury of Vulcan. She gave him leeway to ravage
So that the present-day fire be medicine for the sickness
Causing the House of the Lord to yearn with thirst never changing;
So that this ruin would give a reason for building a new house.
None is shining more brightly than this nowadays in the whole world,
Rising anew and completely after the stone had been dressed,
Already finished below the decor of the roof, it will never
Fear any damage by fire till the day of the Judgment arrives.
Out of this fire arose the salvation for numerous people
Through whose generous help renovation was brought to the building.[1]

GUILLAUME LE BRETON devoted these verses to the great fire of 1194 that completely destroyed Fulbert's cathedral, but spared the Royal Portal and its flanking towers. After the catastrophe had occurred the clerics and laymen of

Chartres in deep despair blamed their own sins for the loss of the Virgin's palace. But this dejection changed suddenly into exuberant joy when it was discovered that the most precious relic of the cathedral, the tunic of the Virgin, had been miraculously preserved. From then on the destruction of the building was regarded as an act of divine providence making it possible to build a more splendid house for the Virgin Mary.[2] It was this feeling that Guillaume le Breton cast into poetic form.

Instantly the rebuilding was undertaken with such energy and speed that in 1220 Guillaume le Breton saw the vaults—at least in part—completed.[3] It may be assumed that the portals of the transept façades were erected between about 1210 and 1220. Yet work on the earliest sculptures, namely those of the north transept, was in all likelihood begun some years before because of the desire to finish the new church as soon as possible.

The original architectural plan for the two transept façades grew in complexity while work was in progress. At first single entrances must have been planned for both transept wings, and the north façade was built accordingly. But when in about 1213 the south façade was started, the plan was revised and the south wing was given three portals. The north façade was then brought into harmony with the new layout, and two lateral doorways were broken into its walls. Finally, porches were added to both façades. This work was started on the north side about 1220, and on the south side in 1224 (figs. 43, 64).[4]

The change in the architectural layout necessarily affected the plan for the sculptural decoration. Originally the program must have been limited to single portals, as the architect had planned it. The northern portal was the first one to receive is sculptures carved between about 1205 and 1210. At the very time when it was decided to give the south transept three entrances, an enlarged iconographic program had to be devised for both transept wings. The actual decoration of the lateral doorways on the north side was begun only after the completion of the south portals. Finally, additional provisions had to be made for the sculptures of the porches.

While realizing their tasks the planners of the program were confronted with two special problems. In the first place, they perceived with their eyes, right from the outset, the sculptures of the Royal Portal, and they perceived with their minds the message these sculptures had conveyed to the churchgoers for almost two generations. In their own enterprise did they consider what had been represented before? Secondly, with the gradual amplification of the program, they had to expand a smaller nucleus of forms and ideas into a wider system. Was the result of this enlargement just patchwork, or did the enlargement intensify the meaning of the original core? A study of the transept sculptures should, therefore, include these two particular problems: the relation of the program of the twelfth century to that of the thirteenth and the relation of the later parts of the transept wings to the earlier parts.

The core of the iconographic program, as it must have been foreseen originally for the central portals in the north and south, honors Christ and the Virgin in the two tympana. In the north, the crowned Virgin is enthroned on the right side of Christ the King, who blesses her (fig. 47). In the south, Christ is the Judge of mankind, while Mary, together with John the Disciple, intercedes for humanity (fig. 76).

By comparison with the Royal Portal, the Virgin has moved to the center of the iconographic program. This is only in harmony with the general trend of the time and reflects the growing veneration of Mary. The cathedrals of Laon and Paris, both dedicated to the Virgin—one antedating with the sculpture of its west façade the Chartres transept by some years, the other somewhat later in its final façade plan than the first program for the Chartres transept—illustrate this point. At Laon as at Paris each of the three tympana on the west façade presents the Virgin to the churchgoer: within the Incarnation cycle, triumphantly enthroned with her Son in heaven, and as Intercessor on the day of judgment.[5]

The Virgin was given a prominent role also at Chartres, but her importance is more strongly emphasized. At Laon and Paris she is co-ordinated with Christ by her place and size in the scene of her Triumph, while in the Last Judgment she is subordinated to her Son by smaller size. At Chartres the belief in her power finds stronger expression. In both scenes she is as large as Christ.

The gradual amplification of the iconographic program opened for its authors opportunities that did not exist at Laon or Paris. When the successive stages of the work at Chartres were completed, six portals had been decorated with hundreds of figures and figure scenes (and in addition the porches built in front of the transept wings). The planners fully explored whatever possibility presented itself. Sometimes they remained within the broad stream of a firmly established iconographic tradition. At other times they proved to be bold inventors.

They assigned scenes of climactic impact to the central tympana and enhanced their meaning by subsidiary scenes in the lateral tympana. They made the sculptures of each portal parts of a specific ideological unit and, at the same time, ramifications of one general idea: the idea of Christ's relation to the Virgin Mary and to the Church, who is His Bride and His Body and whose primary members are the saints on earth and in heaven. The main structure of the iconographic program is based on concepts of St. Paul, while the meaning of its parts may be explained by liturgical texts.

CHAPTER II   The Sculptures of

the North Transept and its

Porch

I   TO START the interpretation with the earliest works
among the transept sculptures, the central portal of the north façade (fig. 44):
the Triumph of the Virgin in heaven, with the additional scenes of her Death
and Resurrection on the lintel, had been sculptured before on the church
façades at Senlis (*ca.* 1175; figs. 45, 49), Mantes (*ca.* 1180), and Laon
(*ca.* 1190; fig. 46).[1] The Chartres tympanum is, therefore, only a link in the
evolution of a theme then extremely popular for churches dedicated to the
Virgin Mary (fig. 47). What are its literary, what its formal sources?

At an early date apocryphal writings had supplied certain details lacking
in the canonical books of the New Testament, by giving an elaborate account
of Mary's death and resurrection. The Greek narrative mentions at the end
how a host of saints and Old Testament personages worship the Virgin in
heaven.[2] The Latin narratives do not go beyond the actual Assumption.[3] None
of these legends says, however, that Mary was crowned and allowed to sit
enthroned with her Son in heaven. Two passages of the Old Testament,
however, became famous when they were interpreted as specific predictions of

the Virgin's Triumph: "Come from Lebanon, my bride, come from Lebanon, come and thou shalt be crowned" (Cant. 4:8); and "The queen stood at thy right side in clothing of gold" (Ps. 44:10 [45:9]).⁴ Thus explained, these passages apparently closed the gap still extant in the apocryphal stories. They may be considered ultimate literary sources for the Triumph of the Virgin.

The ultimate formal sources for the representation of Christ and the Virgin enthroned side by side go back to the art of Antiquity, where gods and goddesses were shown enthroned side by side, and emperors, who shared the rule, also were shown sharing the throne.⁵ This type of representation entered the court art of Byzantium. On official coins, from the late sixth century on, the empress is enthroned next to her husband and partakes of his power and honor.⁶ Pervaded by religious ideas, the ceremonial art of the Byzantine court thus fostered for the imperial pair on earth a pictorial type similar to the image of the holy pair in heaven.

The representation of events from the end of Mary's life no doubt received a tremendous stimulus when in the sixth century the Dormition of the Virgin *(Koimesis)* was celebrated for the first time in the Eastern churches. Her death became a familiar subject in illuminated manuscripts, in ivories and, on a larger scale, in mosaics.⁷ Her Triumph in heaven was vividly described in homilies but, as far as I know, not represented in Byzantine art.⁸

It was due to the initiative of Pope Sergius (687–701) that the feast was introduced into the West under its original title: Dormition of the Virgin. About one hundred years later its name was changed to Assumption of the Virgin.⁹ This indicates a definite shift in emphasis. Instead of Mary's departure from earthly life, her glorious entry into heaven for eternal life is stressed as object of the celebration.

To say precisely when and where the Triumph of the Virgin received for the first time its monumental form in Western art is not possible. Emile Mâle has suggested that the representation made its appearance about 1140–43 in the apse mosaic of Santa Maria in Trastevere at Rome, and that this mosaic was derived from a stained-glass window commissioned by Abbot Suger for Notre-Dame in Paris.¹⁰

Western art, however, provides earlier representations which can be considered direct ancestors for the Roman mosaic and the Senlis tympanum. They are small in size, to be sure, but possibly suggest larger prototypes. On opposite pages of an Ottonian sacramentary a crowned Mary, holding a cross-staff like the Church, sits on the right-hand side of Christ.¹¹ Could this type of representation possibly reflect a ceremony customary in Rome during the vigil of Assumption day? The famous image of Christ which was kept in the chapel of Sancta Sanctorum was carried in the annual procession. At Santa Maria Maggiore it was, in all likelihood, placed on a throne next to an image of the Virgin Mary.¹²

The actual Coronation of the Virgin was represented in English art as early as the first half of the twelfth century on the tympanum of the church at Quenington (Gloucestershire) and on a capital from Reading Abbey.[13] Decorating either a church or an architectural member of minor importance, these reliefs most likely reflect a model of greater prominence no longer existing.

It is, therefore, by no means certain that the tympanum at Senlis is the earliest of its type carved in stone on a monumental scale. One may say with greater confidence that this very tympanum, combined with the Death and Resurrection of Mary, exerted a powerful influence on later representations.

While the historical meaning of the Virgin's Triumph is ultimately derived from the interpretation of biblical passages, its immediate roots lie in the liturgy. The bulk of the lessons for the feast day and the octave of Mary's Assumption were drawn from a letter traditionally ascribed to St. Jerome, very likely a fabrication made under the name of the Church Father by Paschasius Radbertus in the ninth century. This letter not only quotes the famous sentence from the Song of Songs; it also can explain why in the tympanum Mary is crowned like a queen and why the architectural framework surrounding the pair in heaven is not just a compositional device but, above all, an architectural symbol: "The Queen of the world is translated today from earth . . . and already has reached the palace of heaven." It also explains that Mary is accorded the honor of being enthroned with her Son, for "with joy the Savior lets her share His throne," or again: "Elevated in a manner one cannot describe she rules for ever with Christ."[14] In the central tympanum of the Royal Portal the idea of Christ's kingship had been expressed by the symbol of the crown held by Angels above His head. On the north transept Christ is actually shown as King wearing a crown, but this concept of kingship is less austere. He allows his mother to reign with him in heaven and she is thus given the right to plead with her son for the sake of mankind.

The monumental composition of the Triumph of the Virgin dominates two smaller scenes on the lintel, her Death and Resurrection. Mary's death had been represented often before, either by itself or in conjunction with her soul lifted up, if not actually carried to heaven.[15] The lintels of Senlis and Chartres follow therefore a traditional type (figs. 49, 47). The Apostles are grouped around her bed, while (at Chartres) Christ receives her soul. The Resurrection is added to this scene. Angels raise Mary's body from the tomb, reuniting it with her soul. One might say that the shape of a lintel was too long to be formally suited for one scene only. But there also were strong theological reasons for including the Resurrection. The apocryphal stories describe Mary's Resurrection, but they were never officially recognized by the Church. Throughout the middle ages, therefore, theologians were in doubt as to whether the Virgin was translated into heaven with soul and body or only with her soul. Pseudo-Jerome, for instance, disapproving of apocryphal legends, stated the question, but did not give an unequivocal answer: "But in what manner or at which time or by what persons her most holy body was taken away from there, or whither it was brought, or whether she was resurrected is not known, although some people would hold that she is already resurrected and, together with Christ, endowed with blessed immortality in heaven."[16] A treatise ascribed to St. Augustine, however, and following it a number of theologians—Bishop Fulbert was foremost among them—affirmed the belief in the Resurrection of Mary's body.[17] In a more dramatic vein Elizabeth of Schönau, the German mystic of the twelfth century, described how she suffered mental agony until the Virgin appeared to her and said that she was resurrected in soul and body.[18] Thus, to confound the doubters and to reassure the believers, the Resurrection of Mary is added to the scene of her Death on the lintel. Made visible is this miraculous event which only in 1950 was declared a dogma.

In the innermost archivolt the Hierarchy of Angels frames the pair, for according to Pseudo-Jerome, "Mary was worthy to be exalted over the choirs of the angels," and "rightly she surpassed the dignity of angels and archangels."[19]

The outer archivolts contain Christ's Ancestors according to the flesh, the Tree of Jesse. "But the Mother of God," the letter says, "ascended from the wilderness of the present life, the rod that once came forth out of the stem of Jesse."[20]

Thus the letter of Pseudo-Jerome was not only read during the canonical hours of the Assumption week, but also provided the main literary source for the representation of Mary's Triumph in heaven.

II   BEYOND its historical meaning the glorification of Mary has an allegorical one, for the Virgin typifies the Church who is the Bride of Christ.

Medieval theology had established a perfect parallel between Mary and the Church. According to the Gospels, Mary was both Virgin and Mother of Christ. Having been chosen by the Lord as the vehicle of the Incarnation, she was considered to be the Bride of God.[21]

The Church was likewise defined as the Bride of Christ, so as to give the faithful a clear understanding of her close, permanent, and loving union with the Savior. St. Paul had admonished husbands to love their wives "even as Christ also loved the Church, and gave Himself for it" (Eph. 5:25). According to the Book of Revelation, the Holy City, the New Jerusalem, obviously symbolizing the Church, came down from heaven "prepared as a bride adorned for her husband" (Rev. 21:2).

Like Mary, the Church was called virgin and mother, since every day she gives birth to her members. To quote but one of the innumerable passages that refer to this likeness between Mary and the Church: "As the Mother of Christ conceived as Virgin, gave birth as Virgin, and remained a Virgin," said

Ivo of Chartres, "so the Mother Church, the Bride of Christ, daily brings forth the Christian people in the word through the bath of water, so as to remain a virgin."[22]

After the fire of 1194 the desire to identify the Cathedral of Chartres with the Virgin Mary, her patron saint, materialized in a significant change in the liturgy. Henceforth one ceased to celebrate on October 17 the special office for the Dedication of the Church, and celebrated instead a Commemoration of the Virgin Mary.[23]

The early Fathers of the Church had interpreted the Song of Songs as the loving union between Christ and the Church or between Christ and the human soul. Later on, some passages were occasionally related to the Virgin Mary. It was, however, in the twelfth century that Solomon's nuptial song began to be generally explained more broadly. It was said that the bride in the Song of Songs could be understood as both the Church and the Virgin Mary.[24] Thus the exegesis went beyond the confines of conceptual ecclesiology and took a more concretely humanized aspect. This change, in keeping with the growing worship of the Virgin, may well have contributed its share to the popularity enjoyed from the later twelfth century onwards by the representation of the Triumph of the Virgin, who also typifies the Church. A commentary ascribed to Alan of Lille, for instance, interpreted the Song of Songs in this manner: "As the Song of Love, namely the nuptial song of Solomon, refers specifically and spiritually to the Church, nevertheless, whatever we will explain as best we can under divine inspiration, is brought back most specifically and most spiritually to the glorious Virgin."[25] The interchangeability of Mary and the Church was stressed repeatedly in a commentary on the Song of Songs most likely written by Peter of Roissy, chancellor of the School of Chartres between 1208 and 1213.[26]

The interpretation of Mary as the type of the Church was also recognized in the liturgy. According to the *Glossa ordinaria* the Forty-fourth Psalm is sung on the day of the Virgin, because what is said in general about the Church, may be specifically related to Mary.[27] John Beleth stated it more elaborately in his *Rationale divinorum officiorum,* written about 1160: "During this feast of the Assumption psalms etc. are sung especially about the Blessed Virgin, which are usually recited on the day of the Dedication of the Church, for as the Church is the mother of all saints and has the name of virginity, that is to say of mind and faith, which is better than that of the body, so she is called the bride of Christ. Therefore it was said: 'I have espoused you to one husband, that I may present you as a chaste virgin to Christ' (II Cor. 11:2), and so the Blessed Mary is truly called the Virgin and the most saintly of saints."[28]

The concept of the Church had appeared in a rudimentary state in the Incarnation cycle of the Royal Portal where the Holy Animals and the participants in the Presentation of Christ refer to the members of the Church. On the north transept this concept is more decisively realized. Honored by

Christ, the Virgin Mary typifies the Church, His Bride.

While the tympana of Senlis, Laon, and Chartres conform to the same iconographic scheme, the sculptor of the left tympanum on the west façade of Notre-Dame in Paris both simplified and amplified the representation (*ca.* 1220; fig. 48). He restricted the main scene to its bare essentials. He omitted the canopy, but made Mary's Coronation more explicit, because an Angel performs this function. In a radically simplifying manner he eliminated the scene of Mary's Death, or rather made the witnesses of her death, Christ and the Apostles, part of the Resurrection scene. By the addition of a lower lintel, on the other hand, he enriched the subject matter and clarified the allegorical meaning of Mary's Triumph. The Ark of the Covenant stands underneath a canopy in the center of the lintel as a symbol of both the Old Testament and the Church.[29] Three Kings and three Prophets flank it. They allude to *regnum* and *sacerdotium,* on whose harmony the Church securely rests.

About ten years later the sculptor of the right tympanum on the west façade of the cathedral at Amiens harmonizes all the earlier achievements. He reconstitutes the traditional composition. Once more the scenes of Death and Resurrection are represented. But in part he also simplifies. He eliminates the Kings in the lower lintel. Moses and Aaron have their places next to the Ark. Then follow two Prophets on either side.[30]

Still later tympana add more personal traits to the well-established theme. On the south transept of Strasbourg Cathedral Christ is more intimately related to His mother; He Himself places the crown on her head. On the Porte Rouge of Notre-Dame in Paris the pair of heavenly rulers is related to Louis IX and Margaret of Provence. Humbly kneeling they frame the central group.[31]

At Senlis, and also at Chartres, the union of Christ and the Church— allegorically implied in the Triumph of the Virgin—is supported, as it were, by statues flanking the doorway. Eight of the twelve statues at Chartres are derived from Senlis and possibly from Laon (where they are no longer preserved). Yet these statues are differently arranged on the façades at Senlis and at Chartres.

At Senlis two separate rows of four figures lead from the time of the Old Testament to the era of grace, if we follow their temporal sequence on either side (fig. 49). On the left-hand side the cycle begins with Abraham sacrificing Isaac (next to the entrance); then follow Moses, Samuel, and John the Baptist. On the right-hand side the series starts with David (farthest away from the entrance) and continues with Isaiah, Jeremiah, and Simeon holding the Child. Although the historical sequence of the group on the left runs from the doorway to the outside, and that of the group on the right from the outside to the doorway, a meaningful correspondence exists between the statues next to the entrance. Here Abraham and Simeon are shown with children: Isaac prefigures Christ's sacrifice, and the Child Jesus in the arms of Simeon prefigures His own sacrifice.

At Chartres the complexity of the arrangement disappears and the figures are lined up in a continuous chronological order from the left to the right (figs. 50, 51): Abraham, Moses, Samuel, and David on the left side; Isaiah, Jeremiah, Simeon, and John the Baptist on the right side. This group is enlarged because of the desire to make the statues correspond in number to the twelve Apostles who flank the central portal in the south. At the beginning and end respectively Melchizedek and St. Peter are added. They extend the chronological sequence on either side. Yet disregarding time, Elisha and Elijah are placed next to Melchizedek and St. Peter so that they form a frame for the group of ten.[32]

Apart from the order achieved by the chronological arrangement of the figures, further structural clarity is gained by the juxtaposition of certain statues: of King and Prophet (David–Isaiah), of King-Priest and Priest (Melchizedek–St. Peter), of two Prophets (Elisha–Elijah).

The twelve statues flank the *trumeau* with St. Anne holding the Infant Mary in her arms. The relic of St. Anne's head had been taken by Count Louis of Chartres in 1204 during the sack of Constantinople and presented to the cathedral by the Countess Catherine. This precious possession must have caused the planners to give the statue of the saint a special place of honor. At the same time, it made it possible to show Mary as a child immediately underneath those events that are crowned by her final Triumph in heaven.

In Chartres, as before in Senlis, and possibly in Laon and Mantes, the statues lining the jambs fulfill a threefold function. First of all, they exemplify the whole history of salvation, the continuity of the pre-Christian and Christian Church. For St. Gregory, the saints before the Law, the saints under the Law, and the saints in the era of grace all were constituted among the members of the Church.[33] St. Augustine had even specified these sons of promise and grace as Abraham and Moses as well as the prophets and the holy men down to John the Baptist.[34] His list coincides with the series of statues at Senlis and the nucleus of the Chartres group. Secondly, the figures bear witness to the betrothal of the Lord and the Church in different periods of history. Lastly, they prefigure Christ or refer to Him, the priest and sacrifice of the Eucharist. They stress the fact that through the Eucharist the Church is united with Him.

They are the witnesses of the Church whom the Lord betrothed three times, according to the allegorical interpretation that St. Jerome gave of Hosea's marriage (Hos. 2:19, 20): "We ask why he repeats three times the word betrothal. At first he said: 'I will betroth thee unto me for ever.' A second time: 'I will betroth thee unto me in righteousness, and in judgment, and in loving-kindness, and in mercies.' And not satisfied with this ending, he added a third sentence: 'I will even betroth thee unto me in faithfulness, and thou shalt know the Lord.' The first time He betrothed her in the person of Abraham or in Egypt, so as to have a wife for ever. The second time on mount Sinai, giving her as dowry the righteousness and judgment of the law and, combined with the law, loving-kindness so that she would be led to captivity when committing sins, and would be called back home when doing penitence, and thus receive loving-kindness. . . .

"This harlot, therefore, who was at first bound by the bridegroom's vow to be embraced for ever, so as never to relinquish the tie of matrimony, is received again by the Law because she had left and committed adultery in Egypt. Since she broke it when the prophets, the companions of the bridegroom, as it were, were slain, the Son of God came in the last days, the Lord Jesus. When He was crucified and resurrected from the dead, she was betrothed, yet not in the righteousness of the law but in the faith and grace of the Gospel, so that by knowing the only-born she may also know the Father."[35]

This allegorical interpretation was sharpened in a sermon of Hildebert of Lavardin, bishop of Le Mans and archbishop of Tours: "Christ is the bridegroom, His bride the Church, whom He betrothed three times, as he says through Hosea: 'I will betroth thee unto me for ever; yeah, I will betroth thee unto me in righteousness and in loving-kindness, and I will betroth thee unto me in faithfulness.' Three times her bridegroom says that He will betroth her: for the first time, in the era of the patriarchs who kept His ring inviolate and received the dowry of the natural law and of some heavenly precepts . . . ; for the second time, in the epoch of the prophets, when He gave them as wedding gifts the justifications and the judgments of the law of Moses and added loving-kindness to it, asking them to repent so as to escape the misery of captivity; for the third time, He betrothed her in the advent of His Son, when He declared the faith in the Trinity through the Gospels, and accepted as gifts the evangelical precepts and the sacraments; and then He liberated her from the hands of her enemies, namely from the demons who had totally violated her, that is to say, spoiled her through the state of idolatry. But when He came Himself and betrothed her for the third time, He cleaned her from the blood of sins and made her immaculate, as He says through Ezekiel: 'I washed thee with water and I thoroughly washed away thy blood from thee, and I anointed thee with oil, and shod thee with badger's skin. I girded thee about with fine linen, and I decked thee also with ornaments. And I put a crown on thy head and thou wast made my bride' " (Ezek. 16:9–12). The passage ends: "She is crowned with the diadem of eternal beauty and thus made lovable to the bridegroom."[36] If interpreted along these lines, the jamb statues at Chartres represent witnesses of the eras in which the Lord espoused the Church. After her earlier aberrations she is finally crowned in the image of Mary and resides triumphantly with Christ in heaven.

At the same time, the statues refer typologically to the death of Christ re-enacted in the Eucharist, in which Christ is both priest and sacrifice. Of all the sacraments the Eucharist most strongly unites the Church with Christ. Abraham prefigures God the Father, Isaac the sacrifice of Christ.[37] Moses not only anticipates the giver of the New Law by holding the tablets of the Old

Law. Significantly he points to the brazen serpent raised on a column and thereby refers typologically to Christ elevated on the cross.[38] Offering a lamb, Samuel prefigures Christ the priest; by his action he prefigures the Eucharist. King David holds crown, spear, and nails. He had predicted the Passion.[39] Isaiah had prophesied His birth and death, Jeremiah His suffering. Simeon, who holds the Infant Jesus in his arms, had foreseen His death, for He told Mary that she would suffer. John the Baptist presents the Agnus Dei to the churchgoer.

In Senlis, but not at Chartres, the small semi-nude figure of a man kneels at John's feet (fig. 49). He obviously refers to the sacrament of baptism, by which the Christian is made a member of the Church. St. John is the last, from a historical point of view, within the group to the left of the portal. Simeon has the same place among the figures on the other side. Holding the Child in his arms, he alludes to the self-sacrifice of Christ to be re-enacted in the Eucharist, by which the members of the Church receive true life. Thus both groups of statues are terminated by personages who refer to the two most important sacramental concepts.[40] With John the Baptist farthest away from the entrance and Simeon next to it, the churchgoer entering the cathedral is led, as it were, from Baptism to Eucharist.

The same basic idea had been represented before in an Ottonian miniature, an illustration of the Song of Songs. The personification of the Church receives a long procession of saints which proceeds from the sacramental scene of Baptism to the Crucifixion of Christ.[41]

The planners of Chartres omitted the baptismal aspect, but they sharpened the eucharistic concept (figs. 50, 51) that had played such an important role in the Incarnation cycle of the Royal Portal. Melchizedek "who brought forth bread and wine" for Abraham (Gen. 14:18) is the king-priest, prominent prototype of Christ (Heb. 5:10). His counterpart is St. Peter, dressed in the garb of the high priest. Unlike the other statues of the Old Testament, Melchizedek does not simply allude to the self-sacrifice of Christ. In anticipation of the Eucharist, he holds in his hands its actual elements, the host and the chalice with wine. These elements were likewise shown to the beholder by St. Peter, before they were broken off, with the exception of the foot of the chalice. As vicar of Christ on earth and continuing the priesthood of the Old Testament, St. Peter is the foremost member of the clergy which continues to administer the Eucharist. Melchizedek stands on a lamb, as it had been offered from the time of Abel on and as it refers to Christ, the Agnus Dei. The feet of St. Peter rest on the rock, the foundation of the Church.

Thus ten of the Chartres figures are related to both Christ and the Church, His Bride. This double relation is confirmed by the statues of Elisha and Elijah. Each Prophet prefigures a particular moment of Christ's life, Elisha its beginning, Elijah its end. Elisha prefigures His Incarnation. He lay upon the dead son of the Shunammite to bring him back to life, as Christ, "being in the

form of God, thought it not robbery to be equal with God, but made himself
of no reputation, and took upon him the form of a servant, and was made in
the likeness of men" (Phil. 2:6, 7).[42] Elijah prefigures the Ascension of Christ
for he was taken up to heaven in a chariot of fire.[43] The reliefs of the pedestals
refer to the Church. The Shunammite at Elisha's feet typifies the Holy Church
who humbly begged the Lord through the fathers for the redemption of
mankind.[44] This idea is reiterated on the pedestal underneath Elijah. Here the
small figure of Elisha receiving the mantle of his ascending master stands for
the Church as she preserves the faith in the Incarnation of Christ after His
Ascension.[45]

In this way the sculptures of the central portal, like their predecessors on
other church façades, form part of a comprehensive system that combines two
ideas: the relation of Christ to His mother in glory, and His relation to the
Church, His Bride, throughout the three eras of religious history.

As the Triumph of Mary-Ecclesia had undergone an iconographic
evolution from the late twelfth century to the first half of the thirteenth, so did
the cycle of jamb statues accompanying it. The Chartres group amplified the
number of figures compared with Senlis, clarified their arrangement, and
stressed more strongly the eucharistic concept.

On the façade of Saint-Nicolas at Amiens (*ca.* 1210), now destroyed,
the Senlis core of figures was enlarged, not as in Chartres by Melchizedek and
St. Peter, but by a King and a Queen.[46] They were most likely King Solomon
and the Queen of Sheba. As traditional prototypes of Christ and the Church,
the earthly King and Queen at Amiens linked the lower group more strongly to
the King and Queen of heaven.

Since on the west façade of the cathedral at Amiens no doorway was
dedicated exclusively to the Incarnation of Christ, the right portal combines
the Triumph of Mary-Ecclesia with scenes from the Incarnation (*ca.*
1220–30). The jamb statues represent the Annunciation, Visitation, the
Presentation of Christ and Adoration of the Magi. Thereby the idea of
witnesses who exemplify the successive epochs of Church history is given up,
but the relation to the Old Testament is preserved by the addition of Solomon
and the Queen of Sheba to the figures of the New Testament.[47]

III   A NEW problem faced the planners of the north façade at Chartres
when they decided to add lateral doorways to the central portal (figs. 52, 57).
They had to enlarge the original program of representation into a more
comprehensive scheme. How did they do it? The left portal of the cathedral
at Laon (*ca.* 1190) provided a partial answer to their problem (fig. 56).[48]
The planners of Chartres adopted from it the subject matter for the left-hand
tympanum and lintel. Thus, they represented on the lintel the Nativity of

Christ and the Annunciation to the Shepherds; on the tympanum they showed
the Adoration of the Magi, to which they added the scene of the three sleeping
Magi (fig. 53). The events preceding the Nativity and showing the mystery of
the Incarnation—that is, the Annunciation and Visitation—were represented
by pairs of statues, and related to Old Testament prophecies by the addition
of Isaiah and Daniel (figs. 54, 55). These six figures are so arranged that the
two sides balance each other and a hierarchical progression towards the door
takes place. Each side begins at its outer end with a Prophet and terminates at
the entrance with the Virgin Mary.

What was the reason, one might ask, that prompted the planners of
Chartres to duplicate most of the scenes already existing in the Incarnation
cycle of the Royal Portal? (The situation was different at Laon, where no such
repetition had taken place.) The answer may be given by the letter of Pseudo-
Jerome. The Virgin, so the letter says, was accorded the privilege of glorification
because she was the mother of Christ.[49] Therefore at Chartres, as before at
Laon, her very quality as instrument of the Incarnation was made visible on the
left portal so as to illustrate an integral part of the liturgy for the feast of the
Assumption.

Within this particular context the doctrine is represented once more, but
less explicitly than on the Royal Portal, that Mary is the Mother of Christ
as God and man. The direct influence of Pseudo-Jerome is obvious: "For in
such manner we must believe in the Mother of the Lord and give honor to her
who gave us God and man; neither man without God nor God without man,
but one and true God and man, Jesus Christ."[50] In a later passage this dogma is
explained by the Nativity and the Adoration of the Magi: "Therefore the fact
that the Virgin conceived and gave birth is not devoid of the power of the
Word, and likewise, it is not devoid of the truth of the flesh that He lies in
swaddling clothes and rests in the manger. Furthermore, the fact that He is
adored by the Magi with the star as their guide shows His Godhead."[51] The
influence of this passage may be seen in the star that stands prominently above
the Adoration scene. (At Laon the star, now missing, was held by an Angel.)

The Chartres tympanum and its lintel do not exactly coincide with the
Laon model, and there are, it seems, specific reasons for that. Not only were
the figures of an Angel and of Joseph in the tympanum replaced by the sleeping
Magi; not only was the Annunciation shifted to the jambs; more important,
the hieratic type of the Virgin holding the Child was eased and the ideographic
axial relation of the central group in the tympanum to the Nativity scene was
given up.

The planners of the Incarnation tympanum at Laon were not confronted
with the difficulty that an earlier cycle of the same kind existed on their
cathedral. They chose, therefore, a clear structural layout similar to that of
the Incarnation tympanum on the Royal Portal (fig. 56). The Virgin is
represented as Theotokos–*Sedes Sapientiae* underneath a canopy. Thereby the

group is hieratically frozen and singled out within the historical scene of the Adoration. As on the Royal Portal, the idea of Christ's two natures and of the eucharistic reality is stressed at Laon by a meaningful central axis and an altar-like manger.

The situation was different when the Incarnation tympanum on the north façade of Chartres Cathedral was created (fig. 53). There was no need to repeat exactly what had been achieved before on the Royal Portal. Consequently, the emphasis was shifted from an ideographic system to a narrative sequence of scenes embodying ideas. The newborn Babe does not lie on an altar underneath the Child adored but, as Pseudo-Jerome simply states, "He lies in swaddling clothes and rests in the manger," while Mary points lovingly with her hand to Him. Not separated by a canopy from the three Magi, both the Virgin and Child turn strongly towards them, and are actively related to the worshipers.

Even the choice of the subject matter for the archivolts indicates the influence of Pseudo-Jerome, but this influence is not the same at Laon and at Chartres. At Chartres the second archivolt and the lowest sections of the third archivolt contain the Wise and Foolish Virgins.[52] They illustrate one of the primary parables of the Last Judgment and traditionally were associated with this event. At Laon they frame the tympanum of the Last Judgment. At Chartres they seem at first glance out of place; but they are mentioned in the letter of Pseudo-Jerome: "Yet there are wise and foolish virgins. Therefore, my beloved, imitate the blessed and glorious Virgin whom you love and whose feast you celebrate today on earth."[53] In a sermon on the Virgin, Fulbert of Chartres had established an even more definite relation between the parable and the Virgin Mary, whom he calls "the queen of all wise virgins."[54]

In part the subject matter of the Laon and Chartres archivolts is similar. Both show cycles of personified Virtues who have victoriously overcome Vices. At Chartres the group comprises the three theological Virtues, the four cardinal Virtues, and Humility. "If you look at her (i.e. the Virgin Mary) more attentively, there is no virtue, no beauty, no candor and glory which does not shine forth from her," says Pseudo-Jerome. And then he continues: "Her foremost virtue is the foundation and preserver of all virtues, Humility herself, of whom she gives praise: 'For He hath regarded the humility of His hand-maiden; for, behold, from henceforth all generations shall call me blessed' " (Luke 1: 48).[55]

IV   THE planners of Chartres worked out a highly original kind of program for the right portal. Not only were most of the figures and figure scenes new on a church façade, but the ideological system achieved by their combination was equally bold in concept (fig. 57).

The tympanum shows the suffering Job on the dung heap, tortured by the Devil, while his wife and his three friends argue with him (figs. 58, 59). On the lintel the Judgment of Solomon is about to be carried out. The two inner archivolts contain scenes from the lives of Samson and Gideon, and of Esther and Judith. The outermost archivolt is dedicated in its entirety to the story of Tobit and Tobias (figs. 60, 61). Along the jambs stand Balaam, the Queen of Sheba, and King Solomon on the left side; Jesus Sirach, Judith, and Joseph are on the right side (figs. 62, 63). The entire program is drawn from the Old Testament. The various figures have been explained—in a rather spotty manner—as prototypes of Christ and Mary.[56] Yet it seems that they illustrate various aspects of one idea. They were chosen so as to prove typologically the union of Christ and the Church, who has to endure hardships.

In order to illustrate graphically both the indissoluble unity of Christ and the Church and the subordination of the Church to Christ, Paul had called Christ the Head and the Church His Body (Eph. 1:22f.; 4:15; Col. 1:18, 24). In accordance with this simile, the suffering Job in one person prefigures Christ and the Church. In his famous commentary on the Book of Job, St. Gregory had said: "One must also know that our Redeemer showed Himself to be one person with the Church He has assumed. It is namely said of Him: 'Who is the head, namely Christ' (Eph. 4:15). And on the other hand, it is written of His Church: 'and the body of Christ, which is the Church' (Col. 1:24). The blessed Job, therefore, was the prototype of the Mediator even more truly. He prophesied His passion not just with words but also by His suffering. Since he tends to express the Redeemer in words and deeds, sometimes his body becomes suddenly meaningful. We see, therefore, signified by the actions of one person our belief in Christ and the Church as one person."[57] In another passage St. Gregory states: "Job means 'the one who is suffering.' It is no wonder that by this suffering the Passion of the Mediator is expressed or the distress of the Church, who is tortured by the manifold weariness of the present life."[58] The Church Father says of Job's suffering: "From the sole of His foot unto his crown he received wounds, since the raging tempter afflicts the Holy Church, His body, with persecution not only at the extremities but up to the highest members."[59]

Job's wife who provokes him to malediction was interpreted by St. Gregory as "the life of the flesh," and the three friends are the heretics "who under the disguise of counseling make it their business to seduce him."[60]

According to this explanation, the scene in the tympanum prefigures the various attacks on Christ's Body, which is the Church, and its successful resistance to these onslaughts. As the left tympanum complements Mary glorified in heaven by showing her as the instrument of the Incarnation, so the right tympanum complements Mary-Ecclesia, the Bride of Christ, by showing the Church as His Body. The iconographic coherence of the three tympana is made clear by two devices: the representation of Christ (or the Logos) flanked by two Angels in each tympanum, and a group of Angels in each of the innermost archivolts.

The two Pauline concepts of the close union between Christ and the Church could not have been more clearly illustrated side by side. "As they are called bridegroom and bride," states the *Glossa ordinaria,* "so also head and body. Whether one says, therefore, head and body or bridegroom and bride, understand them as just one. For out of two becomes one person, as it were, namely out of head and body, out of bridegroom and bride"[61]

At this point one should remember two facts. First, the representation of the two concepts was not planned at the same time, but resulted from the amplification of the original program. Second, the Church theologically seen, is the Body and Bride of Christ both on earth and in heaven.

In the tympana the two concepts are not made visible in the totality of their meaning, as far as the existence of the Church on earth and in heaven is concerned. In other words, the Church as Bride of Christ is shown in heaven, but not on earth. The Church as Body of Christ is shown on earth, but not in heaven. It was obviously impossible to make the two concepts visible in the totality of their meaning when they were translated from theological definitions into stone sculptures. What is actually represented may be termed a selective illustration in consonance with the concept that the Church reigns in heaven and is militant on earth. The earlier tympanum accentuates the triumphant character of the Church as the Bride of Christ reigning with Him in heaven. The later tympanum accentuates the militant character of the Church as the Body of Christ attacked on earth. In the Book of Job we read: "Warfare (*militia*) is the life of man on earth" (7:1). The close connection between the two parts of the Church was stressed in the liturgy. When the priest celebrates the Mass, he prays for the union of the Church militant and the Church triumphant.[62]

The Judgment of Solomon corroborates the idea of the afflicted Church. According to a sermon ascribed to St. Augustine, the true mother typifies the Church, the false mother the Synagogue. King Solomon symbolizes Christ. He gives to each mother what she deserves.[63] In a more dramatic manner St. Bernard scolds the false mother: "And thou, impious Synagogue, hast given us this son according to a mother's duty, but without the love of a mother . . . Thou hast cast Him off thy bosom and hast thrown Him out of the city and raised Him above the earth, telling, as it were, the Church out of Gentiles and at the same time the original Church who is in heaven: 'Let it be neither mine nor thine, but divide it' " (I Kings 3:26).[64] In this way the false mother, the Synagogue, in the lintel is contrasted not only with the right mother, the Church, but also with the Mother of Christ in the Nativity of the left-hand lintel, so that an antithesis between the two lintels is established. (The allegorical meaning of Solomon's Judgment was explicitly represented about 1230 on the south transept of Strasbourg Cathedral. Here King Solomon is shown on the *trumeau,* flanked by statues of the Church and the Synagogue on the walls).[65]

The Suffering of Job and the Judgment of Solomon demonstrate the successful endurance of the Church against temptations of the Devil, of the flesh, of heresies, and against her antagonist, the Synagogue.

The five narrative cycles of the archivolts develop further this idea (figs. 60, 61). They refer typologically to Christ and the Church, according to the standard commentaries of the Venerable Bede and Hrabanus Maurus which were to a large extent incorporated in the *Glossa ordinaria.* Yet while tympanum and lintel refer to the afflictions of the Church, the archivolt scenes make it clear that all the suffering and every struggle will lead to final victory. In their temporal sequence and their climactic endings at the top of the archivolts, the cycles of Samson and Gideon, of Esther and Judith correspond to the biblical stories from which they were selected.

To begin with the cycles of Samson and Gideon: the four scenes of each series balance each other in form and meaning. The two heroes of the Old Testament were considered to be prototypes of Christ, Samson prefiguring His death and victory, Gideon His conquering of the world in the sign of the cross.[66]

Each cycle starts with a sacrifice at which an Angel appears. Praying for a son, Manoah offers a kid with meat, when the Angel who prefigures the future sacrifice of Christ ascends in a flame (Judg. 13:19, 20).[67] Gideon presents a kid with unleavened cakes beneath an oak tree. He prefigures Christ under the shadow of the cross, and then the Angel departs out of his sight (Judg. 6:19–21).[68]

In the next scenes Samson kills the lion (Judg. 14:5, 6) and Gideon brings an offering on the former site of an altar dedicated to Baal (Judg. 6:25–27). Both overcome evil in this way.[69]

While Samson experiences a miracle, when he extracts honey from the mouth of the lion (Judg. 14:8, 9), Gideon beholds the miracle of the fleece bedecked with dew while the earth besides is dry (Judg. 6:36–38). One scene symbolizes the salvation of the Gentiles. They had honey because they believed. Once they belonged to the body of wilderness, but now they are Christ's.[70] The fleece bedecked with dew prefigures the mystery of grace accorded first to the Jews, while the rest of the world lacked it.[71]

The two topmost scenes represent the final triumph. Samson carries off the gates of Gaza (Judg. 16:3). He prefigures the Resurrection and Ascension of Christ, after He had destroyed the gates of hell.[72] Gideon holds two kings of Midian as captives (Judg. 8:12). They are the philosophers and heretics, the members of the Devil.[73]

While these two cycles prefigure Christ's work of salvation, the scenes from the lives of Esther and Judith show two heroines as prototypes of the Church because of their successful struggles against enemies. Esther overcomes the danger of Haman through humble pleas. Judith vanquishes Holofernes through a heroic deed. According to Hrabanus Maurus, the Book of Esther contains as in a mystery the sacraments of Christ and the Church. Judith formerly had been married to Manasseh. He typifies either the Law of the decalogue or pagan rites.[74]

In the first scene on the left side, Ahasuerus marries and crowns Esther (Esther 2:17). His wife had been Queen Vashti, the Synagogue, but now Esther is made queen in her stead.[75] Then Mordecai who typifies the teachers of the Gentiles, mainly St. Paul, kneels besides Haman.[76] Turning away, Haman holds the letter that will give him the power to persecute the Gentiles (Esther 3:8ff.). With complete disregard for the literal meaning of the text, Haman is interpreted as the Jews who did not accept as proof for their own heresy the books of the divine law, who tried to reject the conversion of the Gentiles and condemned the Gospel as contrary to the divine precepts.[77]

Mordecai is shown mourning in the following scene. He typifies the teachers of the Church (Esther 4:1). They fast in time of persecution; they pray and wake with tears and repentance so that they may be saved by the dignity and the prayers of the true queen, the Church, who partly is wandering on earth and partly ruling with Christ in heaven.[78]

Then Esther humbly asks Ahasuerus to save her people (Esther 5:1ff.). Ahasuerus, who typifies Christ, liberates the faithful from the hands of their enemies because of the daily prayers of His bride, the Church.[79]

Finally, Mordecai gives to a messenger the new letter that revokes Haman's decree (Esther 9:20–22). The letter stands for the doctrine of the Gospel. The preachers will spread it throughout the world.[80]

In the first scene on the right side, Judith leaves an elder in charge of the gate, as the Church entrusts the fortress of God to the priests (Jth. 8:10 ff.).[81]

Then before setting out for her great task, she put on a hair garment, thus repenting her sins. She laid ashes on her head, remembering her frailty. And then she kneels in prayer, hoping to be heard by the Lord because of her humility (Jth. 9:1ff.).[82]

Beautifully dressed she leaves the city with her maid (Jth. 10:3 ff.), as the Church shines with the beauty of all her virtues.[83]

She kneels before Holofernes (Jth. 10:20), the Antichrist, thus giving honor to the earthly power according to the law and not because of adulation.[84]

In the scene of her final triumph, she hands over to her maid the head of Holofernes (Jth. 13:10, 11), for the Church leaves to the faithful a reminder of the finished battle.[85]

There is again formal or iconographic correspondence between some juxtaposed reliefs of the two cycles. This gives order to the total composition. While Mordecai has fallen on his knees, Judith kneels in prayer. The correspondence is more outspoken when Esther kneels before Ahasuerus, and

Judith before Holofernes. Not unlike the topmost scenes of Samson and Gideon, the two last events in the cycles of the women stress final triumph. Mordecai displays the letter that assures the spread of the right faith. Judith holds the head of the enemy of the Church.

In the innermost archivolt, Angels display symbols that accompany and sum up, as it were, the ideas of the adjoining cycles. In the lowest part, two Angels hold sun and moon, symbols of Christ and the Church; the next ones hold stars, symbols of the saints.[86] Although sun, moon, and stars differ in clarity, there is one clarity illuminating everything, as the letter of Pseudo-Jerome defines it and as it is shown by the torches in the hands of two Angels on either side.[87] Further up, sword and shield are displayed, symbols of struggle. The last pair of Angels hold crowns, symbols of the final victory achieved by Samson and Gideon, by Esther and Judith.

The cycle of Tobit and Tobias occupies the whole outer archivolt and acts as frame for the four other cycles. It has to be read clockwise from the left to the right. If interpreted in accordance with the commentary of the Venerable Bede, the cycle comprises the sacraments of Christ and the Church, and gives an all-inclusive illustration of the final salvation of the Jews by Christ and the Church.

Tobit symbolizes Israel. While the Gentiles worshiped idols, he served the Lord in the right faith. He served Him with just works as the first two scenes show, where Tobit prepares a meal and buries a dead man (Tob. 2:1 ff.).[88] But then he is blinded in his sleep, for he was not indefatigable (Tob. 2:10, 11). Israel's blindness was apparent just before the advent of the Lord, when the Jews were under the Roman yoke and violated the precepts of the divine law by their sinful life.[89] Tobit's wife who comforts him is the Synagogue.[90]

The following reliefs show how he sends out his son, namely Christ, the messenger of the paternal will, and blesses him, while the Angel Raphael stands by (Tob. 5:5 ff.).[91] Tobias and the Angel depart (Tob. 6:1), and Tobias catches a fish (Tob. 6:2–5), as the Lord apprehended the Devil who wanted to catch the dying, but instead was caught and conquered by the dying.[92]

Then Tobias embraces Raguel, who typifies the Gentiles out of whom the Church is taken, and he asks the older man for the hand of his daughter Sara, prototype of the Church (Tob. 7:1 ff.).[93] The young couple prays to the Lord (Tob. 8:1 ff.) because God accepts the Church out of the Gentiles and asks her to renounce the Devil, with all his works and pomps, and to confess the faith in the Holy Trinity. The fire burning in a vessel symbolizes the burning of the innermost parts of the body with live coals. This brings remission of sins.[94]

Then the Devil is chained by the Angel (Tob. 8:3), for the demon is repulsed by the water of baptism. He is bound so that he can do no harm to the faithful. He can tempt them at times, enabling them to prove themselves, but he cannot conquer them; they will not give up the right faith.[95] At the end, Tobit is healed by his son with the gall of the fish (Tob. 11:13–15). When the Jews will have realized the most bitter malice of the most wicked enemy they will regain the light.[96]

Seen together, Samson and Gideon, Esther and Judith conquer all the dangers by which the Church felt threatened: evil (lion), heresies (Midianites), the Jews (Haman), and the Antichrist (Holofernes). While in the cycles of Esther and Judith the Synagogue, or Israel, is either ideologically implied as predecessor of the Church (Queen Vashti, Manasseh) or actually shown as her antagonist (Haman), the story of Tobit and Tobias reconciles in a consolatory manner the relation of the Church and Synagogue. Only the continuity of the Old Testament (Tobit-Israel, his wife-Synagogue) and the New Testament (Tobias-Christ, Sara-Church) is stressed. No antagonism is apparent, and the cycle ends with the salvation of Israel.

The six jamb statues complete the iconographic program of the tympanum and the archivolts (figs. 62, 63). Formally they were made part of the program. The four male statues were placed underneath the cycles of Samson and Gideon, Tobit and Tobias. The two women stand underneath the scenes of Esther and Judith.

Balaam on the ass predicted that a star would rise out of Jacob (Num. 24:17). This means that the Church will rise from Christ.[97] Solomon and the Queen of Sheba who came to hear his wisdom prefigure Christ and the Church.[98]

It does not seem to be a mere accident that Jesus Sirach corresponds in position to Solomon. Hrabanus Maurus points out that the Book of Solomon is called Ecclesiastes, and the Book of Jesus Sirach is Ecclesiasticus. Ecclesiastes refers primarily to Christ, Ecclesiasticus to the Church.[99] As if in confirmation of this concept, the pedestal underneath Jesus Sirach shows the building of the Temple, prefiguring the Church.

Judith stands opposite the Queen of Sheba. The two prototypes of the Church are thus brought into definite relation to each other. Joseph, finally, prefigures Christ. He fled from Potiphar's wife, the Synagogue, sculptured on the pedestal.[100]

Thus tympanum, lintel, archivolts, and jamb statues alike serve the same purpose. They show and were, therefore, meant to prove typologically the truth about Christ and His Body, the Church, who has to endure hardships but will achieve victory in the end.

The three tympana of the north transept are interwoven in meaning. Seen from left to right, they represent Mary as Mother of Christ; Mary triumphantly enthroned with her Son—the Church as the Bride of Christ; and the Church as the Body of Christ. Each tympanum, in turn, is related to the statues in the lower zone not only in meaning but also by "personal union." At the left, the Virgin is shown on the tympanum, its lintel, and along the jambs. On the main doorway, the central axis contains Mary as Child and Mary glorified. On the right, Solomon and Judith appear in both the upper and lower zones. In this way a complete unity of the parts of the iconographic program has been achieved although the program itself was not conceived at one and the same time.

V   STARTING in about 1220, a tripartite porch was added as an afterthought to the north transept façade (fig. 43). Its sculptural decoration comprises small figures or figure scenes in the archivolts, large statues for the piers, and reliefs underneath these statues.[101] The additional iconographic program both widens and further intensifies the tripartite program of the doorways.

In the center, the idea of Christ's relation to Mary glorified and the Church, His Bride, is amplified by the outer archivolts. Here the whole story of the Creation of the World and the Fall of Man is narrated word by word.[102] This series of scenes is in manifold ways linked to the cycle of the central portal.

While in the central tympanum Christ is glorified after His Ascension, the archivolt shows Him as the eternal Logos. The days of the creation were interpreted as the various epochs of Church history, as they are directly exemplified by the jamb statues.[103]

The creation of Eve from Adam's rib prefigures, according to medieval exegesis, the creation of the Church from the wound of Christ sleeping the sleep of death on the cross.[104] Because of the original sin, Adam and Eve were placed in opposition to Christ and the Virgin Mary as well as to Christ and the Church. Paul had contrasted the first Adam, a living soul, with the last Adam, a quickening spirit (I Cor. 15:45). Eve brought death, Mary gave life to the world.[105] While the first parents brought forth mankind for death, Christ and the Church are parents bringing forth mankind for life.[106]

On the left side the motif of showing the virtues of the Virgin in the archivolts of the tympanum is widened by the fourteen Beatitudes of Body and Soul in the outermost archivolt.[107]

The idea of representing the cycles of the Active and the Contemplative Lives in the inner archivolt of the left bay is derived from the liturgy.[108] On the day of Mary's Assumption the Gospel story of Christ's visit to the house of Mary and Martha was read as one of the lessons for the canonical hours. Of the two sisters Martha symbolizes the active life, Mary the contemplative life. Both kinds of life were practiced by the Virgin Mary in an exemplary manner.[109] The various stages of the Active Life are exemplified by six women who work the flax till the linen is spun. The different stages of the Contemplative Life are exemplified by six nuns holding a book, opening and reading it, praying, meditating, and contemplating the Divine.[110]

The archivolts of the right bay contain the Signs of the Zodiac, the Labors of the Months, and the four Seasons. They duplicate the cycle of the Year on the Royal Portal.[111] Yet, as on the Incarnation portal of the north façade, this is not a thoughtless repetition. The relation of the stars in heaven to life on earth is mentioned in the final account of God's creation in the Book of Job (38:33): "Knowest thou the ordinances of heaven? Canst thou establish the dominion thereof in the earth?" The cycle of the Year is thus related specifically to the tympanum of Job.

It is well-nigh impossible to identify more than one pair among the large statues still preserved. At the extreme right stand St. Potentien, who founded the Church of Chartres, and St. Modeste, its first female martyr.[112] It seems likely that the whole series of statues forms a parallel to the statues of the central portal, that is, that they lead from the time of the Old Testament to the era of grace, from prototypes of Christ and the Church to the early members of the Church of Chartres. The statues are arranged in pairs. Some pairs comprise one male and one female figure, in consonance with the pair glorified in the central tympanum; others consist of a King and a Prophet, in harmony with the two statues next to the central entrance, King David and Isaiah.[113]

The reliefs underneath the statues tell for the most part the story of Samuel, David, and the Ark of the Covenant. Once more a varied relation is established: between a Prophet and a King of the Old Testament; typologically between Samuel and David, on the one hand, and Christ, on the other hand; between the Ark of the Covenant and the Church.[114]

The four statues once decorating the left bay of the porch were destroyed during the French Revolution, but we know their identity from descriptions. They summed up some basic concepts of the total iconographic program. They represented the figures of the Church and the Synagogue, her predecessor and antagonist, and their Old Testament prototypes, Rachel and Leah.[115]

In its final stage the iconographic program of the north façade and its porch complements the program for the Royal Portal. Concepts which had been clearly presented before are not emphasized again. The hypostatic union of the two natures in the person of Christ is less strongly stressed, Divine Wisdom no longer proclaimed. The reality of the Eucharist, made evident on the Royal Portal by the *corpus verum* of Christ, is not reiterated but typologically it is widened by the reference of the statues in the center to the death of Christ and the sacrament of the Mass. The eternity of Christ was not actually exemplified on the Royal Portal. It is made visible on the north transept by the cross-haloed figure of Christ the Logos, as He creates the world and witnesses the Suffering of Job.

One idea which had appeared only in a general and incipient manner on the Royal Portal is sharpened and enlarged on the north transept. Indeed, it becomes the primary theme: the Church as the Bride of Christ, glorified in heaven after the eras before and under the Old Law, and the Church as Christ's Body attacked by various enemies.

VI   AS AT the time when the Royal Portal was decorated, certain groups of heretics comprising not just the lower classes but also members of the upper ecclesiastic hierarchy and of the high nobility threatened again, and threatened most dangerously, the orthodox beliefs of the Church at the end of the twelfth and the beginning of the thirteenth century.

The heretical tenets are for the most part known through the writings of their opponents. Shortly before 1200 these tenets were recorded by Alan of Lille, and then summarized according to various sects by Bernard Gui late in the thirteenth century.[116] These treatises may give a distorted view of the actual historical situations. Yet they are valuable in interpreting the anti-heretical meaning of the sculptures, because the program must have been devised by orthodox theologians. According to the sources the heretics denied that Mary had been the true mother of Jesus Christ and a woman of real flesh. They called their own sect the Virgin.[117] In Senlis, Laon, Mantes, Chartres, and in many later churches the death of what was mortal in Mary, her Resurrection and final Triumph in heaven were represented. These scenes visibly refuted the beliefs of the heretics. One and the same Mary also typified the true Church, while the heretics believed in two churches, one good, namely their own sect, the other evil, namely the Roman Church, which they called the mother of fornication, great Babylon, harlot, the Church of the Devil, and the Synagogue of Satan.[118]

With disgust and horror a chronicler complains that the names of Mary and the Church were falsely used by the sect of the Poplicani. In 1200 two women were burnt among some heretics at Troyes. They had been given by their friends the names of Holy Church and St. Mary for the sole purpose of deceit, as the chronicler angrily explains, for it enabled members of the sect to say ambiguously: "I believe what the Holy Church and St. Mary believe."[119] To the orthodox believers the tympana of the churches showed the true Mary and the true Church.

Heretics also did not believe that Christ was born of the Virgin and that He had assumed a real human body. To them His Incarnation, Passion, and Resurrection meant a mere simile.[120] At Laon and Chartres-North a whole portal is dedicated to the cycle of the Incarnation. And among the Angels framing the tympanum at Chartres two stand on dragons, the fallen angels, prototypes of the heretics.

The exemplary value of the Old Testament was also under strong attack. Abraham was considered evil, because he wanted to sacrifice his own son at the command of an evil God. Moses was wicked, and this for a number of reasons. He had doubted the power of God, slain a man, married an Ethiopian, and led the army into death for mankind. Isaac was sinful, for he lied when he pretended that his wife was his sister. David was called an adulterer and murderer, and a good many other patriarchs were condemned for similar reasons.[121] "Why did the patriarchs of the Old Testament descend to hell, if not because of their tremendous sinfulness?"[122]

At Senlis the trust in the virtues of Old Testament heroes is reaffirmed by showing them together with personages of the New Testament, with Simeon and John the Baptist—and in Chartres also with St. Peter.

In 1204, during a dispute with orthodox spokesmen at Carcassonne, the Cathari asserted their belief that the world had been created by the evil principle. This belief was also fully recorded by Bernard Gui. The Manichaeans of modern times, he said, believe in two gods, one good, the other evil; not the heavenly Father but Satan, the evil god, the god and prince of this world, has created all visible and invisible things.[123] The outer archivolts of the central porch demonstrate that it was truly the Logos who had created the visible world. The same Logos had espoused the Church before and under the law.

Although the French heresies had grown up for the most part in the south and southwest, and persisted most strongly in these regions, they gained adherents in the north. In 1183 Archbishop William of Reims, uncle of King Philip Augustus, and Count Philip of Flanders, uncle of Queen Elizabeth, tried to bring back to the Church a large group of Poplicani in Arras.[124]

The Church of Chartres took an active part in combating the heresy of the Albigensians. In 1210, Renaud of Mouçon, bishop of Chartres, set out with the bishop of Beauvais and the counts of Dreux and Ponthin to assist Simon de Montfort in his lengthy siege of Termes.[125]

If viewed in relation to the struggle against heresies, the program of the north façade and its porch does not simply make visible certain basic beliefs about the Church and Christ. It fulfills the added function of actually refuting some of the most important tenets of contemporaneous heretical groups. Seen from this particular point of view the program may be interpreted in analogy to the complaints voiced by Pope Innocent III. While Christ, he wrote to Archbishop Guido of Aix in 1198, has chosen the Church as His Bride, who serves Him, her Head, in the unity of faith, the heretics deprave the evangelical, apostolic, and prophetic doctrines.[126]

VII   IN 1198 some clerics belonging to the diocese of Paris set out on an intensive campaign of preaching penitence and doing missionary work.[127] Empowered by the pope with a preaching license, a simple priest, Fulk of Neuilly, became prominent through his successful conversion of sinners to the right way of life. He also brought heretics back to the Church or stamped them out ruthlessly. He dealt a serious blow to the Cathari when he discovered Terric, the heresiarch of the Nivernais, in a cave near Corbigny and caused him to be burned. The priest's fame as converter and miracle worker spread throughout northern Europe. French, German, and English chroniclers reported the success of his missionary work. He chose as helpers among other men Robert of Courçon and Peter of Roissy, "a very erudite man" who only a few years afterwards, in 1208, became chancellor of the School of Chartres and held this position until 1213. (That he gave up his missionary work was resented by some chroniclers, who accused him of accumulating wealth by his preaching.[128])

Peter of Roissy wrote a commentary on the Book of Job, in which he interpreted Job, as St. Gregory had done before, as both Christ and the Church.[129] He could very well have been the author of the iconographic program in its enlarged form at Chartres. It certainly seems possible that he suggested the representation of Job's Suffering—which, as far as I know, had never before been represented in a tympanum—as a suitable reminder of the dangers to which the Church was exposed in his own time. Peter of Roissy not only had interpreted the suffering of Job in writing. Associated with Fulk of Neuilly, he must have had close knowledge of the struggle against heretics, if he did not actively participate in combating them. While he was head of the School of Chartres he must have been consulted when the iconographic program had to be expanded shortly after 1210.

CHAPTER III   The Sculptures of

the South Transept and its

Porch

     I   THE CYCLE of the south façade of Chartres is more unified in meaning and more generalized in concept than its counterpart on the north side (fig. 64). The sculptural decoration for the central portal and the lateral doorways was planned as a whole, and not in successive stages. Its program complements the idea of the Church as the Bride and the Body of Christ. It represents in historical terms the Christian Church on earth and in heaven, and its end in time on the day of the Last Judgment. The three tympana and the statues flanking the portals clearly and comprehensively express these concepts. The central portal shows along the jambs the twelve Apostles grouped around Christ on the *trumeau* (figs. 65–67). The left portal is dedicated to the Martyrs (figs. 68, 69), the right one to the Confessors (figs. 70, 71).[1] The central tympanum reveals the Last Judgment, and the archivolts of the three tympana show in their upper parts the Church in heaven.

     If one follows the history of the Christian Church here represented, one has to begin in the center with Christ the Teacher, and end in the center with Christ the Judge. Christ who by His teachings founded the Church and admits the faithful into the cathedral is surrounded by the Twelve who spread His word and established the Church throughout the world. The Martyrs gave their lives for Christ and the Church. The Confessors affirmed their faith in Christ and His Church through their virtuous lives. The Church on earth, whose exemplary members are the various ranks of saints, will come to its temporal end on the day of judgment to reign forever with God.

Compared with the variety of Old and New Testament statues flanking the three portals of the north façade, the jamb figures of the three portals on the south show greater unity. All of them are saints of the actual Church. Balancing each other, the Martyrs and Confessors flank the Apostles. The Twelve are related to both groups. They may be considered as confessors, since they confessed Christ while spreading His word and as martyrs since they died for His sake and hold as attributes the instruments of their martyrdom. They fulfilled the charge given to them by Christ: to not fear those who kill the body, but cannot kill the soul; and to confess Him before men, so that He will confess them before His Father (Matt. 10:28, 32).

Through ideological and formal ties the tympana of the lateral portals are related to the central tympanum and to each other. As on the west and north façades, the coherence of the iconographic program is made evident by the common motif of Christ between Angels in each tympanum. Again, the readings for the canonical hours provide the key to an understanding of the individual parts of the program.

To start with the left tympanum (fig. 72): the martyrdom of St. Stephen sets a perfect example of how to attain right judgment and eternal life. He is led out of Jerusalem and while he beholds the Son of man in a vision, he asks forgiveness for the sinners who kill him. This supreme proof of self-forgetful love for one's enemies establishes, according to the sermon read on the day of the saint, a perfect example for those who desire right judgment from the Lord.[2] Thereby the scene is ideologically linked to the central tympanum: "Recall what Truth itself has promised you in the Gospel, what care it has provided for you in some way: 'For if you forgive men their trespasses,' it says, 'your heavenly Father will also forgive you. But if you forgive not men their trespasses, neither will your Father forgive your trespasses (Matt. 6:14, 15).' You see, brethren, in what manner we will be judged by the Lord, because it is left to our power by the grace of God."[3]

In the vision of St. Stephen (Acts 7:54 ff.), the fact that the Son of man wears a crown and holds a palm branch, as Christ does in the tympanum, is not mentioned. However, these motives may be explained quite specifically by the sermon: "Blessed will be he who follows him (i.e., St. Stephen) eagerly and who imitates him, for he will receive the palm branch of pudicity and the crown of martyrdom."[4]

. The tympanum on the right side is also thematically related to the Last Judgment (fig. 73). Scenes from the lives of two confessors, St. Martin and

St. Nicholas, exemplify good deeds as they should be performed by the faithful so that they will be admitted to the kingdom of heaven on the day of the Last Judgment. The action of St. Martin is but one of the deeds of mercy. He cuts his mantle in half and gives part of it to a beggar. Then in his sleep he sees the Lord wearing the part of the mantle the poor man had received. The relation of the whole story to the Last Judgment is obvious. The lesson for the day of St. Martin quotes the very words that Christ had spoken, when indicating what He would say to the elect on the day of judgment: "The Lord truly remembered His words (who had said before: 'Inasmuch as ye have done it unto one of the least of my brethren, ye have done it unto me') and professed that He was clothed in the person of the poor man. And so as to confirm the testimony of such a good deed, He was willing to show Himself in the same garment that the poor man had received."[5]

The good deed of St. Nicholas is equally an act of mercy. In order to spend his wealth for the sake of God, he secretly throws pieces of gold into the house of a noble but impoverished man who, in his despair, wanted to abandon his three daughters to the sins of the world. Above this scene the saint performs miracles even after his death. The sick are healed through the oil and water that flow from his tomb.[6]

The lateral tympana show that there is only one kind of supreme sacrifice for the sake of God, namely death, but several kinds of good deeds. The subject matter of the left tympanum is concentrated on the martyrdom suffered by St. Stephen after he had been appointed deacon. The right tympanum stresses variety. It is dedicated to two saints and contains four scenes that are at variance. While the deed of St. Martin and his subsequent vision are parts of one story and while he is shown only as a knight before he was baptized, St. Nicholas is represented both as a young layman and as a bishop resting on his tomb. In formal harmony with compositional principles of the north façade, a number of calm scenes in one lateral tympanum is balanced against a single dramatic event in the other tympanum.

A third saint is added to the two Confessors in the lowest tier of the archivolts. Three scenes from the life of St. Giles, the hermit (figs. 74, 75), not only contribute something new to the stories of St. Martin and St. Nicholas; they also form definite links between the three tympana.

At the left, St. Giles gives his garment to a poor and sick man, who was miraculously healed when he put it on. This event combines the deed of St. Martin, to which it forms a close parallel, with the healing power of St. Nicholas. In the adjoining scene the saint shelters a hind who had nourished him with her milk, and protects her from a hunting king and his servant. St. Giles was then inadvertently wounded by an arrow. This demonstrates that confessors, like martyrs, suffer gladly, because the saint refused the medical help offered by the king. The scene on the right-hand side is related to the idea of the Last Judgment. Through the intercession of the saint, King Charles

Martel is forgiven a sin so grave that the king did not confess it to the hermit. An Angel appears to the saint while he celebrates Mass; the Angel presents to him a scroll on which is written the king's sin to be forgiven by the saint's prayer, if the king will repent and never do it again.[7]

While the scenes from the legend of St. Giles add entirely new stories to the tympanum, the lowest archivolt sections of the left-hand tympanum merely contain an expansion of St. Stephen's story. To the left his dispute with the Jews is represented as the starting point for his martyrdom. On the right side the scene of the stoning is enlarged and Saul is shown as he guards the clothes of those who are killing the saint. Saul is the foremost example of a sinner who was to be saved by the prayer of St. Stephen.

Thus the lateral tympana (and their extension into the archivolts) were conceived as parts of one ideological system through their relation to each other and to the Last Judgment. St. Stephen who prays for his enemies demonstrates that those who forgive will be forgiven. St. Martin and St. Nicholas, and likewise St. Giles, set examples of good deeds as an exhortation to those who desire to stand the probe of the Last Judgment.

The archivolts of the lateral tympana are linked in yet another way. While their lowest tiers illustrate actual scenes, their upper sections show on a more conceptual level various classes of saints, removed from any particular place or definite moment. The specific example set by St. Stephen, the protomartyr, is generalized in the archivolts into a representation of four groups of saints, among them the Innocents and the Martyrs of the Book of Revelation, who made their robes white in the blood of the Lamb (Rev. 7:14).[8]

The place accorded these saints in the upper parts of the archivolts close to Christ in heaven indicates in itself that they represent the souls of the saints in heaven. "And I saw the souls of them that were beheaded for the witness of Jesus, and for the word of God . . . and they lived and reigned with Christ a thousand years" (Rev. 20:4). The use of the past tense in the last sentence proved to be important for the interpretation of the passage. The *Glossa ordinaria* states explicitly that the martyrs will not only live and reign with Christ in the future, but live and reign with Him at the present time, right after their death.[9]

The examples given by St. Martin, St. Nicholas, and St. Giles are similarly broadened in the archivolts of the right tympanum into an ideal representation of saints who vary in rank.

II   BY SIZE, place, and meaning the lateral tympana are subordinated to the central and climactic scene of the Last Judgment (figs. 76, 77).

On the Royal Portal the Second Coming of Christ included the idea of the Last Judgment, because the twelve Apostles chosen by the Lord to judge the twelve tribes were made part of the scene. What had been a mere idea is fully developed into the actual drama of the Last Day on the south transept but, as in the tympana of Saint-Denis (*ca.* 1137–40) and Laon (*ca.* 1180), with great restraint and with a strong desire to soften the terrifying aspect of the ultimate event confronting mankind at the end of the world.[10]

In His prediction of the Last Day, Christ had called the Judge at first the Son of man (Matt. 25:31) and then had called him king (Matt. 25:34). As at Saint-Denis and Laon the representation of Christ in the tympanum combines both concepts.

Seated between two Intercessors, He is humble in His attitude, for He reveals past suffering, while exerting the power of the supreme Judge. As in the earlier tympana His right breast once pierced by the spear is bare. His hands and feet show the wounds made by the nails. The idea of His Passion is visibly enhanced by the instruments of martyrdom surrounding Him. While kneeling and flying Angels hold the spear, the column and the lash of the flagellation, the crown of thorns, and the nails, two Angels in the apex of the tympanum present a small cross above His head.

Within the context of the Last Day it is revealed once more to all the living who enter the cathedral, and to the stone figures shown rising from their tombs, that the Son of God had also become the Son of man when He assumed human nature in addition to His divine nature so as to redeem mankind by His death.[11]

At the same time, all the ranks of Angels surround Him in the archivolts and stress His coming in glory (Matt. 25:31). Furthermore, the cross above Christ's head, the sign of the Son of man which shall appear in heaven (Matt. 24:30) is not only the symbol of martyrdom but also the standard of His victory over death.[12] Lastly, the fact that the cross is presented by Angels was interpreted in analogy to the honor accorded a king. As the crown and other insignia are carried before the worldly ruler to make known his coming when he enters a city, so the cross and other insignia are shown by Angels when Christ appears for the Last Judgment with the whole Hierarchy of Angels.[13]

The Chartres master followed an old tradition when he combined the Judge with the insignia of martyrdom. Yet he established a new relation between Christ and the cross by harmonizing elements taken from earlier tympana. At Saint-Denis Christ had been placed exactly in front of a large cross (fig. 78). Thereby the idea that judge and sufferer are identical was made visible while the gesture of His outstretched arms is grandiose and powerful. In the Last Judgment of Laon, Christ is disengaged from the cross (fig. 79). Diagonally held by an Angel at His left side, the cross is small in size and thus reduced to a mere symbol. Christ raises His hands meekly, while showing His wounds and judging. Now His past suffering is stressed by His whole humble attitude rather than by the size of the cross or by a parallel between His arms and those of the cross.

The Chartres master adopted the attitude of Christ and the small size of the cross from the Laon tympanum. Like the sculptor of Saint-Denis he placed the cross along the central axis, but above Christ's head. By virtue of this synthesis he established a definite central axis and thereby an ideographic relation between a humble Judge and the cross symbol.

At Saint-Denis — and still at Laon — groups of Apostles had flanked Christ and the Intercessors. The Chartres master eliminated these groups from the tympanum, with the result that he achieved a new clarity of composition and strengthened the idea of mercy within the context of the Last Judgment.

Greater importance thus is given at Chartres to the Angels bearing the instruments that had caused Christ to suffer. In the tympanum of Saint-Denis all the Angels were relegated to the upper zone. At Chartres two Angels assume prominence by their size and their place on the same stage as their Master.

The representation of the two Intercessors reflects to an even greater degree the new emphasis on mercy. It forms the high point of an evolution that had begun at Saint-Denis.

In the Last Judgment of Beaulieu (*ca.* 1130) Christ was surrounded by the twelve Apostles, His helpers on the Last Day.[14] There was no one to supplicate for mankind. At Saint-Denis the Virgin was given a place next to the right side of Christ. As Intercessor, as helper of the just ones and of repentant sinners, she has joined the Apostles. And there is a second Intercessor forming her counterpart to the left of Christ. His head, like those of the other figures in the tympanum, is no longer the original one but the poor work of a restorer. Yet it may be assumed that he is John the Disciple who was given the same place in the later tympana of Chartres, Paris, and Amiens. Otherwise, only eleven Apostles would sit with Christ in heaven, obviously an iconographic impossibility.

At an early time Byzantine art had established the norm that the Virgin Mary and John the Baptist flank Christ and intercede for mankind. This Deësis group was at first represented by itself. Later on it was made part of the Last Judgment. In the mosaic of the Last Judgment at Torcello the Virgin and John the Baptist stand next to the Judge, while two groups of Apostles, six on either side, surround the Deësis.[15]

At Saint-Denis—and, later on, at Laon—John the Disciple, not John the Baptist, shares with the Virgin Mary the privilege of direct intercession. This seems to reflect the desire to associate with the Virgin a saint to whom she was more intimately linked than to John the Baptist. The only contact the New Testament mentions between the Virgin and the Baptist occurred at the time when he was still unborn. When Mary entered the house of her cousin Elisabeth and greeted her, the babe leaped in Elisabeth's womb (Luke 1:40, 41). The link between the Virgin Mary and John the Disciple, on the other hand, was very close and tender, as the Gospel according to John tells us. Both Mary and John stood by the cross. It was at this time, just before His death, that Christ entrusted the disciple whom he loved to the Virgin as if he were her son, and the Virgin to John as if she were his mother. "And from that hour that disciple took her unto his own home" (John 19:26, 27). These passages gave impetus to the idea of representing John the Disciple, in analogy to the Baptist, as the second Intercessor on the Saint-Denis tympanum. He still remains one of the Twelve but is privileged in his relation to the Virgin Mary and in his function of interceding for mankind. In the center of the tympanum they balance one another on either side of Christ and the cross, as they had balanced one another in representations of the Crucifixion. Within the context of the Last Judgment, biblical sources began to influence art at the time when the veneration of the Virgin Mary was growing rapidly.

The Chartres sculptor, in consultation with his theological adviser, went one decisive step further than his predecessors. No longer did he give the College of Apostles a place in the tympanum. No longer did he combine the Lord and the Intercessors with those assisting their Master in judging. He showed only the Deësis and Angels in the sphere of heaven. By this restraint he not only created a clearer composition, but also emphasized a pious belief that extended the close association between the Virgin and John the Disciple to the time after their death. Early apocryphal legends had either mentioned that John's tomb was found empty or stated that it was filled with manna.[16] This gave rise to the belief that John like the Virgin Mary had ascended to heaven. Pseudo-Jerome mentions this, yet more for the sake of the record, with only a weak stamp of approval and certainly without any enthusiasm: "Very many assert the same (i.e., the ascension) with regard to the blessed John the Evangelist, her servant. To him who was a virgin, the Virgin was entrusted by Christ. In his sepulchre, we are told, was found nothing but manna."[17]

The case is entirely different with Bishop Fulbert of Chartres. An ardent early champion of the veneration of the Virgin in the eleventh century, he firmly and unequivocally expressed his belief in the ascension of John. He even made it a special point to mention that the Virgin and John are equally glorified in heaven: "Therefore Christian piety believes that Christ, God and Son of God, resurrected His Mother in glory and exalted her above the heavens, and that the blessed John, the virgin and Evangelist, who served her on earth, was deemed worthy to share her glory in heaven."[18]

Bishop Fulbert establishes such a strong link between the Virgin Mary and the Disciple in heaven, that this might well have fostered the decision of the Chartres planners to give an exclusive place to two Intercessors who had both retained a state of virginal purity, had both stood by the cross, were intimately linked to one another, according to Christ's last wish, and were finally allowed to ascend to heaven and to partake of the same glory in heaven.

In one more important aspect the Chartres tympanum differs from the earlier works at Saint-Denis and Laon. There the Intercessors were allowed to sit next to Christ and to address Him directly with their prayers but the Judge overpowered them by His symbolically larger size. At Chartres, the Virgin and the Disciple were given the same size as Christ. This reflects a stronger belief in the power of their intercession.

Such a concept apparently seemed too humanized for other theologians and sculptors who planned and carved later tympana. At Notre-Dame in Paris (*ca.* 1220), Christ is once more larger in size and thereby more powerful than the Intercessors.[19] This indicates a different concept rather than just the desire to have a larger figure in the center of a more pointed tympanum. The Intercessors not only are subordinated by size; they also kneel in more humble attitudes and are, furthermore, separated from Christ by two standing Angels. The planners of the Last Judgments in Amiens and Reims (*ca.* 1230) did not want to separate the Intercessors from the Judge. They devised a composition that harmonizes elements of the tympana at both Chartres and Paris. As in Chartres the Intercessors are allowed to be close to Christ, but as in Paris they remain smaller in size and kneel in devout prayer.[20]

The humanized concept of Christ the Judge and Sufferer is strengthened at Chartres by the lateral tympana (figs. 72, 73). At the left He appears as the Son of man in the image of a victorious Martyr. On the right He humbles Himself by His willingness "to show Himself in the same garment that the poor man had received."

The planners responsible for the Last Judgment portal aimed throughout at a mitigation and, at the same time, a new clarity of meaning. In earlier Gothic tympana the Apostles were contained in the tympanum (Saint-Denis) or in the tympanum and the lowest sections of the archivolts (Laon). Their place was close to Christ the Judge. As a retinue of judges they enhanced His power. In Chartres they were for the first time placed along the jambs. Here they are close to Christ the Teacher. Here they hold in their hands attributes of martyrdom and make it clear to the beholder that they were willing to give their lives for Christ.

Composition and meaning of the Last Judgment were infused with the spirit of calmness in yet other ways. At Saint-Denis and Laon the Resurrection of the Dead with all its strong transitory movements takes place underneath Christ and His retinue. The master of Chartres, however, relegated these scenes to the peripheral sphere of the archivolts, thus freeing the central section of expressive restlessness. He adopted from the Laon tympanum the place for the Separation of the Blessed and Damned in the lintel, yet he changed irregularity of composition into stability and consonance. The two groups are perfectly balanced around the central figure of St. Michael.[21] Their centrifugal direction balances the centripetal poses of the Intercessors. Finally, the Hierarchy of Angels in the archivolts forms a calm frame for the whole event.

The control of composition is equaled and strengthened by the restraint of emotional factors. The Damned are resigned to the fact that they are being led to hell. On either side the Resurrected rise from their tombs in the attitude of prayer. There is no suggestion that many of them are awakened to a terrible fate. Apart from the nude symbolizing Luxury, the Sinners held by devils appearing in the lowest parts of the right archivolts are calm in their attitudes (fig. 65).

If one looks at the Last Judgment in its entirety, one realizes that it was not meant to overwhelm the churchgoer emotionally. Like the tympana of Saint-Denis and Laon it was not meant to strike terror into his heart, for it is pervaded by the spirit of calm justice and by the hope for mercy. It was meant to show him a Judge humble in attitude. It was meant to show him that the Virgin Mary and John the Disciple are willing to help repentant sinners. It allowed him to reflect about himself and about the event that will face him at the end of the days. In addition, the lateral tympana were meant to show him examples of forgiveness and good deeds, as they will enable man to stand the probe of the Last Judgment.

Although separated from the Royal Portal by two generations, the portal of the Last Judgment makes it evident that the principle of an ideographic central axis as the early workshop had established it still remains valid. In the Incarnation tympanum of the Royal Portal a tripartite central axis had clarified the composition and its iconographic structure. The sculptures of the Last Judgment portal also are arranged around a central axis, this time quadripartite (fig. 65). It comprises Christ the Teacher, St. Michael weighing the souls, Christ the Judge, and the sign of the cross. It embodies the very essentials of Christ's importance for the actual Church. He had established the Church by His teachings and after He has redeemed mankind by His death He will be the Judge at the end of the days.

At the same time, the central axis shows the victory over the Devil and over death. Triumphantly and yet calmly Christ the Teacher stands on the lion and the dragon. He fulfills the prophecy of the thirteenth verse of the Ninetieth Psalm (according to the *Vulgate*) that He will, through the members of the Church, trample underfoot the two animals, symbols of the Devil.[22] Archangel Michael defeats the Devil in the Weighing of the Souls, and Christ beneath the standard of victory has conquered death.

III   ANGELS frame the Last Judgment in the archivolts. They correspond to the Martyrs and Confessors in the archivolts of the lateral tympana and are thereby iconographically related to them. Angels and saints together exemplify the Church in heaven, seen in relation to Christ the Teacher *(trumeau),* the Sufferer and Judge (tympanum), according to Heb. 12:22–24: "But ye are come unto mount Sion, and unto the city of the living God, the heavenly Jerusalem, and to an innumerable company of angels, to the general assembly and church of the firstborn, which are written in heaven,[23] and to God the Judge of all [i.e., Christ according to medieval commentators], and to the spirits of just men made perfect, and to Jesus the mediator of the new covenant [i.e., the giver of the Gospels], and to the blood of sprinkling [i.e., the suffering of Christ], that speaketh better things than that of Abel." It should be added here that in the archivolts the saints in heaven are restricted to the Martyrs and Confessors. When a porch was built in front of the façade the Community of Saints was widened into the Community of All Saints. In the archivolts the "missing" classes appear: Patriarchs and Prophets, Apostles and Virgins.[24]

Herewith the history of the Christian Church comes to an end. Founded by Christ, spread throughout the world by the Apostles, testified to by the Martyrs and Confessors, it ceases its temporal existence on the day of judgment to last forever in a newly created world.

The iconographic program of the south transept, like that of the north façade, contradicts heretical beliefs. Some sects did not think that the living could benefit from the prayers of the saints. Alan of Lille defends the orthodox tenets, for otherwise the daily prayer of the Church to the saints would be fruitless, and the litanies would make no sense. The Church prays even for the schismatics and heretics, as St. Stephen interceded for his enemies.[25]

IV   IN 1224 work was begun on the porch in front of the south transept (fig. 64). The groups of statues representing Martyrs and Confessors were extended at each side by one pair of saints, with the archivolts above them enlarging the groups of saints in heaven.[26] In contrast to the earlier classes of saints framing the tympanum of St. Stephen, the added archivolt shows various ranks within the Church in hierarchic order, and comprises a King in addition. (The original archivolts of the Confessors tympanum from the beginning had exemplified the hierarchic order of saints.) Through these additions a more definite ideographic consonance with the Hierarchy of Angels in the archivolts of the central tympanum was established. The decoration of the porch proper comprises various cycles of reliefs and archivolt figures. These, too, complement the original core of the subject matter and intensify its meaning.

Scenes from the lives of Martyrs and Confessors on the outer piers illustrate comprehensively and specifically the actions and sufferings of a great number of saints.[27] The cycle of Virtues and Vices on the inner piers, derived from the façade of Notre-Dame in Paris, enriches the idea of salvation or damnation by the allegories of moral conflict.[28] The cycle of the twenty-four Elders, also on the inner piers, strengthens the apocalyptic idea of the Last Judgment.[29]

The decoration of the vaults links the lateral bays of the porch more closely with the Last Judgment by a cycle of Wise and Foolish Virgins (bay of the Martyrs),[30] by a cycle of the Apostles (bay of the Confessors), and by outer archivolts containing Angels.

The archivolts of the central bay add three more classes of saints: the Patriarchs, the Prophets, and the Virgins.[31]

On the day of All Saints "the bishop reads the first lesson about the Trinity, the dean the second about the Blessed Mary," as it was prescribed in a thirteenth-century *Ordinarium* for the Church of Chartres, "the cantor the third about the Angels, and other persons shall read the remaining lessons: the fourth about the Patriarchs and Prophets, and about the blessed John the Baptist, the fifth about the Apostles, the sixth about the Martyrs, the seventh about the Confessors, the eighth about the Virgins, the ninth about all the saints."[32] In the litany as well, Christ was implored to have mercy and to hear the prayers, and then the whole hierarchy of saints (the Virgin Mary, the nine orders of Angels, Patriarchs, etc.) was asked to pray for the members of the Church.[33]

Corresponding to the liturgy, Christ and all the ranks of saints, who could provide salvation for the faithful, were carved in stone on the south transept and in its porch, a visible promise for those who entered the cathedral.

V   THE decoration of the six portals of the transept wings had resulted in a perfect consonance between their iconographic programs. The two Pauline similes of the Church as the Bride and the Body of Christ represented on the north transept are complemented in the south by another Pauline concept, that of the Church exemplified by the Community of Saints on earth and in heaven.

How did the additional sculptures planned for the porches affect the coherence and balance of meaning which had been achieved before the two façades were amplified?

The two porches differ strongly in the kind of sculpture chosen to decorate the piers (figs. 43, 64). In the north porch the emphasis is on large statues; in the south it is on small-scale reliefs. In spite of these differences, the iconographic program of each new sculpture cycle is not just geared to that of its portals, but anchored to the other side by a transfer of ideas.

Corresponding to the statue of St. Anne with the Infant Mary in her arms on the northern *trumeau*, in the left gable of the south porch, the Virgin's mother is shown, holding a vase with a lily, symbol of the Immaculate Conception.[34] Corresponding to Mary, the Mother of Christ and Queen of heaven, in the north, the Virgin appears also in the south, holding the Child (central gable) and receiving a scepter from an Angel (right gable).[35]

Corresponding to Christ the King in the central tympanum of the north, groups of Kings stand high up in arcades on the front and the sides of the south porch. Corresponding to Christ the Judge in the south, Christ is enthroned in the central gable of the north porch and, similarly, two Bishops are seated in the lateral gables.[36]

The Patriarchs and Prophets of the north transept are echoed in the archivolt groups of the same classes on the south side. In this way the subject matter of the porches strengthens the coherence between the meaning of the transept sculptures.

The programs of the transept wings and their porches at Chartres represent in their totality the climax of an evolution that had begun in Senlis and was carried further at Laon. In Senlis the plan was restricted to the Triumph of Mary-Ecclesia who is Christ's Bride. At Laon this motif appears in conjunction with the Incarnation cycle and the Last Judgment, the very beginning and the very end of the Christian Church on earth.[37] At Chartres— and only here—the Triumph of Mary-Ecclesia was complemented by two other concepts, that of the Church as the Body of Christ, and of the Community of Saints. The program for the west façade of Notre-Dame in Paris, in its final plan, corresponds—in substance, although not in actual arrangement—to that of Laon.[38]

At Reims the abandoning of the original plan and the complete reorganization of the west façade accounts for the lack of clarity within the iconographic program as a whole. The Old Testament statues destined for a portal of the Virgin received a place on the right portal and are, therefore, not connected to the Virgin's Triumph which was carved at a later date for the central gable. The Suffering of Job prefiguring the Church as the Body of Christ was set among scenes from the lives of saints, but it is not, in its present place on the north transept, related to the idea of the Church as the Bride of Christ.[39]

In contrast to Reims, the program for the west façade of the cathedral at Amiens was carried out as planned. With only three doorways to be decorated, the Last Judgment is flanked by the Triumph of Mary–Ecclesia and the Community of Saints.[40] Any allusion to the Church as the Body of Christ is missing. Only at Chartres, it seems, were the various concepts of the Church represented in a truly comprehensive manner. Only at Chartres does the history of the universal Church clearly unfold itself to the beholder in all its ramifications from the beginning of the world to the end of time.

CHAPTER IV   Form and Meaning

BECAUSE OF the different phases of sculptural decoration, various workshops
were active on the transept wings between about 1205 and 1220, and on
the porches between about 1220 and 1235.

Wilhelm Vöge's theory that the sculptures of each portal were carved by
a different workshop still seems to be valid basically, with the modification that
some continuity linked the workshops of the central portals. The statues,
tympana, lintels, and archivolts differ stylistically according to the time of their
creation and according to the individuality and artistic quality of their
sculptors.[1]

I   COMPARED with the jamb statues of the Royal Portal, the statues
of the six portals steadily increase in the degree of humanization. The earliest
among them, the statues of the central portal on the north side, reveal a
definite change in form, stance, and relation to each other (figs. 50, 51).

Gone is the columnar shape, the architectural elongation, the harmonious unity of pure line and volume. The statues have gained bulk. Their proportions are less drawn out. Drapery folds are no longer bound as a dense linear pattern to bodily forms. Fewer in number, they project three-dimensionally and add volume to the figure. Yet there still remains the balance between vertical (now fluted) folds that stabilize the postures of the statues, and curved folds that define the bulk and, in part, the forms of the figures.

Still addorsed to columns, the statues are no longer dependent on them. Their manner of standing becomes increasingly natural. At first this has symbolic implications, for their feet rest on little figures or objects that denote good or evil. The figures carved at a later date stand with greater freedom on horizontal pedestals, small sections of a stage; some even shift their weight, thus being balanced in their own right, as St. Theodore and St. George (figs. 68, 69). The strict parallelism between statues and columns is replaced by a freer interplay between them. The human dignity of the figures is stressed by more natural shapes. Yet the columns to which they remain attached deny their complete autonomy and make them still an integral part of the façade.

The statues of the Royal Portal had remained self-contained entities within the uniform system of columnized figures because of their tectonic immobility, their vertical outlines and frontal poses. Their relation to each other was an ideal, not a natural, relation. On the transept wings, most of the figures turn their heads, thus glancing in different directions. Their arms are not only less firmly bound to the body and thereby less immobilized; they also vary in position. This causes variations in the fall of the drapery and differentiates the figures from one another, whereas the statues carved by the Head Master of the Royal Portal had been unified through equal position of the arms. This increasing freedom of attitudes loosens the static severity of the whole composition and the self-containment of the figures on the transept wings. Some statues even form pairs. The figures of the Annunciation and Visitation communicate with each other by turn, glance, and gestures so that the void between them becomes activated (figs. 54, 55).

On the Royal Portal the main columns lining the jambs and the intermediate ones had remained separate entities. Not only were there no links between them, but they were kept distinctly apart by different ornamental motifs on the lower shafts. On the transept wings these lower shafts throughout have the same spiral shape, and the columns are tied together by rings. This device draws even those statues that remain frontally immobilized into a more unified whole.

The statues of the Royal Portal were totally removed from any specific time. The same principle still governs most of the later statues, but the element of time does enter. Abraham looks toward the Angel (below the canopy of Melchizedek) at the moment when the heavenly messenger intervenes in the sacrifice of Isaac (fig. 50). Samuel is just ready to immolate the lamb. Simeon holds the Child in his arms on the day of the Presentation in the Temple (fig. 51). The Angel Gabriel announces the birth of Christ to the Virgin, and Mary meets Elisabeth (figs. 54, 55). But the moments chosen by the artists do not imply any element of transitoriness. There is no indication of an actual space in which time could pass. Existing in an ideal sphere among ideal assemblies of persons who lived at different times, some figures are shown in particular moments of their lives, but these moments are made permanent.

The statues of the Royal Portal were differentiated according to their sex and age, their royal and nonroyal status, but the books, scrolls, and rods they hold are attributes of a general kind. These attributes do not establish the identity of the statues; instead, they stress the unity of the various groups. The identity of the figures, therefore, must have depended primarily on names once inscribed on scrolls and books.

The statues of the transept wings still form ideal groups, but their individuality is now more precisely described. This is achieved through the greatest possible variety of means. Some statues show their identity by specific actions and attitudes based on the text of the Bible (Abraham, Samuel, Simeon, Annunciation and Visitation). Others are defined by inscribed scrolls, differentiated according to rank by liturgical garments (Martyrs and Confessors), or characterized from without by attributes and pedestal figures.

The attributes do not conform to a single type. First of all, they fulfill different functions. In the hands of Old Testament statues prefiguring Christ, they are related to His future self-sacrifice. In the hands of the Apostles, they refer to the disciples themselves. Second, in part they are of general nature and indicate only a certain rank (e.g., the croziers), while the actual identification of the figures is provided by the pedestal reliefs. In part they are specific enough to establish the identity of the figures. Third, they are in meaning like rungs of a ladder reaching from the natural to the symbolic realm. Natural attributes are the books held by four of the Martyrs; the weapons of the soldier saints, Theodore and George; or the tablets of the Law in the hand of Moses (figs. 50, 68, 69).

The croziers of the holy Popes and Bishops symbolize, as they do in the actual life of the Church, the power of the higher clergy, the shepherds of the Lord's flock, and the authority of the doctrine (figs. 68 f., 70 f.). In addition, because of the sharpness of their lower ends they were interpreted as symbolic weapons against rebels and heretics.[2] This meaning is made evident where some Confessors use their croziers as spears to pierce the forces of evil underneath their feet.

The crosses, swords, and other objects held by the Apostles are by themselves real instruments of martyrdom (figs. 66, 67). Yet they are transformed into symbols of suffering and of victory over death, some of them because they are small in size (e.g., the crosses), all of them because they are carried by the victims and not by the torturers.

Some objects are a priori symbolic, such as the discs with the Agnus Dei (John the Baptist) and the cross (Jeremiah; fig. 51). Unlike the attributes of the Apostles, these objects refer not primarily to the figures holding them but to the death of Christ.

The spear, crown, and nails (now broken off) shown by King David have an intermediate place between the two last classes of attributes (fig. 50). Natural in size and shape like some attributes of the Apostles, they were meant to refer prophetically, like the cross disc of Jeremiah, to Christ's Passion.

Of all the statues, those of the central portal on the north side are, like their predecessors at Senlis, identified in the most varied manner by actions or attributes of very different kinds. From this point on a trend towards using the same species of attributes develops. All the attributes of the Apostles, though different, are those of martyrdom. The Martyrs and Confessors hold books or croziers. On the Incarnation portal on the north side the two Prophets show scrolls, and scrolls are also given to the statues of the Job portal.

Small pedestal reliefs are used as additional identification for some statues, and as exclusive identification for others. These reliefs, too, have a wide range of meaning. A good number of them represent specific evildoers who had caused the death of some saints and resisted others. Because of their small size and particular place they appear powerless and their actual defeat is made obvious where they are pierced by croziers. Other pedestal sculptures have a merely descriptive or symbolic meaning.[3]

Within the general stylistic evolution of the jamb figures individual characteristics bear witness to the number of artists active in each workshop. The twelve Apostles show a high degree of unity in their design. The statues of the central portal on the north side must have been carved by a greater number of artists. Marked differences are noticeable (figs. 50, 51). They range from the "neo-Romanesque" emotional intensity of John the Baptist, the ascetic thinness of St. Anne and King David, to the greater bulk and coarseness of Abraham.

Stylistic differences apparent among members of one workshop also exist between contemporary workshops. On the south transept the six Martyr statues originally planned share the equal size, the frontal pose, and the restraint that seems to reflect the influence of the Head Master (figs. 68, 69). The Confessor statues are somewhat more differentiated by variations in size, slight turns of heads, or by the motif of crushing with their croziers specific kinds of evil underneath their feet (figs. 70, 71). On the north transept the figures of the Annunciation and Visitation groups, although actually intercommunicating, remain perfectly static in pose and are balanced through similarity of body volumes (figs. 54, 55). The statues of the Job portal, although not drawn together into groups, are imbued with inner life, because of their energy-filled yet controlled attitudes, their swelling forms, and the deliberate differentiation of body volumes (figs. 62, 63). These differences between the statues of the lateral doorways seem accidental, but they correspond to the kind of tympana with which they are co-ordinated. Where only one martyrdom scene is represented, the Martyr statues form a homogeneous whole. Where the good deeds of the three Confessors—St. Martin, St. Nicholas, and St. Giles—are shown, the Confessor statues underneath vary considerably. The calmness of the Visitation and Annunciation groups corresponds to the quiet scenes in the Incarnation tympanum, while the inherently active quality of the statues decorating the Job portal is in harmony with the drama in the tympanum.

The master of the Annunciation and Visitation had a predilection for perfect control of drapery design. He arranged multiple folds evenly. They have a purity that indicates the belated influence of the Head Master of the Royal Portal. The sculptor of the statues on the portal of Job, on the other hand, was extremely bold and vigorous in his freer, more dramatic design of the drapery.

I I   LIKE the jamb statues, the tympana differ according to time and the individual styles of their artists. The Incarnation tympanum obviously was carved by a minor artist (fig. 53), while the tympanum of Job shows the same extraordinary boldness of design characteristic of the large statues underneath (fig. 58). Its balance is one not of static parts but of dramatic contrasts: between the active Devil and a meekly suffering Job, between the angular pattern of this group and the softer curves of the flanking figures, between the drama on earth and the calm group in heaven. Aside from differences in artistic quality, the tympana of the transept wings are of greater variety than those of the Royal Portal. On the earlier façade the unity of the Christological idea had found its formal counterpart in identical accents, in Christ assuming the same hieratic position with the same gesture in each tympanum. The tympana of the later cycles evince outspoken differences. Four tympana show Christ in frontal immobility, but in compassionate attitudes and with different gestures (Last Judgment tympanum; tympana of the Martyrs, of the Confessors, and of Job). In the other two He is in posture, gesture, and glance actively related to other figures (Triumph of the Virgin, Adoration of the Magi).

The central tympana share not only the compositional balance of central groups and kneeling Angels, but also the dominance over the lintel scenes, for in the tympana the power of Christ and the glory of Mary-Ecclesia are shown (figs. 47, 76). The lateral tympana, on the other hand, vary in emphasis. While this is, no doubt, due to different artistic aims, it also corroborates the specific meaning of the different scenes. In the lateral tympana individuals, and not Christ, are the main actors: a dying Saint, an Old Testament Hero plagued by the Devil, and Confessors performing good deeds.

In the tympanum of St. Stephen the emphasis is placed on the impressively large figure of Christ, who thereby strengthens the promise of eternal life to the saint in the hour of death (fig. 72). In contrast, the Logos, a passive witness to the Suffering of Job, is not larger than the human beings and is even smaller than the defiant Devil (fig. 58). The dramatic scene on earth, in conjunction with the equally dramatic Judgment of Solomon attracts, therefore, the primary attention of the beholder. It is only the place of the Logos in the apex that implies His ultimate power. Similar principles govern the design of the Confessors tympanum where good deeds of exemplary men are the main theme (fig. 73). The Incarnation tympanum, on the other hand, has an even distribution of accents (fig. 53). While the formal unity characterizing the layout of the tympana on the Royal Portal thus has been lost, individualizing differentiation has been gained.

Other changes achieve greater unity in the definition of space and greater equality in the relation of figures to each other. The subtle gradation in the degree of spatial description differentiating tympana, lintels, and archivolts of the Royal Portal is given up in favor of a greater unison of parts. On the Royal Portal settings were confined to the periphery, to the secular scenes in the lateral archivolts. On the transept wings elements of actual setting enter even the tympana and lintels where individual men assume the role of the main actors (trees in the Job scene, gate in the Martyrdom of St. Stephen, wall with window in the lintel of St. Nicholas). The back plane of the Confessors tympanum serves as a real wall. On a hook attached to it hangs half of St. Martin's cloak.

The more volumetric carving of the figures has its parallel in the deeper stages accorded them on tympana and lintels. On the Royal Portal the lintel figures had existed on narrow undescribed stages, but they did not interact with space either because of their immobile attitudes (Nativity lintel) or because of arches confining and stabilizing their heads. On the transept wings the relation of figures to a stage space is more definite. They exist in different planes (Separation of the Blessed and Damned, Judgment of Solomon). Their poses are not self-contained and the figures interact with space through turns and gestures.

As on the Royal Portal a series of arches span the width of some lintels, but their stage-defining function has increased. The arches have become completely independent of the figures, since they do not enclose their heads. They are also separated from the back wall and act as mere curtain fringes in the foreground.

In the sculptures of the transept wings, unlike those of the Royal Portal, the relation between figures does not increase with subtle gradation from the center towards the periphery. In the tympana of the Royal Portal Christ was given an immobile and frontal pose. On the north transept He interacts with the Virgin in the scene of her Triumph and He turns towards the adoring

Magi. On the west façade the intercommunication of the lintel figures was restricted. The witnesses of Solomon's Judgment, the three daughters of the impoverished man, on the other hand, are dramatically related to each other by poses and gestures. The Blessed and the Damned of the Separation scene, although calm in their attitudes, are tightly massed together and thus are closely connected with their own kind.

III   WHEREVER the sculptors of Chartres represent a scene for which a compositional scheme had been established not many years before on another church façade, they prove to be no mere imitators. The Triumph of the Virgin illustrates their attitudes and aims.

The tympana of Mantes, Laon, and Chartres are derived iconographically from Senlis, but none of them is a strict copy (figs. 45–47).[4] It seems that the masters of these tympana used earlier representations as working formulas to develop more valid solutions for the architectural framework, the relation between the main group and the Angels, between tympanum and lintel scenes.

The sculptors of Mantes and Laon tightened and unified the composition of the Senlis relief. The Chartres master went one step further in basic clarification. At the same time he also synthesized elements that were at variance with each other in the other tympana, thus creating the effect of normative validity.

The architectural framework of the Senlis tympanum may be interpreted as a symbol of the palace in heaven. By its compartmental design it separates rather than unites the figures placed within it. The elastically swinging curves of the large double arch give individual emphasis to Christ and Mary, while adjoining arches separate them from the attending Angels. The master of Mantes had different aims. In order to unify the main group he contracted the wide double arch into a steeper trefoil arch, yet he still retained the separation of the main group from the Angels.[5] The sculptor of Laon further transformed the framework for the purpose of total unity. He broadened the trefoil arch which now encompasses and ties together all the figures.

The Chartres master harmonized these earlier achievements. He adopted from Senlis the motif of separating the Angels from Christ and Mary by columns, and keeping the Angels apart from the realm reserved for the heavenly pair. He took over from Mantes the trefoil arch, changing it into a canopy that encloses and accentuates Christ and Mary. By crenellating the arch, adding architectural forms to its top, and covering the background with wavy cloud lines, the Chartres master made the function of the canopy as a symbol of the heavenly palace clearer than it had been in other tympana.

The arrangement of attending Angels underwent the same process of gradual simplification and clarification. In the tympana of Senlis, Mantes, and

Laon, four Angels had their place on the same stage as the main group. Hierarchically smaller than Mother and Son, the Angels next to them are standing. The Angels on the outer sides, at Senlis and Mantes, are seated; the sculptor of Laon transformed the sitting pose of the Angels in the corners into one of kneeling. This accentuates the movement towards the center in perfect consonance with the function of the trefoil arch and the swinging curves of the Angels' wings. The sculptor of Chartres eliminated the standing Angels altogether. He made the kneeling Angels as large as Christ and Mary, thus simplifying and clarifying the composition. In comparison to Laon, the curvilinear movement from the corners to the center has decreased. But this decrease is compensated for by the addition of two small flying Angels who by their direction accentuate Christ and Mary, and by the verticality of their wings accentuate the apex of the tympanum.

Other changes indicate the same tendency towards clarification and simplification. At Senlis, the Virgin Mary although turning towards Christ was not related to Him by gesture. A dramatic tension exists between their calm attitudes, on the one hand, and, on the other hand, their active drapery rhythms and the lively movements of the lintel figures. At Laon (where the original lintel reliefs no longer exist) the relation of Christ and Mary becomes closer. She turns her head more definitely and points with her left hand, although in a very restrained manner, towards Him. At Chartres, their relation becomes more intimate. The Virgin bends towards her Son and both her arms are extended towards Him in the gesture of submission. In contrast to the figures at Senlis, the poses and drapery design here are in consonance. While their attitudes have become less static, those of the lintel figures have become more so. With the differences existing at Senlis thus evened out, a perfect harmony among the three scenes is created at Chartres.

This balance may be seen in yet another detail. At Senlis the soul of Mary is taken up by two small flying Angels in the Death scene (fig. 49). In the Resurrection scene a large Angel holds the crown to be placed on Mary's head. This dynamic diagonal balance between two small Angels in the sky and a larger one on the ground, holding respectively Mary's soul and her crown, was translated at Chartres into a perfect balance. Two flying Angels are given the task of holding a crown in the Death scene, and Mary's soul in the Resurrection scene. This strengthens the harmony between the two compositions, a harmony achieved—in contrast to Senlis—by similarity in the arrangement of the figures on the stage and a continuous row of Angels in the clouds.

While this synthesis of earlier compositional types does not basically affect the meaning of the Virgin's Triumph, the Last Judgment at Chartres (fig. 76) shows both synthesis (attitude of Christ, size and place of the cross) and radical changes (elimination of the Apostles from the tympanum, size of the Intercessors). This not only gives a new lucidity to the composition and clarifies the essence of the Last Judgment to the beholder; above all, it strengthens the idea of mercy and gives a more hopeful aspect to the scene.

IV   HOW does the humanization as it characterizes the sculptures of the transept wings differ in degree from the incipient humanization evident in the sculptures of the Royal Portal? Towards the middle of the twelfth century the School of Chartres was one of the most important seats of learning in France. Sixty or seventy years later the center of gravity shifted to the University of Paris. Here the Aristotelian concepts—that universal ideas have reality within visible forms, that the soul is the form of the body—had taken firm roots. The ascendancy of these concepts may well be reflected in the sculptures of the transept wings at Chartres.

Similar in poses and gestures, the jamb statues of the Royal Portal were primarily manifestations of the same idea, while inner attitudes differentiated them from one another. Differentiated in poses, gestures, attributes, pedestal figures and, in addition, by specific actions, the statues of the transept wings are primarily particular personalities, while they express specific ideas. The statues of the Royal Portal were related as a whole group to the three tympana. The statues on the north and south sides are specifically co-ordinated with individual tympana.

In the jamb statues of the Royal Portal, the idea still prevailed over natural forms and shaped them. In the statues of the transept wings, a balance between their greater physical reality and their ideal relation to the façade was achieved.

On the transept façades, Mary is more intimately related to her Son, and Christ is more closely linked to individuals. Each of the three central tympana shows His power, while He is enthroned in heaven. The Royal Portal reveals the apocalyptic vision of the almighty God and King, aloof in His attitude and enclosed by a mandorla. In the later representations at Chartres the concept of his might is mitigated. On the north façade He reigns in heaven, but allows the Virgin Mary, the Intercessor for mankind, to rule with Him and He blesses her. In the south He is the supreme Judge appearing with all the holy Angels, but His wounds and insignia remind us of past self-sacrifice, and He suffers the intercession of His mother and of John the Disciple.

On the transept façades He is even compassionately related to individuals. Mournfully He witnesses the Suffering of Job, He appears to St. Stephen in an act of personal grace, and He reveals to St. Martin the true value of the gift to the poor man. As Teacher of mankind Christ has stepped down, as it were, from the exalted height of the tympana and stands closer to those who enter the cathedral. And as the supreme Judge does not differ in size from the Intercessors, so is the Teacher not larger than the Apostles surrounding Him.

He is just one, although the central, member of the whole group. On the west façade of Amiens, on the other hand, His power is stressed anew, for He towers in size over the Intercessors in the tympanum of the Last Judgment, and as Teacher over the Apostles along the jambs. While the lateral tympana of the Royal Portal illustrate the Christological dogma, three of the four lateral tympana on the transept wings show man as he wins reward by suffering or by performing good deeds.

Lastly, the incipient differentiation of human attitudes on the Royal Portal is carried further in the later phase. The master of the archivolts on the portal of Job explores emotional possibilities to the fullest degree. Judith kneels on the ground in an attitude of innermost humility (fig. 61). Manoah and his wife pray with moving intensity (fig. 60). Blind Tobit—whether he sits with his head bent sidewards, as if listening, or lovingly and eagerly touches with his groping hands the head of his returning son—was carved by an artist who knew about the behavior and the feelings of a blind man (figs. 60, 61).

The sculptures of the transept wings thus evince a greater degree of humanization than the earlier works. But one should not forget: it was the Head Master who had taken the bold step in a new direction when he began to give his sculptures inner animation. It was left to the masters of the transept wings, and to the masters of other church façades, to follow his lead and go farther in the same direction.

Although the total program of the transept cycles is the result of a change in the original plan, the two façades are balanced iconographically and by formal means. An over-all harmony is achieved because each tympanum shows the Lord flanked by Angels who emphasize Him.

There exists a perfect balance between the corresponding figures of Christ on the north and the south sides: between Christ the King (Triumph of the Virgin) and Christ the Judge; between the Logos (tympanum of Job) and the Son of man (tympanum of St. Stephen), both witnessing martyrdom and holding palm branches (now broken off); between Christ receiving gifts on earth (Adoration of the Magi) and Christ receiving a gift in heaven (tympanum of the Confessors); and in addition, between Mary-Ecclesia and Mary the Intercessor, both humbly bending towards Christ.

On either façade four calm scenes (Incarnation and Confessors tympana) are balanced against a smaller number of dramatic events (tympana of Job and St. Stephen).

V   WHAT the masters of the Royal Portal achieved proved fruitful for later generations. The transept façades show the adaptation of basic elements from the Royal Portal: the leitmotiv of Christ flanked by two Angels, and the particular balance of the lateral tympana. The restrained attitudes of the

Martyrs, and the controlled drapery design of the statues in the later Incarnation portal reflect the style of the Head Master. The principle of a multipartite central axis that had given order to the Incarnation tympanum of the Royal Portal and revealed specific ideas was used again for the portal of the Last Judgment where it fulfills the very same function.

The total sculptural decoration of the cathedral thus forms in the very end an organic and integrated whole, because the planners of the transept wings were well aware of certain principles of composition that had been evolved on the Royal Portal. These compositional devices clarify and heighten the coherence between successive iconographic programs that complement each other in the representation of Christ, of the Virgin Mary, and of the Church.

If one considers the three façade programs as an ultimate unit, one realizes that they depict, like a *Summa,* the total essence of Christ in all its conceptual ramifications. Each façade glorifies Him. On the west side He is shown as Divine Wisdom, as God and man, who was born so that His body could provide the substance of the Eucharist, who ascended to heaven and will return at the end of the days. On the transept wings He is shown as the eternal Logos, as the Son of man, as Teacher, as King and Judge. The purpose of His Incarnation to redeem mankind through His death, as it had been prefigured by actions and attributes of Old Testament personages, is revealed at the beginning of His earthly life by the altar-like manger on which the Child is placed. His same purpose is revealed once more at the end of time when the Judge shows His wounds.

The Virgin Mary, the Lady of Chartres, was honored in the lateral tympanum of the Royal Portal as Theotokos and *Sedes Sapientiae.* She received a prominent place on the transept wings. In the scene of her Triumph she is glorified in her own right and as the type of the Church. In the Last Judgment she intercedes for mankind.

The Church is shown as the Bride of Christ and as His Body. She is shown triumphant and militant. She is exemplified by her foremost members, the Community of Saints.

The concept of harmony between *regnum* and *sacerdotium* as the best guarantee for the welfare of the Church is still another thread linking the various cycles. The Old Testament statues of the Royal Portal prefigure this harmony, as they form the foundation of the sculptural decoration. Encompassing front and sides of the cathedral, the Gallery of Kings, and the Bishops in the tabernacles of the buttresses reaffirm this concept at a later time, as they terminate the sculptural decoration in the upper part of the cathedral.

Each of the nine doorways of the cathedral is flanked by statues. Larger in size than the churchgoers, they protect the entrances while bearing witness to Christ, Mary, and the Church.

The iconographic programs were not conceived simply as general systems of ideas. They make visible theological truths as they were stressed in the liturgy year after year, and as they were defended against the tenets of heretics.

The planners of the three cycles at Chartres drew inspiration from many sources: from the two Testaments and from legends, from the dogmas of the Church, from theological exegesis, from political and philosophical concepts. Where they did not create new kinds of representation, they proved to be great synthesizers of the ideological and artistic heritage. They also were quick in sensing changes of thought and history occurring in their own time.

Ideas promulgated by the great teachers of the School of Chartres over the span of two centuries remain alive in the sculptural decoration. This establishes an indissoluble link between a great center of learning and a great center of art. Early in the eleventh century Bishop Fulbert had expressed his strong liking for the apocryphal story of Mary's infancy, as it was to be represented on the friezes of the Royal Portal. He had extolled the close relation between the Virgin Mary and John the Disciple in heaven, as it was to become visible in the Last Judgment tympanum. Bishop Ivo not only had stressed again and again the necessity of harmony between *regnum* and *sacerdotium;* he also had seen this idea translated into practice. His concept might well be reflected in the statues of royal portals. Like other teachers of the School of Chartres, Thierry had fostered the study of the liberal arts and he also demonstrated their application to the understanding of theological truths. Thereby he made the liberal arts acceptable as framework for the Incarnation cycle. New psychological notions of William of Conches about the relation of soul and body, and new philosophical definitions of the difference between individuals, as Gilbert de la Porrée formulated them, are related to the new inner animation and differentiation of the Head Master's statues. Finally, Peter of Roissy reaffirmed St. Gregory's interpretation of the body of Job as the Church and, in all likelihood, caused its representation on the north transept.

After the churchgoer has entered the cathedral he may, at the crossing of nave and transept, look at the interiors of the three façades. In their stained-glass windows he may see, represented in colors aglow with light, some of the ideas carved in stone on the outside: in the west, the Kings and Prophets in the Tree of Jesse window, the *Sedes Sapientiae* and the earthly life of Christ in the adjoining windows; in the north, an even closer "replica" of the sculptural cycle decorating the central portal, namely St. Anne holding the Infant Mary among witnesses of the Old Testament, and in the rose window the Ancestors of Christ, in harmony with the Tree of Jesse in the archivolts; in the south, the Return of the apocalyptic Christ in the rose window, and the idea of continuity between the two Testaments in the Evangelists sitting on the shoulders of Prophets. Thus ideas radiating outwards, as it were from the portals of the cathedral also radiate inwards into the interior and permeate with their colors the room where the religious services take place.

Notes

Introduction

1. Urbs quoque Carnotum, quam civis tam numerosus,
    Tamque potens clerus et tam predives opimant,
    Ecclesieque decus, cui scemate, mole, decore,
    Judicio par nulla meo reperitur in orbe:
    Quam, quasi postpositis specialiter omnibus, unam
    Virgo beata docet Christi se mater amare
    Innumerabilibus signis, gratoque favore,
    Carnoti dominam se dignans sepe vocare;
    Cujus et interulam cuncti venerantur ibidem,
    Qua vestita fuit cum partu protulit agnum,
    Qui mundi peccata tulit, qui sanguine mundo
    Mundum mundavit a primi labe parentis;
    Qui thronum mundum sibi sanctificavit eamdem,
    Sic ut virgo manens matris gauderet honore.

(Willelmi Brittonis Philippis, II, vss. 391 ff.; *Oeuvres de Rigord et de Guillaume le Breton,* ed. H.-F. Delaborde, Paris, 1885, II, pp. 55 f.) These verses are a poetical translation of a passage in the *Miracles of the Blessed Virgin,* performed in the Cathedral of Chartres, written *ca. 1210:* " . . . pia Dei genitrix ac perpetua virgo Maria, que se urbis et ecclesie dominam Carnotensis multis pridem miraculis quibusdam fidelibus visibiliter apparendo et colloquendo fuerat protestata . . . ostendens quod locum illum, quasi singulariter diligeret ac precipue, et eamdem ecclesiam tanquam speciale domicilium sibi elegerat in terris. Nec mirum sane si eam pre ceteris diligat ecclesiis, que tanto dilectionis sue ab antiquo pignore insignata est, illa videlicet insigni et sacrosancta camisia, quam eadem virgo dum Dei filium suo gestaret in utero induit, et quam ipsa in puerperio, juxta multorum assercionem fidelium, circa renes beatissimos dicitur habuisse" (A. Thomas, *Les miracles de Notre-Dame de Chartres, Texte latin inédit* [*Bibliothèque de l'Ecole des Chartes,* XLII], 1881, pp. 508 f.).

2. The siege of Chartres in 911 is mentioned in various chronicles. See, for instance, *Historia Francorum Senonensis* (*Monumenta Germaniae Historica* [cited as *Mon. Germ. Hist.* afterwards], *Scriptores,* IX, p. 365); Hugh of Fleury, *Modernorum regum Francorum actus* (*ibidem,* IX, p. 380); William of Malmesbury, *Gesta regum Anglorum (ibidem,* XIII, p. 134).

The salvation of the city in 1119 was recorded by Abbot Suger (*Vie de Louis VI le Gros,* ed. and trans. H. Waquet, Paris, 1929, pp. 198, 200).

3. The story made its appearance in the *Vieille Chronique* commissioned in 1389 by Bishop Jean Lefèvre (*Cartulaire de Notre-Dame de Chartres,* publ. by E. de Lépinois and L. Merlet, Chartres, 1862–65, I. 2, pp. 38 ff.). For a critical evaluation of the *Vieille Chronique,* see M. Jusselin, *Les traditions de l'église de Chartres (Mémoires de la Société archéologique d'Eure-et-Loir,* XV), Chartres, 1914.

The claim made for the priority of Chartres Cathedral over all other churches in France was recognized in official documents. King Charles VII wrote in 1432: " . . . néantmoins en pitié et en faveur de la dicte eglise de Chartres, laquelle est la plus ancienne eglise de nostre royaume, fondée

par prophecie en l'onneur de la glorieuse
Vierge Marie par avant l'Incarnacion de
Nostre Seigneur Jhesucrist et en laquelle
icelle glorieuse Vierge fu aourée en son
vivant" (M. Jusselin, *op. cit.*, p. 24). Yet
even before the *Vieille Chronique* was
composed, a document given by King Jean
II le Bon in 1356 mentions that the church
was founded at a most remote time while
the Virgin was still alive, as it is written
in the old books of the church (*ibidem*,
p. 19 f.).

4. "Curiae coelesti gaudium intulisse
credimus, quod Beatae Virginis Ecclesia,
per Spiritum sanctum concipiens, dilectum
Deo et hominibus pastorem germinavit.
Acclamantibus itaque omnium votis desi-
deratum sibi postulat, et ad dilectum et ad
electum sibi incunctanter aspirat Carnotensis Ecclesia, sponsique desiderio jam
languescens: 'Osculetur me,' inquit, 'osculo
oris sui,'" (J. P. Migne, *Patrologia latina*
[cited as *P. L.* afterwards], CIC, col. 375).

5. *Chronicle* of Robert of Torigni
(*Mon. Germ. Hist., Scriptores*, VI, p. 496).

6. P. du Colombier, *Les chantiers des
cathédrales*, Paris, 1953, pp. 18 f.; E.
Panofsky, *Abbot Suger on the Abbey
Church of St. Denis and Its Art Treasures*,
Princeton, 1946, pp. 214 f.

7. *Monographie de la cathédrale de
Chartres*, 2d ed., Chartres, 1887–92.

8. *L'art religieux du XIIe siècle en
France*, 2d ed., Paris, 1924; *L'art religieux
du XIIIe siècle en France*, 6th ed., Paris
1925; *Notre-Dame de Chartres*, Paris,
1948.

9. The book was published in Strasbourg
in 1894, the article in the *Zeitschrift für
bildende Kunst*, new series, XXV (1913–
14), pp. 193 ff. See now *Bildhauer des
Mittelalters, Gesammelte Studien von Wilhelm Vöge*, Berlin, 1958, pp. 63 ff.

10. For the sculptures of Chartres
Cathedral, see E. Houvet's "Summa photo-
graphica," *Cathédrale de Chartres*, Chelles
(S. et M.), 1919; W. Sauerländer, *Die
Kathedrale von Chartres*, Stuttgart, 1954;
Notre-Dame de Chartres, with introduction
by Chanoine Y. Delaporte, Paris, 1957;
P. Kidson, *Sculpture at Chartres*, London,
1958.

For the Royal Portal, see M. Lanore,
"Reconstruction de la façade de la cathé-

drale de Chartres au XIIe siècle," *Revue
de l'art chrétien*, 1899, pp. 328 ff., and
1900, pp. 32 ff., 137 ff.; E. Lefèvre-
Pontalis, "Les façades successives de la
cathédrale de Chartres au XIe et XIIe
siècles," *Congrès archéologique*, 1900, pp.
256 ff.; A. Mayeux, "Réponse à M. Eugène
Lefèvre-Pontalis sur son article" (*Mémoires
de la Société archéologique d'Eure-et-Loir*,
XIII), Chartres, 1901–4, pp. 414 ff.; E.
Lefèvre-Pontalis, "Nouvelles études sur les
façades et les clochers de la cathédrale
de Chartres: Réponse à M. Mayeux,"
ibidem, pp. 434 ff.; A. Priest, "The
Masters of the West Façade of Chartres,"
Art Studies, I, (1923), pp. 28 ff.; A. K.
Porter, *Romanesque Sculpture of the Pilgrimage Roads*, Boston, 1923, pp. 123 ff.
et passim; M. Aubert, *French Sculpture at
the Beginning of the Gothic Period 1140-
1225*, Florence-New York, 1929, pp. 8 ff.;
idem, La sculpture française au moyen-âge,
Paris, 1946, pp. 176 ff.; *idem*, "Le portail
royal et la façade occidentale de la cathédrale de Chartres, Essai sur la date de
leur exécution," *Bulletin monumental*, C
(1941), pp. 177 ff.; *idem*, "Le portail
royal de Chartres, Essai sur la date de son
exécution," *Miscellanea Leo van Puyvelde*,
Brussels, 1949, pp. 281 ff.; C. Gold-
scheider, "Les origines du portail à statues-
colonnes," *Bulletin des Musées de
France*, XI (1946), no. 6/7, pp. 22 ff.;
H. Giesau, "Stand der Forschung über das
Figurenportal des Mittelalters," *Beiträge
zur Kunst des Mittelalters*, Berlin, 1950,
pp. 119 ff.; W. S. Stoddard, *The West
Portals of Saint-Denis and Chartres*, Cambridge, Mass., 1952; E. Fels, "Die Grabung
an der Fassade der Kathedrale von Chartres," *Kunst-Chronik*, VIII (1955), pp.
149 ff.

For the architecture of Chartres Cathedral, see O. von Simson, *The Gothic
Cathedral (Bollingen Series, XLVIII)*, New
York, 1956. Finally Henry Adams' *Mont-
Saint-Michel and Chartres* should not be
forgotten. Published in 1904, it has capti-
vated readers for more than half a century
because its author had the rare power to
conjure up and recreate the life and the
thoughts of medieval times.

For the transept, see W. Vöge, *op. cit.*;
S. Abdul-Hak, *La sculpture des porches du*

transept de la cathédrale de Chartres, Paris, 1942; G. Schlag, "Die Skulpturen des Querhauses der Kathedrale von Chartres," "*Westdeutsches Jahrbuch für Kunstgeschichte (Wallraf - Richartz Jahrbuch),* XII-XIII (1943), pp. 115 ff.; L. Grodecki, "The Transept Portals of Chartres Cathedral: The Date of their Construction according to Archaeological Data," *Art Bulletin,* XXXIII (1951), pp. 156 ff.; P. Frankl, "The Chronology of Chartres Cathedral," *ibidem,* XXXIX (1957), pp. 33 ff.; L. Grodecki, "Chronologie de la cathédrale de Chartres," *Bulletin monumental,* CXVI (1958), pp. 91 ff.; M. Aubert, *French Sculpture,* pp. 81 ff.; *idem, La sculpture française,* pp. 219 ff.

11. Of fundamental importance for the history of the School of Chartres: Abbé A. Clerval, *Les écoles de Chartres au moyen-âge (Mémoires de la Société archéologique d'Eure-et-Loir,* XI), Chartres, 1895. See also A. Clerval, *L'enseignement des arts libéraux à Chartres et à Paris dans la première moitié du XIIe siècle d'après l'Heptateuchon de Thierry de Chartres,* Paris, 1889; R. L. Poole, "The Masters of the Schools at Paris and Chartres in John of Salisbury's Time," *The English Historical Review,* XXXV, (1920), pp. 321 ff.; *idem, Illustrations of the History of Medieval Thought and Learning,* 2d ed., London, 1920, pp. 95 ff.; L. C. MacKinney, *Bishop Fulbert and Education at the School of Chartres,* Notre Dame, Indiana, 1957; C. H. Haskins, *The Renaissance of the Twelfth Century,* Cambridge, Mass., 1927, especially pp. 101 ff., 135 ff.; G. Paré, A. Brunet, P. Trem-

blay, *La renaissance du XIIe siècle. Les écoles et l'enseignement (Publications de l'Institut d'études médiévales d'Ottawa,* III), Paris-Ottawa, 1933; M. de Wulf, *Histoire de la philosophie médiévale,* 6th ed., Louvain-Paris, 1934–47, I, pp. 178 ff.; E. Gilson, *History of Christian Philosophy in the Middle Ages,* New York, 1955, pp. 139 ff.; M.-D. Chenu, *La théologie au douzième siècle (Etudes de philosophie médiévale,* XLV), Paris, 1957, pp. 20 ff.

Philosophical treatises of the School of Chartres were published by B. Hauréau, *Notices et extraits de quelques manuscrits latins de la Bibliothèque nationale,* Paris, 1890, I, pp. 52 ff.; W. Jansen, *Der Kommentar des Clarenbaldus von Arras zu Boethius De Trinitate (Breslauer Studien zur historischen Theologie,* VIII), Breslau, 1926; J. M. Parent, *La doctrine de la création dans l'école de Chartres (Publications de l'Institut d'études médiévales d'Ottawa,* VIII), Paris-Ottawa, 1938; N. M. Haring, "A hitherto unknown Commentary on Boethius' *de Hebdomadibus* written by Clarenbaldus of Arras," *Mediaeval Studies,* XV (1953), pp. 212 ff.; *idem,* "The Creation and Creator of the World according to Thierry of Chartres and Clarenbaldus of Arras," *Archives d'histoire doctrinale et littéraire du moyen âge,* XXII (1955), pp. 137 ff.; *idem,* "The Lectures of Thierry of Chartres on Boethius' De Trinitate," *ibidem,* XXV (1958), pp. 113 ff.

For documents of the Cathedral of Chartres, see *Cartulaire de Notre-Dame de Chartres,* publ. by E. de Lépinois and L. Merlet, Chartres, 1862–65.

Part One: The Sculptures of the Royal Portal

I   RELATION TO EARLIER CHURCH FAÇADES

1. S. McK. Crosby, *L'abbaye royale de Saint-Denis,* Paris, 1953; W. S. Stoddard, *The West Portals of Saint-Denis and Chartres.*

2. The archivolts of Burgundian tympana are usually flat and, for the most part, ornamented (Perrecy - les - Forges; Saint-

Vincent, Mâcon; Saint-Julien-de-Jonzy; see A. K. Porter, *Romanesque Sculpture of the Pilgrimage Roads,* figs. 84, 92, 111). Aside from Saint-Lazare, Avallon, no more than one archivolt is decorated by figures (La Madeleine, Vézelay; Saint-Lazare, Autun; Charlieu; *ibidem,* figs. 137 f., 47, 80, 110).

In the Languedoc, tympana are deeply recessed, without having adjoining archivolts (Saint-Sernin, Toulouse; Saint-Bertrand-de-Comminges; *ibidem,* figs. 308, 323). Where archivolts occur, they are plain or ornamented (Saint-Pierre, Moissac; Carennac, Beaulieu, Cahors; *ibidem,* figs. 339, 381, 409, 422).

3. See also Saint-Symphorien; Sainte-Croix, Bordeaux; Saint-Pierre, Aulnay; Saint-Hilaire, Melle *(ibidem,* figs. 919, 921, 979, 1011).

4. For the Cathedral of Ferrara, see, D. M. Robb, "Niccolò: A North Italian Sculptor of the Twelfth Century," *Art Bulletin,* XII (1930), pp. 374 ff., especially pp. 394 ff.; T. Krautheimer-Hess, "The Original Porta dei Mesi at Ferrara and the Art of Niccolo," *Art Bulletin,* XXVI (1944), pp. 152 ff., especially p. 160; G. H. Crichton, *Romanesque Sculpture in Italy,* London, 1954, pp. 22 f.

For the façade of Saint-Gilles, see R. Hamann, *Die Abteikirche von St. Gilles und ihre künstlerische Nachfolge,* Berlin, 1955.

5. A detailed description of the cutting is given by W. Sauerländer, "Zu den Westportalen von Chartres," *Kunst-Chronik,* IX (1956), pp. 155 f.

6. The different theories are summarized by W. S. Stoddard, *op. cit.,* pp. 14 ff.

7. E. Fels, "Die Grabung an der Fassade der Kathedrale von Chartres," *Kunst-Chronik,* VIII (1955), pp. 149 ff. He suggests that the foundations discovered in part by E. Lefèvre-Pontalis, in part during the excavations of 1938, once supported a central tower with three openings in front of Fulbert's cathedral, comparable to the western tower of Saint-Benoît-sur-Loire (pp. 149 f.). This theory finds its corroboration in several passages of a Chartrain *Ordinarium,* composed in the first half of the twelfth century. On certain days, we are told, processions pass through the middle doorway of the tower *("per mediam portam turris").* Significantly enough, a later *Ordinarium* of the thirteenth century mentions that the same processions pass through the Royal Portal *("per portam regiam").* See Y. Delaporte, *L'ordinaire chartrain du XIIIᵉ siècle publié d'après le manuscrit original (Mémoires de la Société archéologique d'Eure-et-Loir,* XIX), Chartres, 1953, p. 26.

8. Because of the findings of E. Fels,

M. Aubert proposes that the Royal Portal was never actually put into place at its original site ("Le portail royal et la façade occidentale de la cathédrale de Chartres," *Bulletin monumental,* C [1941], pp. 177 ff.; "Le portail royal de Chartres, Essai sur la date de son exécution," *Miscellanea Leo van Puyvelde,* Brussels, 1949, pp. 281 ff.). His opinion about the first façade plan and his reasons for the adjustment necessitated by the new site differ from the theory I would like to propose.

According to Aubert, the first plan for the façade (to be placed between the eastern piers of the towers and therefore somewhat narrower than the present façade) was confined to three sculptured tympana (the lateral tympana planned without lower lintels) and to jamb figures for the central portal only. The more old-fashioned jamb statues (now on the outer jambs), the right tympanum and its lower lintel had been carved, the left tympanum possibly had begun, but nothing had been put into place when this nucleus of sculptures was made part of the new enlarged plan for a façade flush with the towers.

Aubert assumes that the adjustments were necessary because the right portal had to be squeezed in, owing to a discrepancy between the center of the new site and the central axis of the church. The validity of this theory seems open to questions. It presupposes that the master, planning the façade in its final shape, realized the discrepancy only after all the sculptures had been carved. Otherwise it would not have been necessary to cut the upper lintel on the right side and the archivolts at the bottom. According to Aubert, these parts were carved only after the change in plan.

Furthermore, if we follow his arguments, the left portal would not have to be squeezed in. And yet, here too the tympanum was narrowed and the archivolts were cut off at the lower ends. Could all this not be explained by assuming that the first project had foreseen two lintels and the archivolts? Being carved but not yet put into place when the plan was changed, they had to be cut drastically to fit the new site. See also P. Kidson, *Sculpture at Chartres,* pp. 8 f.

W. S. Stoddard *(op. cit.,* pp. 16 f.) proposes anew the theory of E. Lefèvre-Pontalis that the façade was moved forward only after the fire of 1194.

9. M. Schapiro, "The Romanesque Sculpture of Moissac, Part I (2)," *Art Bulletin,* XIII (1931), pp. 464 ff., figs. 92, 93, 107, 108.

10. A. Katzenellenbogen, "The Central Tympanum at Vézelay, Its Encyclopedic Meaning and Its Relation to the First Crusade," *Art Bulletin,* XXVI (1944), pp. 141 ff., figs. 1, 5, 6.

For the façade of Saint-Gilles, see R. Hamann, *op. cit.,* pls. 1–5.

II THE TYMPANA AND CAPITAL FRIEZES

1. "Thesaurus enim regni, sacrificium Dei, myrrha est sepulturae" (St. Ambrose, *De fide,* I. 4; *P. L.,* XVI, col. 558). See G. Vezin, *L'adoration et le cycle des mages dans l'art chrétien primitif,* Paris, 1950; A. Grabar, *L'empereur dans l'art byzantin (Publications de la faculté des lettres de l'Université de Strasbourg,* fasc. 75), Paris, 1936, pp. 233 f.

2. A. K. Porter, *Romanesque Sculpture of the Pilgrimage Roads,* pp. 125 ff.; E. Mâle, *L'art religieux du XIIe siècle en France,* pp. 116 f.; H. Beenken, "Die Tympana von La Charité sur Loire," *Art Studies,* VI (1928), pp. 145 ff. Mâle and Beenken regard the lintels of La Charité as copies of the Chartres scenes. Yet they are more *retardataire* in style than the Chartres lintels. The proportions of the figures are stockier, their poses less stabilized and more restricted since parts of their bodies are kept parallel to the back plane. Some halos press against the molding. The drapery design is less controlled.

3. M. Aubert, *French Sculpture at the Beginning of the Gothic Period,* pl. 30.

4. That Christ is represented as God and man was suggested by Abbé Bulteau, *Monographie de la cathédrale de Chartres,* II, p. 73.

5. A. Katzenellenbogen, "The Sarcophagus in S. Ambrogio and St. Ambrose," *Art Bulletin,* XXIX (1948), pp. 249 ff., figs. 3, 4.

6. To name just a few examples: fresco of the fifth century at Bawit (J. Maspero, *Fouilles exécutées à Baouît* [*Mémoires publiés par les membres de l'Institut français d'archéologie orientale du Caire,* LIX], Cairo, 1943, pl. XXI); Bernward Gospels of the early eleventh century (Hildesheim, Cathedral Treasure, MS 18, fol. 174r; F. J. Tschan, *Saint Bernward of Hildesheim,* Notre Dame, Indiana, 1952, III, fig. 73); tympanum of Anzy-le-Duc (A. K. Porter, *op. cit.,* fig. 98).

7. "Longe est super omnes coelos, sed pedes habet in terra: caput in coelo est, corpus in terra" (St. Augustine, *Enarratio in Psalmum XC; P.L.,* XXXVII, col. 1163). See E. H. Kantorowicz's magnificent book *The King's Two Bodies, A Study in Mediaeval Political Theology,* Princeton, 1957, pp. 70 ff.

8. A. Grabar, "The Virgin in a Mandorla of Light," *Late Classical and Mediaeval Studies in Honor of Albert Mathias Friend, Jr.,* Princeton, 1955, pp. 305 ff.

9. *Sermo IV (P.L.,* CXLI, cols. 320 ff.).

10. *De miraculis Beatae Mariae Virginis,* prologue *(P.L.,* CLXXIII, col. 1379).

11. A. Grabar, *Ampoules de Terre Sainte,* Paris, 1958, pp. 16 ff. See pls. I, IV, VIII, and X. Grabar suggests the imperial art of Rome and Byzantium as the source for these representations (p. 53). Because of the complete lack of evidence, he rejects, at least for the time being, the theory that these compositions reflect a monumental painting or mosaic of one of the sanctuaries in the Holy Land (pp. 46 ff.).

12. M. van Berchem and E. Clouzot, *Mosaïques chrétiennes du IVme au Xme siècle,* Geneva, 1924, figs. 143, 173, 178.

13. *Ibidem,* fig. 221.

14. For the Theotokos as part of the Adoration of the Magi, see, for instance, portal of Saint-Ours, Loches (A. K. Porter, *op. cit.,* fig. 1113).

For the Theotokos flanked by Angels, see, for instance, ivory kettle in the Treasure of Milan Cathedral (A. Goldschmidt, *Die Elfenbeinskulpturen aus der Zeit der karolingischen und sächsischen Kaiser,* Berlin, 1914–26, II, pl. Ia); tympanum of Corneilla-de-Conflent (A. K. Porter, *op. cit.,* fig. 528).

For the Theotokos group alone, see, for

instance, west portal at Donzy; south transept, Mozac; altar-frontal, Old Cathedral in Marseilles; altar-frontal from Carrière-Saint-Denis, now in the Louvre (A. K. Porter, *op. cit.*, figs. 113, 1223, 1284, 1485 f.). This type of representation is discussed fully by M. Lawrence, "Maria Regina," *Art Bulletin,* VII (1924-25), pp. 150 ff.

15. E. Kitzinger, *Early Medieval Art in the British Museum,* London, 1940, p. 101.

16. For an Ottonian example, e.g., see Codex Aureus from Echternach (Gotha, Landesbibl., MS I.19, fol. 36r; A. Goldschmidt, *Die deutsche Buchmalerei,* Florence-Munich, 1928, II, pl. 46). Several examples of eleventh-century miniatures are reproduced by C. Rohault de Fleury, *La sainte Vierge,* Paris, 1878, I, pls. XXI, XXIII, XXVI.

17. "Gratiae plenus erat idem homo Christus Jesus, cui singulari munere prae caeteris mortalibus datum est, ut statim ex quo in utero virginis concipi et homo fieri inciperet, verus esset et Deus" (*Homilia VII, P.L.,* XCIV, col. 43). "Unde oportet . . . , ut qui humanam Redemptoris nostri nativitatem hodie annua devotione recolimus, et divinam pariter et humanam ejus naturam non annuo, sed continuo semper amplectamur amore" (*ibidem,* col. 44). The homily forms part of the twelfth century Lectionary of the Chapter of Chartres Cathedral (*olim* Bibl. de la Ville, MS 138, fols. 23v ff.).

18. "Ergo Dominus nostrae per omnia memor salutis, non solum homo fieri, cum Deus esset, sed etiam cum dives esset, pauper fieri dignatus est pro nobis, ut nos sua paupertate, simul et humanitate divitiarum et divinitatis suae donaret esse participes" (*Homilia XV, ibidem,* col. 80). See MS 138, fols. 34 ff.

19. "Unde et eadem gloriosa semper virgo Maria non solum hominis Christi sed et Dei genitrix recte credenda et confitenda est" (*Homilia VII, ibidem,* cols. 43 f.).

20. "Solemnitatem nobis hodiernae celebritatis, quam quadragesimo dominicae nativitatis die debitis veneramur officiis, maxime ejusdem Domini Salvatoris nostri, simul et intemeratae genitricis ejus humili-

tati dedicatum sacra Evangelii lectio designat" (*Homilia XV, ibidem,* col. 79).

21. "Qui bene etiam in Bethlehem nascitur: Bethlehem quippe domus panis interpretatur. Ipse namque est qui ait: 'Ego sum panis vivus, qui de coelo descendi.' Locus ergo, in quo Dominus nascitur, domus panis antea vocatus est, quia futurum profecto erat, ut ille ibi per materiam carnis appareret, qui electorum mentes interna satietate reficeret" (*P.L.,* LXXVI, col. 1104). See MS 138, fols. 17v ff.

22. "Unde et natus in praesepio reclinatur, ut fideles omnes, videlicet sancta animalia, carnis suae frumento reficeret" (*loc. cit.*).

23. John Chrysostom, for instance, says that the body of the Lord will lie on the table, not wrapped in swaddling clothes as before, but clothed by the Holy Spirit (*Eulogy of St. Philogonius; Patr. graeca,* XLVIII, col. 753). According to a treatise ascribed to St. Germanus, the altar is, and is called, manger and tomb (*Historia ecclesiastica et mystica contemplatio; Patr. graeca,* XCVIII, col. 389). See also Walafrid Strabo, *Expositio in quatuor Evangelia:* "Positus in praesepio, id est corpus Christi super altare" (*P.L.,* CXIV, col. 896).

24. *Ordo Romanus XIV,* 67; *P.L.,* LXXVIII, col. 1182.

25. H. de Lubac, *Corpus mysticum,* 2d ed., Paris, 1949. See also M. Lepin, *L'idée du sacrifice de la messe d'après les théologiens depuis l'origine jusqu'à nos jours,* Paris, 1926; F. Holböck, *Der eucharistische und der mystische Leib Christi in ihren Beziehungen zueinander nach der Lehre der Frühscholastik,* Rome, 1941.

26. Paschasius Radbertus, *Liber de corpore et sanguine Domini (P.L.,* CXX, cols. 1267 ff.), written in 831, dedicated in a second edition to Charles the Bald in 844; Ratramnus of Corbie, *De corpore et sanguine Domini (P.L.,* CXXI, cols. 125 ff.). See H. de Lubac, *op. cit.,* pp. 39 ff.; M. Lepin, *op. cit.,* pp. 6 ff.

27. W. Koehler, *Die karolingischen Miniaturen,* I (*Die Schule von Tours, Text,* II), Berlin, 1933, p. 135, pl. I. 73; M. Schapiro, "Two Romanesque Drawings in Auxerre and some Iconographic Problems," *Studies in Art and Literature for Belle da*

Costa Greene, Princeton, 1954, pp. 331 ff., especially pp. 341 ff.

28. See also the tympana of Vizille (A. K. Porter, *op. cit.,* fig. 1185), Vaudeins, and Bellenaves (R. Hamann, *op. cit.,* figs. 430, 432). At Saint-Gilles where the original tympanum no longer exists the Majestas Domini—or, as R. Hamann *(op. cit.,* p. 89) suggests, the Deësis—dominated the Last Supper.

29. "Solent quidam quaerere quale corpus suum discipulis suis Dominus Christus tradidit. Hoc est passibile an impassibile, mortale an immortale . . . " (Hugh of St. Victor, *De sacramentis,* II. 8. 3; *P.L.,* CLXXVI, col. 462).

30. See also the tympanum at Champagne (R. Hamann, *op. cit.,* fig. 427). Professor Harry Bober was very kind in directing my attention to two miniatures in the Gospel Book of Uta of Niedermünster (Munich, Bayer. Staatsbibl., Cod. lat. 13601, fols. 3v and 4r). They show that already in the early eleventh century the crucified Christ and the Celebration of the Mass were represented side by side. This apparently is a unique type of representation which was shaped by Pseudo-Dionysian ideas, as A. Böckler has brilliantly demonstrated ("Das Erhardbild im Utacodex," *Studies in Art and Literature for Belle da Costa Greene,* Princeton, 1954, pp. 219 ff.).

31. See note 25, *supra.*

32. H. de Lubac, *op. cit.,* pp. 185 f.

33. "Sciendum autem, quod carnis illius vel corporis spiritualis . . . sacramentum est caro vel corpus Christi, quod in ara crucis et in altari sacrificatur, et corporaliter manducatur." "Sed materialis caro Christi, cum sit sacramentum illius spiritualis carnis, tamen vere est caro Christi" *(De sacramento altaris,* IX; *P.L.,* CLXXX, cols. 355 f.).

34. "Item in ps. CIII. Ut educas panem de terra . . . A terreni corporis agro, quem a nobis assumpsit, proferens mysterium coelestis panis . . ." *(op. cit.,* XII; *P.L.,* CLXXX, col. 363).

35. ". . . iste panem vivum e coelo servandum accepit tam sibi quam toti mundo" *(Homilia II super Missus est; P.L.,* CLXXXIII, col. 69).

36. For the iconographic history of the subject, see D. C. Shorr, "The Iconographic Development of the Presentation in the Temple," *Art Bulletin,* XXVIII (1946), pp. 17 ff.

37. See note 22, *supra.* According to St. Ambrose, the Nativity is the beginning of the Church. The shepherds are the priests. The flock symbolizes the people, the night the world *(Expositio in S. Lucam,* II, 6, 7; *P.L.,* XV, col. 1652).

38. "Mater itaque ac propinqui Redemptoris nostri a Nazareth in Hierusalem ad templum Domini deferunt, quia primitiva illa in primis discipulis Ecclesia, a Judaeis repulsa, ejusdem redemptionis dispensationem ad notitiam gentium perduxit" *(P.L.,* LXV, col. 840).

39. E. Mâle, *Notre-Dame de Chartres,* pp. 23 ff.

40. " . . . ipsa Dei sapientia carnem, in qua videri posset, induta est . . . " *(P.L.,* XCIV, col. 40).

41. "Christ the power of God, and the Wisdom of God" (I Cor. 1:24); "Christ Jesus, who of God is made unto us wisdom, and righteousness" (I Cor. 1:30).

42. "Sapientia Dei Patris . . . ipsa est Salomon, quae thronum de ebore sibi fecit, dum sedem in Virgine, qua nil unquam fuit castius, sibi ponit" *(De laude s. Mariae,* c. 3; *P.L., CLVI,* cols. 541 f.). Occasionally, the representation of the *Sedes Sapientiae* bears the following inscription: "In gremio matris Residet Sapientia Patris." See, for instance, the eleventh-century relief of the Adoration of the Magi in the Church of Saint Mary in Arezzo (G. Vezin, *L'adoration et le cycle des mages dans l'art chrétien primitif,* pl. XX) or the twelfth-century Virgin and Child in Beaucaire (R. Hamann, *op. cit.,* fig. 456).

43. See, for instance, the Boethius MS written for Emperor Charles the Bald (Bamberg, Staatsbibl., H.J. IV. 12, fol. 9v); A. Boinet, *La miniature carolingienne,* Paris, 1913, pl. 57; Martianus Capella MS, *ca.* 900, Paris, Bibl. nat., lat. 7900 A; Paris, Bibl. nat., lat. 3110, fol. 60r (M.-Th. d'Alverny, "La Sagesse et ses sept filles," *Mélanges F. Grat,* Paris, 1946, I, pp. 245 ff., pl. III); Martianus Capella MS, *ca.* 1100, French, Florence, Bibl. Laur., Cod. S. Marco 190; Boethius MS, *ca.* 1140, Darmstadt, Landesbibl., MS 2282.

44. See the tituli written by Hibernicus Exul, probably for the palace built for Charlemagne at Saint-Denis by Abbot Fardulf *(Mon. Germ. Hist., Poetae latini medii aevi*, I, pp. 408 ff.). Théodulf of Orléans gives a poetic description of a table with representations of the Liberal Arts and other personifications *(ibidem*, pp. 544 ff.). Wisdom personified and the seven arts are described in verses of the Codex 397 of Saint-Gall. They refer in all likelihood to the palace built by Abbot Grimold at Saint-Gall (P. Clemen, *Die romanische Monumentalmalerei in den Rheinlanden*, Düsseldorf, 1916, p. 745).

45. Floor mosaics in the choir of Saint-Remi at Reims, destroyed in the eighteenth century, and in Saint-Irénée, Lyon (P. Clemen, *op. cit.*, pp. 179, 181).

46. P. Abrahams, *Les oeuvres poétiques de Baudri de Bourgueil*, Paris, 1926, pp. 196 ff.

47. Plato, for instance, thought that the philosopher who holds conversation with the divine order becomes himself orderly and divine, as far as the nature of man allows it *(Republic* 500C).

48. For a comprehensive history of the seven liberal arts in the middle ages, see G. Meier, *Die sieben freien Künste im Mittelalter (Jahresbericht über die Lehr- und Erziehungsanstalt des Benediktiner-Stiftes Maria-Einsiedeln im Studienjahre 1885/86, 1886/87)*, Einsiedeln, 1886-87; P. O. Kristeller, "The Modern System of the Arts: A Study in the History of Aesthetics (I)," *Journal of the History of Ideas*, XII (1951), pp. 496 ff.; M.-Th. d'Alverny, *op. cit.;* E. R. Curtius, *European Literature and the Latin Middle Ages* (Bollingen Series, XXXVI), New York, 1953, pp. 36 ff.

For the representation of the liberal arts, see P. d'Ancona, "Le rappresentazioni allegoriche delle arti liberali nel medio evo e nel rinascimento," *Arte*, V (1902), pp. 137 ff., 211 ff.; E. Mâle, *L'art religieux du XIIIe siècle en France*, pp. 75 ff.

49. "Est enim philosophia amor et studium et amicitia quodammodo sapientiae, sapientiae uero non huius, quae in artibus quibusdam et in aliqua fabrili scientia notitiaque uersatur, sed illius sapientiae, quae nullius indigens, uiuax mens et sola

rerum primaeua ratio est. est autem hic amor sapientiae intellegentis animi ab illa pura sapientia inluminatio et quodammodo ad se ipsum retractio atque aduocatio, ut uideatur studium sapientiae studium diuinitatis et purae mentis illius amicitia" *(In Isagogen Porphyrii commenta*, I. 3; *Corpus scriptorum ecclesiasticorum latinorum*, XLVIII, p. 7). See Plato's statement that the philosopher is a lover, not of part of wisdom only, but of the whole *(Republic* 475B).

50. "Haec igitur sapientia cuncto equidem animarum generi meritum suae diuinitatis inponit et ad propriam naturae uim puritatemque reducit. hinc nascitur speculationum cogitationumque ueritas et sancta puraque actuum castimonia" *(In Isagogen Porphyrii commenta*, I. 3; *loc. cit.*). Cf. the Stoic statement that philosophy is the practice of a necessary and befitting way of life (A.-H. Chroust, "The Definitions of Philosophy in the *De divisione philosophie* of Dominicus Gundissalinus," *New Scholasticism*, XXV (1951), pp. 264 f.).

51. For his discussion of the Trivium, see *In librum de interpretatione*, II *(P.L.*, LXIV, cols. 433 ff.). Of the Quadrivium he says: "Quibus quatuor partibus si careat inquisitor, verum invenire non possit, ac sine hac quidem speculatione veritatis nulli recte sapiendum est" *(Institutio arithmetica*, I. 1; *P.L.*, LXIII, col. 1081).

52. " . . . quantum nostrae mentis igniculum lux diuina dignata est" *(De Trinitate*, prologue; Boethius, *The Theological Tractates*, with an English translation by H. F. Stewart and E. K. Rand, London, 1918, p. 2).

53. "Inter omnes priscae auctoritatis viros, qui, Pythagora duce, puriore mentis ratione viguerunt, constare manifestum est haud quemquam in philosophiae disciplinis ad cumulum perfectionis evadere, nisi cui talis prudentiae nobilitas quodam quasi quadrivio vestigatur, quod recte solertiam intuentis non latebit" *(Institutio arithmetica*, I. 1; *P.L.*, LXIII, col. 1079).

54. "Hoc ergo omnes artes agunt, hoc intendunt, ut divina similitudo in nobis reparetur, quae nobis forma est, Deo natura; cui quanto magis conformamur, tanto magis sapimus. Tunc enim in nobis incipit relucere, quod in ejus ratione semper

fuit: quod quia in nobis transit, apud illum incommutabile consistit" *(Didascalion,* II. 1; *P.L.,* CLXXVI, col. 751).

55. "Ordo vero discendi talis est ut, quia per eloquentiam omnis sit doctrina, prius instruatur in eloquentia. Cujus sunt tres partes, recte scribere, et recte pronuntiare scripta, quod confert grammatica; probare quod probandum est, quod docet dialectica; ornare verba et sententias, quod tradit rhetorica. Initiandi ergo sumus in grammatica, deinde in dialectica, postea in rhetorica; quibus instructi, et ut armis muniti, ad studium philosophiae debemus accedere. Cujus hic ordo est, ut prius in quadrivio, id est in ipsa prius arithmetica, secundus in musica, tertius in geometria, quartus in astronomia. Deinde in divina pagina. Quippe cum per cognitionem creaturae ad cognitionem Creatoris perveniamus" *(De philosophia mundi,* IV. 41; *P.L.,* CLXXII, col. 100, where it is falsely printed under the works of Honorius Augustodunensis).

The idea that the liberal arts provide for the human mind the means of a gradual ascent from the material to the immaterial, is, of course, much older. St. Augustine, for instance, said that he intended to write about the liberal arts because he wanted to arrive at, or lead to, incorporeal things through corporeal things as if by some definite steps *(Retractationes,* I. 6; *P.L.,* XXXII, col. 591).

56. "Habebat enim connexas disciplinas easque theologie seruire faciebat, et cohibebat omnium regulas infra proprii generis limitem" (John of Salisbury, *Historia pontificalis,* c. 12 [ed. R. L. Poole, Oxford, 1927, p. 28]).

57. "Nos autem non nostra sed precipuorum super his artibus inuenta doctorum quasi in unum corpus uoluminis apta modulatione coaptauimus et triuium quadruuio ad generose nationis phylosophorum propaginem quasi maritali federe copulauimus. . . . Nam, cum sint duo precipua phylosophandi instrumenta, intellectus eiusque interpretatio, intellectum autem quadruuium illuminet, eius uero interpretationem elegantem, rationabilem, ornatam triuium subministret, manifestum est eptatheucon totius phylosophye unicum ac singulare esse instrumentum" (E.

Jeauneau, "Le Prologus in Eptatheucon de Thierry de Chartres," *Mediaeval Studies,* XVI (1954), p. 174).

58. John of Salisbury speaks of "magister Theodoricus, artium studiosissimus investigator" *(Metalogicon,* I. 5 [ed. C. C. J. Webb, Oxford, 1929, p. 16]). A literary epitaph of Thierry, recently discovered in a manuscript coming from Clairvaux, praises him as one who has scrutinized both the Quadrivium and the Trivium by his ever vigilant work, and has made them known to everyone A. Vernet, "Une épitaphe inédite de Thierry de Chartres," *Recueil de travaux offert a M. Clovis Brunel,* Paris, 1955, II, pp. 660 ff., especially p. 669).

59. *De philosophia mundi,* I. 4, 5; *P.L.,* CLXXII, cols, 43 f.

60. "Adsint igitur quattuor genera rationum quae ducunt hominem ad cognitionem Creatoris, scilicet arithmeticae probationes et musicae et geometricae et astronomicae. Quibus instrumentis in hac theologia breviter utendum est, ut et artificium Creatoris in rebus appareat et, quod proposuimus, rationabiliter ostendatur" (N. Haring, "The Creation and Creator of the World according to Thierry of Chartres and Clarenbaldus of Arras," *Archives d'histoire doctrinale et littéraire du moyen âge,* XXII (1955), p. 194). The passage is in part derived from Chalcidius, *In Timaeum Platonis,* 355, as Haring has pointed out *(ibidem,* p. 157, note 2).

61. "Cum igitur unitas omnem creaturam praecedat, aeternam esse necesse est. At aeternum nihil est aliud quam divinitas. Unitas igitur ipsa divinitas." "Quoniam autem unitas omnem numerum creat, numerus autem infinitus est, necesse est unitatem non habere finem suae potentiae. Unitas igitur est omnipotens in creatione numerorum. Sed creatio numerorum, rerum est creatio" *(ibidem,* pp. 195 f.). Haring has rightly translated *unitas* as "the One" except where it has a purely mathematical meaning *(ibidem,* pp. 157 ff.).

62. "Unitas ergo ex se per semel aequalitatem gignit" *(Librum hunc;* W. Jansen, *Der Kommentar des Clarenbaldus von Arras zu Boethius De Trinitate* [*Breslauer Studien zur historischen Theologie,* VIII],

Breslau, 1926, p. 12*). Jansen ascribes this work to Thierry.

"Substantia Patris est unitas. . . . Sicut enim binarius bis vel quaternarius quater arithmetica ratione tetragonum constituit, ita quoque unitas semel tetragonum primum efficit. . . . Et quoniam tetrago natura prima generatio Filii est, et Filius tetragonus primus est. . . . Bene autem tetragonus Filio attribuitur, quoniam figura haec perfectior ceteris propter laterum aequalitatem iudicatur et, sicut in omnibus trianguli lateribus quaedam aequalitas est, triangulus namque latera habet aequalia, ita quoque Filius essendi est aequalitas" *(ibidem,* p. 13*). See also O. von Simson, *The Gothic Cathedral,* pp. 27 f.

63. " . . . . quia dum loquimur de Divinitate, angustias nostrae scientiae transgressi sumus. . . . " *De philosophia mundi,* I. 14; *P.L.,* CLXXII, col. 46).

64. William of Conches: "Unde Plato: intelligentia solius Dei est et admodum paucorum hominum" *(Dragmaticon* 308; H. Flatten, *Die Philosophie des Wilhelm von Conches* [Diss. Bonn], Koblenz, 1929, p. 77).

Thierry of Chartres: "Haec vero comprehendendi vis suo nomine vocatur intelligentia. Quae solius quidem Dei est et admodum paucorum hominum. Qui vero res in puritate sua intellegere possunt, intra homines ceteros quasi dii reputandi sunt" *(Librum hunc;* W. Jansen, *op. cit.,* p. 7*).

65. See note 57, *supra.*

66. "Ibi Doctor cernitur ille Carnotensis, Cujus lingua vehemens truncat velut ensis."

The author of the *Metamorphosis Goliae* describes him in this way as one of the famous masters teaching at Paris (A. Clerval, *Les écoles de Chartres au moyenâge,* p. 171).

67. It is generally assumed that the two Signs were planned originally as part of the zodiacal cycle in the archivolts of the lefthand tympanum, but were put into their present place when the Royal Portal was supposedly reconstructed. Wilhelm Vöge, however, realized that they were planned from the beginning for the place they occupy *(Die Anfänge des monumentalen Stiles im Mittelalter,* p. 3). He did not give any reasons for it, but they are obvious. The Signs could not have fitted into the inner archivolt of the left tympanum, where their legitimate place would be at the very top. But even if one would assume that the inner archivolt originally was meant to frame the outer one—this would leave enough room for the two Signs but would presuppose a wider tympanum—the Signs could not have been used as the top voussoirs. They are carved from one block, while they ought to face one another at a certain angle. And again, if one assumes that this single block was meant to be cut into two parts after the carving, one sees that they would still lack the curvature necessary for the top voussoirs.

But what could their meaning be if they were planned for their present place? One possibility is provided by the mythological explanation given the signs in the Fables of Hyginus. The Gemini are Castor and Pollux, one being mortal, the other immortal. The two stars of the constellation are never visible together but they alternate from day to day *(Hygini fabulae,* c. 80 [ed. H. I. Rose, Leyden, p. 60]). See also Helpericus of Auxerre, *Liber de computo:* " . . . . alterum immortalem, alterum fuisse natum mortalem. Sed is qui mortalis exstiterat, suae mortis objectu fratri immortalitatem acquisisse, id quod in ipsis probare nituntur stellis, quod uno oriente alter occidit" *(P.L.,* CXXXVII, col. 24). Fishes and birds were given a place in the sky because the fishes brought to the shore, and the birds hatched, an egg from which the Syrian goddess was born *(Hygini fabulae,* c. 197, pp. 139 f.). There is an alternate legend, mentioned by Honorius Augustodunensis, that Venus and Cupid were persecuted by Typhon. They were transformed into fishes and thus hid in the waters of the Nile. The two fishes were then transferred as stars to the sky *(De imagine mundi,* I. 103; *P.L.,* CLXXII, col. 143).

We know that the Fables of Hyginus were considered suitable reading material in the School of Chartres (William of Conches, *De philosophia mundi,* II. 5; *P.L.,* CLXXII, col. 59. William also recommended that the treatise of Helpericus should be read; *ibidem,* col. 60). We do not know, however, whether pagan mythology was given a Christian meaning in the teachings of the school. Medieval interpretation occasionally associated signs of the zodiac with personalities of the Old Testament. It would, therefore, be mere speculation to assume that the Gemini would symbolize the two natures *(gemina natura)* of Christ. Such an assumption would also leave unanswered the question why an incomplete zodiacal cycle was planned for the left tympanum.

68. "Gaudentius quidam, de musica scribens, Pythagoram dicit hujus rei invenisse primordia ex malleorum sonitu et chordarum extensione percussa" (Cassiodorus, *De artibus ac disciplinis liberalium litterarum,* c. 5; *P.L.,* LXX, col. 1208). For the identification of the philosophers, see Abbé Bulteau, *op. cit,* pp. 76 ff.; E. Mâle, *Notre-Dame de Chartres,* p. 25.

The iconographic programs for some later church façades show a vigorous experimentation with both the specific places given to the cycles of the Liberal Arts and their particular relation to Philosophy personified. On the north portal of the Abbey Church at Déols, destroyed in 1830, and on a window of the west façade of Laon Cathedral, the cycles retain their exalted places in archivolts (J. Hubert, "L'abbatiale de Notre-Dame de Déols," *"Bulletin monumental,* LXXXVI (1927), pp. 5 ff.; L. Broche, *La cathédrale de Laon,* Paris, 1926, pp. 74 ff.). On the west façade of Sens Cathedral, however, their place in the socle zone suggests that they represent fundamental knowledge subservient to theological truths (L. Bégule, *La cathédrale de Sens,* Lyon, 1929, pp. 35 f.). If the information given by Viollet-le-Duc is correct, an equally fundamental place was accorded the Liberal Arts at Notre-Dame in Paris on the pedestal below the *trumeau* statue of Christ in the central portal *(Dictionnaire raisonné de l'architecture française,* Paris, 1867, II, p. 8).

At Déols, Philosophy personified gave substance to the Liberal Arts. Placed in the apex of the archivolt, she handed scrolls to Grammar and Dialectic who stood immediately underneath her. As an introductory figure Philosophy precedes the cycle at Laon, while in Sens the sequence of the Liberal Arts leads to Philosophy who is thus given the role of a final concept.

The fact that at Déols, and, possibly, at Paris the Liberal Arts were related to Christ corroborates the assumption that on the Royal Portal of Chartres they are also related to Him, the Divine Wisdom, rather than to the Virgin Mary as E. Mâle *(Notre-Dame de Chartres,* p. 24) and O. von Simson *(The Gothic Cathedral,* p. 153) like to assume.

69. In the miniature of the Seven Liberal Arts in the *Hortus Deliciarum* of Herrad of Landsberg, Dialectic holds the head of a dog. An inscription identifies the head as "caput canis" (A. Straub and G. Keller, *Herrade de Landsberg,* Strasbourg, 1879-99, pl. XI bis). See the contrasting attributes given to Dialectic later on by Alan of Lille:

"Dextra manus floris donatur honore,
    sinistram

Scorpius incidens caudae mucrone
    minatur."

(Anticlaudianus, III. 1; *P.L.,* CCX, col. 509.)

70. "Sapientia siquidem fons quidam est de quo egrediuntur flumina, quae irrigant omnem terram, et non modo ortum deliciarum divinae paginae replent sed etiam ad gentes pertranseunt" *(Policraticus,* VII. 10 [ed. C.C.J. Webb, Oxford, 1909, II, p. 660c]).

71. "Non ait: 'Unde hoc sciam,' sed, 'Quomodo fiet,' inquit, 'quoniam virum non cognosco.' . . . Neque enim decebat electam generando Deo virginem dubiam diffidentia sed prudentia cautam existere, quia nec facile poterat homo nosse mysterium quod in Deo manebat a saeculis absconditum" (Bede, *Expositio in Evangelium S. Lucae,* I. 1; *P.L.,* XCII, col. 318).

72. *Tractatus adversus Petrobrusianos (P.L.,* CLXXXIX, cols. 719 ff.). See A. Borst, *Die Katharer (Schriften der Monumenta Germaniae Historica,* XII), Stuttgart, 1953, especially pp. 81 ff.

73. M. Schapiro, "The Sculptures of Souillac," *Medieval Studies in Memory of A. Kingsley Porter,* Cambridge, Mass., 1939, II, pp. 359 ff.

74. See A. Borst, *op. cit.,* p. 83.

75. Peter the Venerable, *op. cit. (P.L.,* CLXXXIX, col. 771).

76. R. Hamann, *Die Abteikirche von St. Gilles,* pls. 6, 32. The importance of anti-heretical tenets in the subject matter of Romanesque sculpture is discussed by E. Mâle. He does not mention, however, the Fall of the Rebel Angels *(L'art religieux du XIIe siècle en France,* pp. 420 ff.).

77. R. Hamann, *op. cit.,* figs. 373-75.

78. Canon 23 (C.-J. Hefele and H. Leclercq, *Histoire des conciles d'après les documents originaux,* Paris, 1912, V, pp. 731 f.).

79. His letter to Adeodadus concerns the two natures of Christ *(P.L.,* CXLI, cols. 196 ff.). His letter to Einardus discusses the Eucharist *(ibidem,* cols. 192 ff.). For the Synod of Orléans, see *Gesta Synodi Aurelianensis (Recueil des historiens des Gaules et de la France,* X, pp. 536 ff.).

80. Letter 109 *(P.L.,* CLXII, cols. 127 f.).

81. *Vita prima,* III. VI, 17, 18 *(P.L.,* CLXXXV, col. 313).

82. Preface to Commentary on Cicero's *De inventione rhetorica ad Herrenium* (P. Thomas, "Un commentaire du moyen âge sur la Rhétorique de Cicéron," *Mélanges Graux,* Paris, 1884, pp. 41 ff.).

83. *Metalogicon,* I. 24 (ed. C.C.J. Webb, Oxford, 1929, pp. 57 f.); G. Paré, A. Brunet, P. Tremblay, *La renaissance du XIIe siècle. Les écoles et l'enseignement,* pp. 190 ff.; H. Liebeschütz, *Mediaeval Humanism in the Life and Writings of John of Salisbury (Studies of the Warburg Institute,* XVII), London, 1950, pp. 90 f.

84. *Metalogicon,* I. 25. The translation is taken from the English edition by D. D. McGarry, Berkeley—Los Angeles, 1955, p. 72.

85. "Pueros conuocat, rationes recte scribendi recteque loquendi prescribit" (Thierry, *Prologue to the Heptateuchon; Jeauneau, op. cit.,* p. 174).

86. ". . . nichil expeditius ad scientiam, et plurimum confert ad uitam, si tamen hanc sedulitatem regit caritas, si in profectu litteratorio seruetur humilitas. Non est enim eiusdem hominis litteris et carnalibus uitiis inseruire" *(Metalogicon,* I. 24 [ed. C.C.J. Webb, p. 57]).

87. See, for instance, the tympana of Charlieu, Saint-Paul-de-Varax, Anzy-le-Duc, Montceaux-l'Etoile, Cahors, and Mauriac (A.K. Porter, *Romanesque Sculpture of the Pilgrimage Roads,* figs. 4, 88, 98, 104, 422, 1246 f.). E. Mâle relates the tympanum to the Ascensions of Cahors and Carennac *(Notre-Dame de Chartres,* p. 26). See also S. H. Gutberlet, *Die Himmelfahrt Christi in der bildenden Kunst von den Anfängen bis ins hohe Mittelalter,* Strasbourg, 1934.

88. In medieval art a zodiacal sign is usually related to the month in which the sun seems to enter the sign, i.e., Aquarius to January, Pisces to February, etc. The zodiacal cycle of Chartres, on the other hand, follows the more unusual pattern of relating a sign to the month in which the sun still seems to remain in the sign, i.e., Capricornus to January, Aquarius to February, Pisces to March, etc. There apparently was a predilection at Chartres for this pattern. It can be found in miniatures of four Missals of the eleventh and twelfth centuries *(olim* Chartres, Bibl. de la Ville, MSS 165, 222, 231; Saint-Etienne, Bibl. munic., MS 104), and in the archivolt cycle of the right bay of the north porch. See Abbé Bulteau, "Etude iconographique sur les calendriers figurés de la cathédrale de Chartres *"(Mémoires de la Société archéologique d'Eure-et-Loir,* VII), Chartres, 1882, pp. 197 ff.; R. Merlet and Abbé Clerval, *Un manuscrit chartrain du XIe siècle,* Chartres, 1893; E. Houvet, *Cathédrale de Chartres, Portail nord,* I, pl. 4.

The same combination of signs and months is made by Wandalbert of Prüm, *De mensium duodecim nominibus signis culturis aerisque qualitatibus (Mon. Germ. Hist., Poetae latini medii aevi,* II, pp. 604 ff.) and by Honorius Augustodunensis, *De imagine mundi,* I. 96 f. *(P.L.,* CLXXII, col. 142).

89. For Autun, see C. Oursel, *L'art de Bourgogne,* Paris-Grenoble, 1953, fig. 56.

90. E. Mâle, *Notre-Dame de Chartres,* pp. 26 f.; *L'art religieux du XIIe siècle en France,* pp. 4 ff.

91. " . . . et ideo apostoli septenario numero expressi sunt, quia per septem dona Spiritus sancti quattuor partes mundi ad fidem sanctae Trinitatis perduxerunt" (Honorius Augustodunensis, *Speculum Ecclesiae; P.L.,* CLXXII, col. 1032).

92. "Enoch placuit Deo et translatus est

in paradisum, ut det gentibus poenitentiam. . . . Hic ergo creditur venturus cum Elia juxta finem mundi, ut hominibus det consilium a peccatis ad poenitentiam convertendi, et sic cum collega suo in persecutione Antichristi solvet debitum lethi" (Hrabanus Maurus, *Commentaria in Ecclesiasticum*, X. 3; *P.L.*, CIX, col. 1084). See also Honorius Augustodunensis, *Elucidarium*, III. 10 *(P.L.*, CLXXII, col. 1163). The identification of the two lintel figures was suggested by A. Priest, "The Masters of the West Façade of Chartres," p. 37. These two standing figures are, on the one hand, subordinated by size to the seated Apostles. On the other hand, they are co-ordinated with them compositionally, because all the heads are on the same level.

93. E. Houvet, *Cathédrale de Chartres, Portail occidental ou royal*, figs. 75-95; E. Mâle, *Notre-Dame de Chartres,* pp. 27 ff.; Abbé Bulteau, *Monographie de la cathédrale de Chartres*, II, pp. 36 ff.; For the small figures decorating the pilasters between the portals, and the doorposts, see E. Houvet, *op. cit.*, pls. 6-9, 11 f.

94. *Sermo IV (P.L.*, CXLI, col. 320). In another sermon Fulbert tells the story of Mary's infancy according to the apocryphal legends *(Sermo V; ibidem*, cols. 324 f.).

95. While the Last Supper is ideologically related to the eucharistic idea of the Nativity and Presentation, the Disciple John leaning on Jesus' bosom is related to the idea of Divine Wisdom as it had entered the homily of Bede for the day of the Nativity: "It is not shown in vain that he leaned on the bosom of the Lord during the supper, but it is shown thereby in a typological manner that he drank the flow of heavenly wisdom which is more perfect than everything else, from the most sacred fountain of His heart." For the Latin text, see *P.L.*, XCIV, col. 38.

III THE JAMB STATUES: *REGNUM* AND *SACERDOTIUM*

1. Vol. I, p. 193, pls. XVI-XVIII.

2. J. Vanuxem, "The Theories of Mabillon and Montfaucon on French Sculp-

ture of the Twelfth Century," *Journal of the Warburg and Courtauld Institutes*, XX (1957), pp. 45 ff., especially p. 57. See also Didron ainé, "Monographie de la cathédrale de Chartres. Description de la sculpture extérieure," *Annales archéologiques*, XXVII (1870), pp. 18 ff., especially p. 26.

Wilhelm Vöge identified the Chartres statues as the ancestors of Christ according to the Gospel of Matthew *(Die Anfänge des monumentalen Stiles im Mittelalter*, pp. 170 ff.). E. Mâle sees in the Saint-Denis statues the heroes of the Old Testament, the patriarchs and kings *(L'art religieux du XIIᵉ siècle en France*, p. 392), in the Chartres statues the kings, queens, and high priests of the Old Law, the ancestors of Christ *(Notre-Dame de Chartres*, p. 20). M. Aubert identifies the Chartres statues as patriarchs, prophets, and the great figures of the Bible, each personifying a book of the Holy Scriptures *(La sculpture française au moyen-âge*, p. 178). S.McK.Crosby calls the Saint-Denis statues kings and queens, the royal ancestors of Christ *(L'abbaye royale de Saint-Denis*, p. 36). See also P. Kidson, *Sculpture at Chartres*, pp. 17 f. Abbé Bulteau forms a notable exception. He identified the crowned figures at Chartres tentatively as (a rather odd medley of) medieval rulers and queens, among them Constantine as well as William the Conqueror and Henry II of England, Bertha, Charlemagne's mother, and Queen Matilda of England *(Monographie de la cathédrale de Chartres*, II, pp. 62 ff.).

3. "The Mosaics of the Cappella Palatina in Palermo: An Essay on the Choice and Arrangement of Subjects," *Art Bulletin*, XXXI (1949), pp. 291 f. Kitzinger's suggestion was accepted by Crosby *(op. cit.*, p. 37).

4. The headless figure on the left portal resembles the Queen on the extreme right side of the Royal Portal at Chartres in the belt, the oval-shaped section underneath the belt, the narrow sleeves, and the mantle fastened by a clasp on one shoulder. The headless figure on the central portal wears the pallium of a medieval ruler and has, therefore, royal status.

5. For the history of the relation between the Abbey of Saint-Denis and the kings of

France, see S. McK. Crosby, *op. cit.*, pp. 7 ff.

An excellent characterization of Suger's personality is given by E. Panofsky in his introduction to *Abbot Suger on the Abbey Church of St. Denis and Its Art Treasures.* See also M. Aubert, *Suger*, Paris, 1950; and O. von Simson, *The Gothic Cathedral*, pp. 61 ff.

6. For the relation of French to Jewish kings, see E. H. Kantorowicz, *Laudes regiae (University of California Publications in History*, XXXIII), Berkeley–Los Angeles, 1946, pp. 56 ff.

7. "Omnipotens sempiterne Deus, creator et gubernator coeli et terrae, conditor et dispositor angelorum et hominum, qui Abraham famulum tuum de hostibus triumphare fecisti, Moysi et Iosue populo tuo praelatis multiplicem victoriam tribuisti, humilem quoque David puerum tuum regni fastigio sublimasti . . . et Salomonem sapientiae pacisque ineffabili munere ditasti, respice, quaesimus, ad preces humilitatis nostrae, et hunc famulum tuum virtutibus, quibus praefatos fideles tuos decorasti, multiplici honoris benedictione condecora" *(Mon. Germ. Hist., Capitularia*, II, p. 461). See also A. Sprengler, "Die Gebete der Krönungsordines Hinkmars von Reims für Karl den Kahlen als König von Lothringen und für Ludwig den Stammler," *Zeitschrift für Kirchengeschichte*, LXIII (1950-51), pp. 245 ff.

For a fundamental discussion of paradigmatic prayers, see A. Baumstark, "Paradigmengebete ostsyrischer Kirchendichtung," *Oriens Christianus*, new series, X/XI (1923), pp. 1 ff.

8. P.E. Schramm, "Der König von Frankreich. Wahl, Krönung, Erbfolge und Königsidee vom Anfang der Kapetinger [987] bis zum Ausgang des Mittelalters," *Zeitschrift der Savigny Stiftung für Rechtsgeschichte, kanonistische Abt.*, XXV (1936), p. 278; *idem*, "Ordines-Studien, II: Die Krönung bei den Westfranken und Angelsachsen von 878 bis um 1000," *ibidem*, XXIII (1934), pp. 203 f.

9. " . . . quatinus predicti Abrahae fidelitate firmatus, Moysi mansuetudine fretus, Iosue fortitudine munitus, David humilitate exaltatus, Salomonis sapientia decoratus, tibi in omnibus complaceat" *(Fulrad Ordo*, § 7). See P. E. Schramm, "Der König von Frankreich," pp. 278 f.; *idem*, "Die Krönung bei den Westfranken und Angelsachsen," pp. 224, 238 f.

10. "Quid enim alium quam novum te dixerim Moysen et praefulgidum asseram David regem?" *(Mon. Germ. Hist., Epistolae*, III, p. 505). An earlier instance is the letter of a bishop written *ca.* 645 to a young king, probably Clovis II or Sigebert III. The king is admonished to follow the footsteps of David and Solomon *(ibidem*, p. 457).

11. *Vita Constantini*, I, 12, 38 f. *(Patr. graeca*, XX, cols. 925, 953).

12. Ratramnus of Corbie states in a letter, for instance, that virtue and wisdom make Charles the Bald comparable to these kings *(Mon. Germ. Hist., Epistolae*, VI, p. 150).

13. A poem of Théodulf of Orléans hails Charlemagne as Solomon, David, and Joseph *(Mon. Germ. Hist., Poetae latini medii aevi*, I, p. 484). Praising Charlemagne, Petrus Diaconus mentions the examples of Noah, Samson, Gideon, and David *(ibidem*, I, pp. 74 f.). Sedulius Scottus addresses Charles the Bald as Solomon, calls his father Isaac, and Charlemagne, Abraham *(ibidem*, III, pp. 180 f.). A poem composed in 888 for the beginning of the reign of King Eudes gives a whole comparative list of Old Testament personalities *(ibidem*, IV, p. 138). See also J. Funkenstein, *Das Alte Testament im Kampf von regnum und sacerdotium zur Zeit des Investiturstreits* (Diss. Basle), Dortmund, 1938; A. Werminghoff, "Die Fürstenspiegel der Karolingerzeit," *Historische Zeitschrift*, LXXXIX (1902), pp. 193 ff.

14. "A primordio etenim unctionis vestrae in Regem, et Davidicam humilitatem, et Salomonis sapientiam, et Job tolerantiam, vestra consecuta est genuina nobilitas" (Letter written in 1161; *Recueil des historiens des Gaules et de la France*, XVI, p. 24).

15. "Rex humilis, Rex pacificus, David et Salomonem
Protulit exemplo, seque suosque regens."

See *ibidem*, p. 715.

16. "Renovantur jam nostro tempore antiqua saecula, et in diebus novae gratiae

vetusti populi miracula reparantur. Processit de Aegypto Moyses, regesque Amorrhaeorum cum subjectis populis delevit. Successit ei Josue, regesque Chananaeorum cum infinitis gentibus Dei jussu prostravit, terramque illam, extinctis impiis, illi tunc Dei populo sorte divisit. Egrediens ab ultimis occiduae plagae finibus, immo ab ipso solis occasu, Rex christianus Orienti minatur, et nefandam Arabum vel Persarum gentem, sanctam Terram rursum sibi subjugare conantem, cruce Christi armatus aggreditur" *(ibidem,* XV, p. 641).

17. A. Alföldi, "Insignien und Tracht der römischen Kaiser," *Mitteilungen des deutschen Archäologischen Institutes, Römische Abteilung,* L (1935), pp. 1 ff., especially pp. 102 ff.

18. E. Wind, "Studies in Allegorical Portraiture I," *Journal of the Warburg Institute,* I (1937-38), p. 138 and pl. 16a.

19. K. Weitzmann, *The Joshua Roll, A Work of the Macedonian Renaissance (Princeton University Studies in Manuscript Illumination,* III), Princeton, 1948, pp. 113 f.; M. Schapiro, "The Place of the Joshua Roll in Byzantine History," *Gazette des Beaux-Arts,* (1949), I, pp. 161 ff. The importance of historical, mythological, and biblical personages as examples for the concept of Byzantine emperorship is discussed by A. Grabar, *L'empereur dans l'art byzantin,* pp. 93 ff.

20. E. Panofsky, *Early Netherlandish Painting,* Cambridge, Mass., 1953, figs. 353, 356.

21. A. Chastel, *Botticelli,* Greenwich, Conn., 1958, pl. VIII. A symbolic relation between similar acts performed by a living person and by the Magi—yet not a personal identification—was established in Byzantine court art. In the famous mosaic of San Vitale at Ravenna, the robe of Empress Theodora, as she brings the chalice with wine to the altar, is embroidered with the figures of the Magi bringing their gifts. Her offering is thus placed in analogy to the biblical scene.

22. E. Wind, *op. cit.,* p. 152, pl. 17.

23. *Ibidem,* p. 153, pl. 18c.

24. A. McComb, *Agnolo Bronzino, His Life and Works,* Cambridge, Mass., 1928, pl. 33.

25. J. Seznec, *The Survival of the Pagan Gods (Bollingen Series,* XXXVIII), New York, 1953, pp. 34 f.

26. A. Rosenberg, *P.P. Rubens,* 4th ed., Berlin-Leipzig, illus. on p. 249.

27. "Despondeo te uni viro virginem castam atque pudicam, futuram coniugem, ut sanctae mulieres fuere viris suis, Sarra, Rebecca, Rachel, Hester, Iudith, Anna, Noëmi, favente auctore et sanctificatore nuptiarum Iesu Christo domino nostro, qui vivit et regnat in saecula saeculorum" *(Mon. Germ. Hist., Capitularia,* II, p. 426). See also the prayer spoken during the coronation of Queen Ermentrude at Soissons in 866 *(ibidem,* p. 455). This paradigmatic benediction, still to be found in the wedding rite of the Roman Missal, is derived from the *Sacramentarium Leonianum* and the *Sacramentarium Gelasianum* (A. Baumstark, *op. cit.,* p. 7).

28. "Reverendae Anglorum reginae Mathildi, Ivo, humilis Carnotensis Ecclesiae minister, in finibus terrae audire sapientiam Salomonis" (Letter 107; *P.L.,* CLXII, col. 125).

29. M.A. Luchaire, *Histoire des institutions monarchiques de la France sous les premiers Capétiens,* 2d ed., Paris, 1891, I, pp. 147 f.; F. Olivier-Martin, *Les régences et la majorité des rois sous les Capétiens directs et les premiers Valois (1060-1375),* Paris, 1931, p. 22. Hugh Capet called his wife *"sociam ac participem nostri regni"* (J. Flach, *Les origines de l'ancienne France, Xe et XIe siècles,* Paris, 1904, III, p. 406, note 1).

30. *Fulrad Ordo,* §§ 2, 16, 28, (P. E. Schramm, "Die Krönung bei den Westfranken und Angelsachsen," pp. 238, 240 f.). Pope Innocent II reminded King Louis VII of his duties that originated in his coronation: "Et quoniam te Deus in regem eligi et ungi voluit ut sponsam suam, sanctam videlicet Ecclesiam, proprio sanguine suo redemptam, defendere et ejus libertatem illibatam servares . . . " (Letter written in 1139; *P.L.,* CLXXIX, col. 497).

31. In 1159 Pope Alexander III urged Queen Constance to give him strong support, because of her devotion to the Church, and to exhort her husband, Louis VII, to do likewise *(P.L.,* CC, cols. 80 f.). A letter written in 1162 asked Queen Adela to imitate her ancestors in her attitude towards

the Church and to exert her influence on the king *(ibidem,* cols. 139 f.).

32. J. Haller, *Das Papsttum,* Stuttgart, 1951, II, pp. 457 ff.

33. "Videmus enim scissum regnum et sacerdotium, quibus tanquam principalibus et fortioribus paxillis tabernaculi Dei status firmiter figebatur, ne ullo impetu procellarum et turbinum everteretur. In tanta scissura, in tanta procella florere et fructificare non potest mater Ecclesia, de qua dicitur: 'Una est columba mea, sponsa mea'" (Letter 214; *P.L.,* CLXII, col. 218).

34. "Quia ergo rex Francorum, utpote homo simplicis naturae, erga Ecclesiam Dei est devotus, et sedi apostolicae benevolens, petimus et consulimus, ut a benevolentia ejus nulla vos subreptio subtrahat, nulla persuasio disjungat. Novit enim paternitas vestra, quia cum regnum et sacerdotium inter se conveniunt, bene regitur mundus, floret et fructificat Ecclesia. Cum vero inter se discordant, non tantum parvae res non crescunt, sed etiam magnae res miserabiliter dilabuntur" (Letter 238; *ibidem,* col. 246).

35. "Cum gloria corporis Christi, videlicet Ecclesiae Dei, regni et sacerdotii indissolubili unitate consistat, constat profecto quia qui alteri providet, alteri suffragatur, quoniam et temporale regnum per Ecclesiam Dei stare et Ecclesiam Dei per temporale regnum proficere omnibus discretis evidenter ostenditur" (Letter 74; *P.L.,* CLXXXVI, col. 1386). Suger wrote this letter in 1149 when rebellion threatened the royal domain. At that time he held the particular position of combining sacerdotal power as abbot, and temporarily delegated regal power as regent of France.

36. "Scimus quia ex autoritate Veteris Testamenti, etiam nostris temporibus, ex ecclesiastico instituto soli reges et sacerdotes sacri crismatis unctione consecrantur. Decet autem ut qui soli prae ceteris omnibus sacrosancta crismatis linitione consociati, ad regendum Dei populum praeficiuntur, sibi ipsis et subditis suis tam temporalia quam spiritualia subministrando provideant" (M. A. Luchaire, *op. cit.,* p. 42, note 2). This is, within the context of actual ecclesiastical policy, a reduction of the coronation prayer: "Unde unxit sacerdotes, reges, prophetas et martyres

. . . " to its older core: "Unde unxit sacerdotes, reges. . . . " See A. Sprengler, *op. cit.,* p. 251.

37. Samuel had anointed Saul (I Sam. 10:1) and David (I Sam. 16:13). Jehu was anointed by Elisha (II Kings 9:1 ff.).

38. "David nihilominus et omnis regum successura series, sive Iuda vel Israel, a prophetis vel sacerdotibus, quod pene idem erat, in regnum eligebantur, ungebantur, et tamen pene omnes eisdem in divinis subiecti memorantur. Ipsi econtra eos in secularibus subditi venerabantur" *(Summa gloria,* c. 12; *Mon. Germ. Hist., Libelli de lite,* III, p. 70). For the examples, see chap. 13 of the treatise.

39. " . . . sic in regno Christi cooperantur sibi in bonum regalis potestas et sacerdotalis dignitas, ita ut omnis David suum habeat Nathan, quem audiat, et omnis Ezechias per sibi contemporaneum regatur Ysaiam et omnis Iosias per suum deploretur Ieremiam" *(Commentarius in Psalmum LXIV; ibidem,* III, p. 465).

40. "Nunc autem sanctorum prophetarum vicem in aecclesia Christi retinent sacerdotes." *(De regia potestate et sacerdotali dignitate; ibidem,* II, p. 485).

41. "Constitutus es, venerabilis Pater, inter filios prophetarum" *(P.L.,* CCVII, col. 1099).

42. E. Panofsky, *Abbot Suger,* pp. 196 ff.; A. Watson, *The Early Iconography of the Tree of Jesse,* London, 1934, pp. 81 f., 112 ff., pls. XXIV f.; E. Mâle, *L'art religieux du XIIᵉ siècle en France,* pp. 168 ff.

43. E. Mâle, *Notre-Dame de Chartres,* pp. 20 ff. For Etampes, see W. S. Stoddard, *The West Portals of Saint-Denis and Chartres,* pp. 27 ff., pls. XXIII f.

44. The sculptural decoration on the southern flank of Etampes Cathedral is more modest than that of the Royal Portal, for it is restricted to one doorway. The jambs show two Kings, two Queens, Moses, and a Prophet. Two figures of nonroyal status—they received the features of Peter and Paul in the thirteenth century—were carved for the same doorway but not incorporated in the final scheme. See W.S. Stoddard, *op. cit.,* pp. 27 ff.

45. The south portal of the Cathedral of Le Mans shows four Kings, two Queens,

two Prophets and, embedded in the embrasures, Peter and Paul. The south door of Bourges Cathedral is flanked by two Kings, two Queens, and two Prophets. At Saint-Germain-des-Prés five Kings, two Queens, and St. Germain, the bishop, had been chosen (B. de Montfaucon, *Monumens,* I, pl. VII). The portal of St. Anne of Notre-Dame in Paris showed four Kings, two Queens, Peter, and Paul *(ibidem,* pl. VIII). See E. Mâle, *L'art religieux du XIIᵉ siècle en France,* pp. 392 ff. For the statues on the façade of Saint-Bénigne in Dijon (Peter and Paul, Aaron and Moses, two Kings, Solomon and the Queen of Sheba) see P. Quarré, "La sculpture des anciens portails de Saint-Bénigne de Dijon," *Gazette des Beaux-Arts,* 1957, II, pp. 177 ff., especially pp. 190 ff.

46. "Rogamus ergo ut pro Ecclesia Dei murum te validissimum opponas . . . " (Letter written in 1130 by Pope Anacletus II to King Louis VI; *P.L.,* CLXXIX, col. 701). The same metaphor is used in letters of Pope Alexander III to King Louis VII: " . . . quomodo te ab ipso nostrae promotionis exordio pro domo Israel murum inexpugnabilem constitueris . . . " *(P.L.,* CC, col. 158); " . . . et decreveris te murum ferreum et praesidium inexpugnabile pro domo Domini opponere . . . " *(ibidem,* col. 168).

47. " . . . firma suo tempore ecclesiae Dei tam in sacerdotali dignitate quam in honore regni columna . . . qui in magna tranquillitate, quoad vixit, praesentem rexit ecclesiam, et murum validissimum pro ea se opponens, ab innumeris perturbationibus eam strenue defensavit" *(Recueil des historiens des Gaules et de la France,* XIV, p. 333).

48. M. Aubert, *French Sculpture at the Beginning of the Gothic Period,* p. 31, pl. 30. W. Vöge *(Die Anfänge des monumentalen Stiles im Mittelalter,* pp. 251 ff.) has identified the two statues as the Church and the Synagogue, but there is not sufficient evidence to sustain this theory.

49. To identify more than a few statues is no longer possible. It is not certain whether they were arranged along the façade according to the original plan, or in what sequence they should be identified. The two Kings and the Queen between them on the right-hand jamb of the central doorway are, in all likelihood, David, Solomon, and the Queen of Sheba.

IV   FORM AND MEANING

1. The Nativity lintel contains in unbroken sequence scenes that happened at different times but together reveal the mystery of the Incarnation. The stage is merely marked off by the projection of top and bottom ledges.

A continuum of crowning arches is used for the single scene of the Presentation. Not projecting to any great degree, the arches neither separate the figures nor mark off the stage at the top. They stress the even rhythm of the two processions and fix the place of each figure by framing its head, thus giving ideal permanence to a solemn moment.

Definitely projecting arches enclose more strongly the groups of Apostles, thereby confining their reaction to the disappearance or reappearance of their Master.

2. *Die Anfänge des monumentalen Stiles im Mittelalter,* pp. 80 ff., 135 ff., 210 ff. Vöge ascribed to the Head Master the statues of the central portal and of the inner jambs of the lateral portals, the central tympanum and its lintel. To a master active at Etampes he attributed the three statues at the extreme left of the façade; to a master coming from Saint-Denis he attributed the three statues of the extreme right. He held a fourth master responsible for the lateral tympana and the archivolts, while the lateral lintels were carved by assistants.

3. The following authors differ in some respects from the attributions given here. A. Priest ("The Masters of the West Façade of Chartres," pp. 28 ff.) agrees with Vöge in attributing the central lintel and the jamb statues of the inner sides of the lateral portals to the Head Master. He gives the two lintels of the right portal to a master who had worked on the friezes of Saint-Gilles. This suggestion was supported by A.K. Porter *(Romanesque Sculpture of the Pilgrimage Roads,* pp. 284 ff.). M. Aubert *(La sculpture française au* *moyen-âge,* pp. 184 ff.) ascribes the lower lintel of the Incarnation tympanum to the sculptor who carved the lateral tympana. He attributes to another workshop the upper right-hand lintel and the two lintels on the left side. See also E. Mâle, *Notre-Dame de Chartres,* pp. 21, 23, 25 ff.; W.S. Stoddard, *The West Portals of Saint-Denis and Chartres,* pp. 20 ff.

4. W.S. Stoddard *(op. cit.,* pp. 22 ff.) suggests that the decoration of the whole façade was created in one campaign, with the Head Master liberal enough to give freedom to the sculptors of his workshop. Stoddard certainly is right in his argument that stylistic differences do not invalidate this theory. Yet it seems to me that differences in the general layout favor the assumption of two campaigns in rapid succession. The Head Master established the principle of complete stillness for the jamb statues of the central portal by having decorated shafts underneath the pedestals. Does it seem likely that he gave leeway to some sculptors in his workshop to place dramatic figures underneath the pedestals, according to the opposite principle of agitation? The theory of a change of artists does not exclude the possibility that sculptors specializing in the decoration of columns remained active even after the new Head Master had taken over direction of the work.

5. E. Panofsky, *Early Netherlandish Painting,* I, p. 15. See also H. Focillon, *L'art des sculpteurs romans,* Paris, 1931, pp. 274 ff.; E. Mâle, *Notre-Dame de Chartres,* pp. 21 f.

In spite of all their stylistic variety, Romanesque jamb figures were always kept in close contact with the wall. At Souillac and Moissac they were even "glued" to the wall with the back of their mantles, but they contrast all the more strongly with the static mass of the façade by their intense lateral movements and the sheer energy of drapery lines (A.K. Porter, *op. cit.,* figs. 344, 360). The Apostles of Saint-Gilles, while bulky in shape and calmer in pose, were kept within the plane of the wall *(ibidem,* figs. 1302-15). Without pushing against their confines, they fill the niches or recesses in which they exist, thus restoring the continuity of the wall sur-

face. The sculptor who carved the Apostles underneath the central tympanum at Vézelay created in a truly experimental manner a variegated relation of the figures to the wall. The figures are flattened against either a straight or a slightly curved plane. St. Paul to the right of the doorway is drawn around a corner (F. Salet, *La Madeleine de Vézelay,* Melun, 1948, pl. 21). One Apostle projects in part from a corner, but remains nonarchitectonic by the liveliness of pose and drapery lines *(ibidem,* pl. 20).

The jamb statues of Lombardy show a steady change in the direction of their diminishing relation to the wall and their growing importance within the sculptural system. On the façade of Modena Cathedral (early twelfth century) Master Wiligelmus had placed Prophets of small size into niches (G. H. Crichton, *Romanesque Sculpture in Italy,* figs. 5a, 5b). Tł s solution was carried out on a larger scale at Saint-Gilles. The Prophets on the façade of Cremona Cathedral *(ca.* 1107-17) are in front of the wall but flattened against it *(ibidem,* figs. 9a, 9b). Working at approximately the same time as the new enterprise at Saint-Denis was in progress, Master Niccolo went further than Wiligelmus and the master of Cremona. On the façade of Ferrara Cathedral *(ca.* 1135) the Prophets still seem lost by reason of their small size and partial superposition within the ornamental richness of sculptural decoration *(ibidem,* figs. 11 f.). They are carved from piers set at an angle, however, so that they are no longer bound to just one plane of the wall. This solution has its parallel in the statues of the Chapter House of Saint-Etienne in Toulouse (A.K. Porter, *op. cit.,* figs. 434-43). Niccolo took the next step at Verona Cathedral (after 1140). Here he made the Prophets larger, thereby increasing their importance (G. H. Crichton, *op. cit.,* figs. 14a-14c). He now let them project from piers set at an angle. The time, it seems, was ripe for a more definite disengagement of the jamb statues from the wall. This decisive step was taken at Saint-Denis.

The stylistic sources of the Saint-Denis and Chartres statues may best be explained in analogy to the sources of the new architectural style. In the design of the Abbey Church, as far as Suger rebuilt it, vocabularies of various regions, primarily Normandy and Burgundy, are molded into an essentially new entity. The columnar statues show the same fruitful fusion and basic transformation of existing ingredients.

Antecedents may be found for the specific place given the statues, for their importance within the sculptural system, and for their close relation to columns.

In Lombardy the idea of placing statues along the jambs of richly ornamented portals had been realized, yet the statues were small in size (western portal of Ferrara Cathedral). See H. Giesau, "Stand der Forschung über das Figurenportal des Mittelalters," *Beiträge zur Kunst des Mittelalters,* Berlin, 1950, pp. 119 ff., especially p. 126. The link to Lombardy is, furthermore, corroborated by the motif of small figures placed in superposed niches. The Wise and Foolish Virgins of the central portal at Saint-Denis (S. McK. Crosby, *L'abbaye royale de Saint-Denis,* pls. 5, 14 f.) are arranged in this way, as were the Prophets carved by Wiligelmus for the façade of Modena Cathedral.

It is in Provence that statues of prominent size calmly flank a portal (Saint-Gilles, Romans).

The motif of relating figures to columns can be traced back to Roman columnar supports, with three figures clustered around them (E. Espérandieu, *Recueil géneral des bas-reliefs, statues et bustes de la Gaule romaine,* Paris, 1913, V, no. 4286; cf. H. Sedlmayr, *Die Entstehung der Kathedrale,* Zurich, 1950, p. 207; W. Paatz, *Von den Gattungen und vom Sinn der gotischen Rundfigur* [*Sitzungsberichte der Heidelberger Akademie der Wissenchaften, Phil.-Hist. Klasse,* 1951, III]).

This motif reappeared in Christianized form at Santiago de Compostela. The altar above the tomb of St. James the Great was supported by four columns with three Apostles addorsed to each column (1105 or 1135; A.K. Porter, *Spanish Romanesque Sculpture,* Florence-Paris, 1928, I, pl. 59; II, pp. 4 ff.). In the sculptured colonnettes from Saint-Quentin-lès-Beauvais, now in the Beauvais Museum, this relation became restricted to that of one figure to a column

(A.K. Porter, *Romanesque Sculpture of the Pilgrimage Roads,* figs. 1431–33). Here a new solution was achieved on a small scale. The Saint-Denis sculptors took the decisive step of giving the columnar statue monumental size and releasing the large jamb figure from its flattened position. The Chartres Head Master achieved a final harmony between the figures and the architectural members so that they seem, in the words of H. Focillon, *"conquis par un surnaturel repos" (op. cit.,* p. 275). P. Kidson has made the important observation that the columnar statues adjacent to the pilasters between the portals of Chartres-West are strongly related to the vertical articulation of the second story (*Sculpture at Chartres,* pp. 9 f.).

Antecedents may also be found for certain elements in the design of the Saint-Denis and Chartres statues. The influence of the Languedoc style has been pointed out rightly by W. Vöge (*op. cit.,* pp. 80 ff.). One should add that the sculptures of the Puerta de las Platerias in Santiago de Compostela anticipate in some respects the style of the Chartres statues carved by the Head Master. The figure of Christ in the center of the wall (early twelfth century) may be called an ancestor of the Chartres statues because of the slender compactness of His shapes, the frontality of His pose, the verticality of drapery lines, but He still remains bound to the wall plane behind Him (A. K. Porter, *Spanish Romanesque Sculpture,* I, pl. 62b). One of the Prophets next to Christ (*op. cit.,* pl. 62b, lower row, left) is very close in his head type, the softness of its forms, and the carving of the hair to the young King on the left jamb of the Incarnation portal.

That the Head Master was open to the influence of Byzantine ivories of the Harbaville Triptych type has also been suggested (O. von Simson, *The Gothic Cathedral,* p. 152, note 36). In the epoch of the crusades such works could well have been brought to France. The ivories, small as they are in size, have in common with the statues of the central doorway the basic concept of lining up frontalized figures in complete immobility, the vertically contained contours, and the control of the drapery design. The degree of abstraction from natural forms might well have appealed to a master who wanted to give his figures immobile monumentality, to clarify their design, and to imbue their forms with human warmth. W. Koehler has suggested the influence of Byzantine mosaics ("Byzantine Art in the West," *Dumbarton Oaks Papers*, I, 1941, pp. 84 f.). See also O. von Simson, *op. cit.*, p. 151.

The only remaining jamb statue from the portal of Saint-Lazare in Avallon (A. K. Porter, *Romanesque Sculpture of the Pilgrimage Roads*, fig. 139) is mentioned by H. Giesau (*op. cit.*, p. 123) as a precursor of the Chartres statues. This statue, however, gives the impression of being a dried out version of the Chartres type inserted as a modern element into a still totally Romanesque system of decoration. Giesau (pp. 120 f.) also believes that the Bourges statues (W.S. Stoddard, *op. cit.*, pl. XXXVII, 4) were carved before those of Chartres. Yet the incipient fluidity in the design of the *Sedes Sapientiae* in the northern tympanum contradicts this theory.

Some initial figures in illuminated manuscripts, primarily of the Citeaux School, resemble the statues of the Head Master. A.K. Porter ("Les manuscrits cisterciens et la sculpture gothique," *Saint Bernard et son temps*, Dijon, 1929, pp. 212 ff.) proposes book illuminations, therefore, as a stylistic source for the columnar figures. Since they differ in the purity of their design from the more restless Saint-Denis statues, they could have influenced only the later Chartres workshop. It seems more likely that the Head Master achieved his aims by clarifying the shapes of the Saint-Denis statues and harmonizing them with the columns, rather than by looking at miniatures. The similarities between miniatures and statues may be explained by the corresponding aims of painter and sculptor, one identifying a human figure with the shape of the initial *I*, the other identifying statue and column.

What conclusions may then be drawn from these observations? Apart from the fundamentally new concept of the columnar jamb statue as it was realized at Saint-Denis, the sculptures of the Languedoc-Santiago region and, possibly, Byzantine art provided ingredients for the

Head Master's style. Yet the essence of his style is not the result of a mere amalgamation of existing ingredients. The statues he carved are governed and shaped by new ideas: the idea of perfect consonance between sculptural and architectural components, between statues and columns, and the idea that statues released from direct contact with the wall should be given inner life.

The stylistic affinity between one of the statues from the cloister of Saint-Denis (*ca.* 1150; now in the Metropolitan Museum of Art in New York) and the jamb figures from the Royal Portal has been discussed by V.K. Ostoia ("A Statue from Saint-Denis," *The Metropolitan Museum of Art Bulletin*, new series, XIII (1954-55), pp. 298 ff.).

To ascribe specific works to the earlier activity of the Head Master is certainly tempting but must remain speculation. R. Hamann (*Die Abteikirche von St. Gilles*, p. 138) suggests that the Head Master as a young man carved the Archangel Michael on the façade of Saint-Gilles. Although this conclusion might be wrong (like A.K. Porter's suggestion that Master Gislebertus of the Autun Last Judgment is identical with Master Gilabertus of the Toulouse Apostles) Hamann's attempt to identify the early style of the Head Master has its merits. The style of a medieval sculptor must have changed, and even radically so, when new artistic ideas came to the fore. Historians of early medieval art are hampered by the lack of documentary evidence. Historians of later art periods are more fortunate. Would they have ascribed to Donatello the statues of St. Mark of Or San Michele and of John the Baptist in the Cathedral of Siena if no documents existed?

6. W.S. Stoddard (*op. cit.*, pp. 11 f.) gives an excellent characterization of stylistic differences in design and carving of the ornaments at Saint-Denis and Chartres.

7. At Etampes the statues are separated from the upper part of the columns by canopies disrupting the vertical movement, and no shafts are placed underneath their feet (W.S. Stoddard, *op cit.*, pp. 27 ff., pl. XXIII, 1, 2). At Le Mans and at Saint-Ayoul in Provins the heads of the statues reach up to the capitals (*ibidem*, pp. 32 ff.,

pls. XXV, 1, 2; XXVI, 1, 2). This emphasizes the importance of the figures at the expense of the columns. At Le Mans the columnar shaft still appears underneath the figures. It is altogether eliminated at Provins. On the south portal of Bourges Cathedral the statues are brought once more into closer contact with the wall. The columns to which they are addorsed are set back into shallow niches. Their architectural quality is in part obscured by rich ornamental design, in part hidden by canopies of equal decorative profusion *(ibidem,* pl. XXXVII, 4). At Angers both capitals and bases are thickened, thus definitely framing the statues at top and bottom (M. Aubert, *La sculpture française au moyen-âge,* illus. on p. 195). Here the figures are tightly contained within the angles of the jambs.

8. The effect of these differences in size has been described beautifully by W. Vöge: "Der Blick hebt sich, wie von selber emporgetragen, und fällt, an den Statuen hinaufgleitend, auf den thronenden Christus, auf die im Halbdunkel dahinter liegenden Gewölbe des Schiffes" *(Die Anfänge des monumentalen Stiles im Mittelalter,* p. 6).

9. M.C. Ross, "Monumental Sculptures from St.-Denis, An Identification of Fragments from the Portal," *The Journal of the Walters Art Gallery,* III (1940) pp. 91 ff.; W.S. Stoddard, *op. cit.,* pp. 7 f.; M. Aubert, "Têtes des statues-colonnes du portail occidental de Saint-Denis," *Bulletin monumental,* CIII (1945), pp. 243 ff.

10. This most important observation was made by W. Koehler *(op. cit.,* pp. 85 ff.). See also E. Panofsky *(Gothic Architecture and Scholasticism,* Latrobe, Pa., 1951, p. 6) who remarks that "this psychology was still based upon the Biblical—and Augustinian—dichotomy between the 'breath of life' and the 'dust of the ground.' "

11. "Anima quippe in quantum est spiritus rationalis, ex se et per se habet esse personam, et quando corpus ei sociatur non tantum ad personam componitur, quantum in personam apponitur" *(De sacramentis,* II. I, 11; *P.L.,* CLXXVI, col. 409).

12. " . . . sed anima magis exercet vires suas in nostris interioribus quam in exteri-oribus; non est igitur corpori apposita" *(Dragmaticon* 303; H. Flatten, *Die Philosophie des Wilhelm von Conches,* p. 162, note 958).

W. Koehler *(op. cit.,* p. 83) gives an excellent characterization of the differences in expression between the head of Christ in Vézelay and the head of a statue carved by the Head Master. Of the earlier head he says that "the dualism of physical shell and animating force prevails. Only when we turn to a head by the great master of Chartres are we confronted with a face in which inner life, animation, actually permeates the countenance." The new character of the Chartres heads cannot be defined better than by the unforgettable sentence of W. Vöge *(op. cit.,* p. 51): "An die Stelle des Greisenhaft - mürrischen, des Tiefsinnig-zerstreuten, des Gewaltsam-gesammelten, tritt das Kraftvoll-gespannte männlicher Energie, das Untadelhafte männlicher Schönheit, das Lachende der Jugend." See also W.S. Stoddard, *op. cit.,* pp. 12 ff.

13. " . . . ut Platonis et Ciceronis non solum accidentales proprietates, verum et substantiales, quibus ipsi sunt . . . " *(Commentaria in librum de Trinitate; P.L.,* LXIV, col. 1256). For this opinion he was attacked by Clarenbaldus of Arras who denounced the famous doctors spreading the notion that individual human beings are human beings because of individual properties. See W. Jansen, *Der Kommentar des Clarenbaldus von Arras zu Boethius De Trinitate,* p. 42*

14. M. Schapiro, "The Romanesque Sculpture of Moissac, Part I (2)," *Art Bulletin,* XIII (1931), pp. 464 ff. See also the beautiful stylistic analysis given by W. Vöge ("Zur frühgotischen Plastik Frankreichs," *Bildhauer des Mittelalters,* Berlin, 1958, pp. 44 ff.).

15. A. Katzenellenbogen, "The Central Tympanum at Vézelay, Its Encyclopedic Meaning and Its Relation to the First Crusade," *Art Bulletin,* XXVI (1944), fig. 7; J. Adhémar, *Influences antiques dans l'art du moyen âge français (Studies of the Warburg Institute,* VII), London, 1939, p. 190.

16. See also the relief of a procession of Isis in the Vatican Museum (F. Cumont,

Les religions orientales dans le paganisme romain, Paris, 1929, pl. VIII, 1); J. Adhémar, *op. cit.,* p. 178.

17. The use of Early Christian motives also is apparent. The decorative plant forms in the spandrels of the arches over the Presentation scene are derived from sarcophagi. This link to Early Christian art is strengthened by the relief discovered at Saint-Denis (S. McK. Crosby, *op. cit.,* figs. 88–90). The motif of Apostles in an arcade, the harmony between the verticality of the columns and the vertical containment of the figures, the spandrel decoration akin to that of Chartres reflect the ultimate influence of a sarcophagus. The principle of organizing and stabilizing the lintel compositions by an architectural framework became at Chartres an important artistic device.

18. M. van Berchem and E. Clouzot,

Mosaïques chrétiennes du IVme au Xme siècle, figs. 15 ff.

19. O. Fischel, *Raphael,* London, 1948, II, figs. 62, 72.

20. O. von Simson suggests that the proportions of the jamb statues on the central doorway correspond to the golden section, and he illustrates his point by placing a scheme conforming to the golden section next to the King at the very right-hand side of the portal *(The Gothic Cathedral,* p. 155, pl. 22b). It should, be pointed out, however, that this principle does not apply to other statues of the same portal. They differ in the total length of their bodies, while the distance from elbow to top of head remains approximately the same.

21. A.K. Porter, *Romanesque Sculpture of the Pilgrimage Roads,* figs. 80 f.

22. *Ibidem,* figs. 344, 360.

Part Two: The Sculptures of the Transept Wings

I   GENESIS OF THE SCULPTURAL CYCLES

1.   Virgo Dei mater, que verbo se docet et re
Carnoti dominam, laudabiliore paratu
Ecclesiam reparare volens specialiter ipsi
Quam dicat ipsa sibi, mirando provida casu
Vulcano furere ad libitum permisit in illam,
Ut medicina foret presens exustio morbi
Quo Domini domus illa situ languebat inerti,
Et causam fabrice daret illa ruina future,
Cui toto par nulla hodie splendescit in orbe;
Que, lapide exciso surgens nova, corpore toto
Sub testudineo jam consummata decore,
Judicii nihil usque diem timet igne noceri;
Multorumque salus illo provenit ab igne,
Quorum subsidiis operis renovatio facta est.

(Philippis, IV, vss. 599 ff.; *Oeuvres de Rigord et de Guillaume le Breton,* II, pp. 121 f.)

2. A. Thomas, *Les miracles de Notre-Dame de Chartres, Texte latin inédit,* pp. 509 f.

3. For the history of the rebuilding of the cathedral, see the interesting chapter "The Palace of the Virgin" in O. von Simson, *The Gothic Cathedral,* pp. 159 ff.

4. The various phases in the building and

decoration of the transept are discussed thoroughly, according to documentary, structural, and stylistic evidence, by L. Grodecki ("The Transept Portals of Chartres Cathedral: The Date of their Construction according to Archaeological Data," *Art Bulletin,* XXXIII (1951), pp. 156 ff.).

The question as to whether the building of the new cathedral proceeded from the west to the east, or from the east to the west, is being hotly debated by P. Frankl ("The Chronology of Chartres Cathedral," *Art Bulletin*, XXXIX [1957], pp. 33 ff.) and L. Grodecki ("Chronologie de la cathédrale de Chartres," *Bulletin monumental*, CXVI [1958], pp. 91 ff.) The issue is of no vital concern to the scope of this study. I am inclined to agree, however, with the arguments brought forward by Grodecki, the champion of the west-to-east theory. He has strengthened his position by a meticulous stylistic analysis of the changes in the design of the buttresses. One can expect that both authors will discuss more fully the crucial problem of the dates to be assigned to the windows in the nave and the choir.

Although Frankl is very positive in his assertion that the transept was built before 1210, he does not suggest a specific date for its portals and statues. He leaves open the question whether the lower part of the northern façade had been constructed by 1210 or not *(op. cit.,* p. 46). Grodecki dates the portals of the transept between 1210 and 1220.

Of fundamental importance for the problem of distinguishing various sculptural workshops is W. Vöge's article, "Die Bahnbrecher des Naturstudiums um 1200" *(Gesammelte Studien,* pp. 63 ff.). See also G. Schlag, "Die Skulpturen des Querhauses der Kathedrale von Chartres," *Westdeutsches Jahrbuch für Kunstgeschichte (Wallraf-Richartz Jahrbuch),* XII-XIII (1943), pp. 115 ff.; S. Abdul-Hak, *La sculpture des porches du transept de la cathédrale de Chartres,* pp. 17 ff.; M. Aubert, *La sculpture française au moyen-âge,* pp. 219 ff.; E. Mâle, *Notre-Dame de Chartres,* pp. 42 ff.; W. Sauerländer, "Beiträge zur Geschichte der 'frühgotischen' Skulptur," *Zeitschrift für Kunstgeschichte,* XIX (1956), pp. 1 ff., especially pp. 21 ff.

5. For Laon Cathedral, see E. Lambert, "Les portails sculptés de la cathédrale de Laon," *Gazette des Beaux-Arts,* 1937, I, pp. 83 ff.

For Notre-Dame in Paris, see M. Aubert, *La cathédrale de Notre-Dame de Paris,* new ed., Paris, 1929, pp. 116 ff.; A. Temko, *Notre-Dame of Paris,* New York, 1955, especially pp. 182 ff.

II THE SCULPTURES OF THE NORTH TRANSEPT AND ITS PORCH

1. See the important article of W. Sauerländer, "Die Marienportale von Senlis und Mantes," *Wallraf-Richartz Jahrbuch,* XX, (1958), pp. 115 ff. Through acute observations he has revealed the stylistic origins of the sculpture at Senlis and Mantes. He has also convincingly dated the two portals. See also M. Aubert, *Monographie de la cathédrale de Senlis,* Senlis, 1910, pp. 99 ff.; *idem,* "Le portail occidental de la cathédrale de Senlis," *Revue de l'art chrétien,* 1910, pp. 157 ff.; E. Lambert, *op. cit.,* pp. 83 ff.; E. Mâle, *Notre-Dame de Chartres,* pp. 44 f.; *idem, L'art religieux du XIIIᵉ siècle en France,* pp. 248 ff.; S. Abdul-Hak, *op. cit.,* pp. 24 ff.; P. Kidson, *Sculpture at Chartres,* pp. 32 ff.; Abbé Bulteau, *Monographie de la cathédrale de Chartres,* II, pp. 170 ff.

P. Wilhelm *(Die Marienkrönung am Westportal der Kathedrale von Senlis* [Diss. Hamburg], Hamburg, 1941) traces various components of the Coronation of the Virgin.

2. M. R. James, *The Apocryphal New Testament,* Oxford, 1926, p. 209.

3. *Ibidem,* p. 216.

4. The first passage is quoted, for instance, in the famous letter of Pseudo-Jerome within the framework of the Assumption of the Virgin Mary *(P.L.,* XXX, cols. 135 f.).

For the second passage, e.g., see Homily 45 in the collection of homilies made by Paulus Diaconus *(P.L.,* XCV, col. 1492): "Ecce enim exaltata est super choros angelorum usque ad dexteram filii, et facta est potens materfamilias in universo domo Domini, et regina coelorum appellata est. Quam potenter ad se traxit versiculum illum propheticum, quo dictum est: 'Astitit regina a dextris tuis in vestitu deaurato, circumdata varietate.' "

5. See the fundamental article of E. H. Kantorowicz, "ΣΥΝΘΡΟΝΟΣ ΔΙΚΗΙ," *American Journal of Archaeology,* LVII (1953), pp. 65 ff. In the West the Empress Theophanu was given the twofold title of "*coimperatrix augusta nec non imperii*

regnorumque consors." See M. Uhlirz, "Zu dem Mitkaisertum der Ottonen: Theophanu coimperatrix," *Byzantinische Zeitschrift,* L (1957), pp. 383 ff., especially p. 385.

6. A. Grabar, *L'empereur dans l'art byzantin,* p. 27.

7. K. Künstle, *Ikonographie der christlichen Kunst,* Freiburg im Breisgau, 1928, I, pp. 564 ff.; O. Sinding, *Mariae Tod und Himmelfahrt,* Christiania, 1903.

8. See, for instance, the encomium of the late seventh or early eighth century ascribed to Archbishop Modestos of Jerusalem (died 634; *Patr. graeca,* LXXXVI, cols. 3277 ff.) or the homilies of St. John of Damascus (died 749; *ibidem,* XCVI, cols. 699 ff.).

9. M. Jugie, *La mort et l'assomption de la sainte Vierge (Studi e Testi,* CXIV), Città del Vaticano, 1944; E. Staedel, *Ikonographie der Himmelfahrt Mariens,* Strasbourg, 1935; J. Hecht, "Die frühesten Darstellungen der Himmelfahrt Mariens," *Das Münster,* IV (1950/51), pp. 1 ff.; A. Weiss, "Die Himmelaufnahme Mariens am Strassburger Münster und die Symbolik der Kathedralkunst, *ibidem,* pp. 12 ff.

10. *L'art religieux du XIIe siècle en France,* pp. 183 ff.

11. Sacramentary of Petershausen, Heidelberg, Univ. Libr., Cod. Sal. IXb, fols. 40v, 41r (A. Goldschmidt, *Die deutsche Buchmalerei,* II, pl. 19). See also Sacramentary of Worms, Paris, Bibl. de l'Arsenal, MS 610, fol. 25v (H. Martin and Ph. Lauer, *Les principaux manuscrits à peintures de la Bibliothèque de l'Arsenal à Paris,* 1929, pl. 2).

12. Professor E. H. Kantorowicz kindly has drawn my attention to the hymn composed for the year 1000 and sung during the procession. The crucial verses are:

Sistitur in solio domini spectabile signum,
Theotocosque suo sistitur in solio.

See *Mon. Germ. Hist., Poetae latini medii aevi,* V, p. 467; *Ordo Romanus XI (P.L.,* LXXVIII, col. 1052); W. F. Volbach, "Il Cristo di Sutri e la venerazione del SS. Salvatore nel Lazio," *Rendiconti della Pontificia Accademia Romana di Archeologia,* XVII (1940–41), pp. 97 ff., especially pp. 116 ff.

13. G. Zarnecki, "The Coronation of the Virgin on a Capital from Reading Abbey," *Journal of the Warburg and Courtauld Institutes,* XIII (1950), pp. 1 ff.

Other representations may have prepared the way for the final formulation of the scene. In the northern tympanum of the Abbey Church of La Charité-sur-Loire, Christ enthroned in a mandorla receives the Virgin who ascends to heaven (A.K. Porter, *Romanesque Sculpture of the Pilgrimage Roads,* fig. 120). A tympanum from Saint-Pierre-le-Puellier, now in the museum of Bourges, shows above the lintel (Annunciation of Death—Death—Carrying to the Tomb) her Burial and Assumption. Four Angels carry the crowned Virgin to heaven (*ibidem,* fig. 1262). In contrast to the Senlis tympanum, both reliefs show the Virgin on her way to glory, but not yet enthroned in heaven.

14. *Epistola IX ad Paulam et Eustochium de assumptione beatae Mariae Virginis (P.L.,* XXX, cols. 126 ff.). For a critical discussion of the possible author of the treatise, see M. Jugie, *op. cit.,* pp. 277 ff.

"Regina mundi hodie de terris . . . eripitur: . . . ad coeli jam pervenit palatium" *(P.L.* XXX, col. 130) " . . . Salvator . . . cum gaudio eam secum in throno collocavit" *(ibidem,* col. 134). " . . . ineffabiliter sublimata cum Christo regnat in aeternum" *(ibidem,* col. 130). "Haec est, inquam, dies, in qua usque ad throni celsitudinem intemerata mater et virgo processit, atque in regni solio sublimata, post Christum gloriosa resedit" *(ibidem,* col. 132). Similar ideas occur in a poem wrongly ascribed to Venantius Fortunatus but already copied in an eighth-century codex:

conderis in solio felix regina superno,

. . . . . .

sic iuxta genitum regem regina perennem,
ornata ex partu, mater opima, tuo.

(In laudem s. Mariae, vss. 261, 265 f.; *Mon. Germ. Hist., Auctores antiquissimi,* IV, pp. 377 f.)

Another source for the letter of Pseudo-Jerome can be found, e.g., in the homily of an anonymous author, included in the collection of patristic homilies made by Paulus Diaconus: "Daughters of Jerusalem, come and see the mother of the Lord with the royal diadem of her glory, with which her Son crowned her on the day of His heart's gladness, on the day of her blessed Assumption to heaven." (For the Latin text, see *P.L.*, XCV, col. 1490.) "For there she is exalted above the choirs of the angels to the right side of Her Son, and she is made the mighty mother in the whole house of the Lord and called Queen of heaven" *(ibidem,* col. 1492).

The famous passage of the Forty-fourth Psalm, *"Astitit regina a dextris tuis, in vestitu deaurato, circumdata varietate,"* was paraphrased in an antiphon sung since the end of the eleventh century at Chartres during the office of Assumption day:

Propterea regum te rex benedixit in aevum,
Et facit a dextris, casta, sedere suis,
Aurea quam fulvo vestis circumdata limbo
Ambit et exornat, riteque condecorat.

(Y. Delaporte, *Les vitraux de la cathédrale de Chartres,* Chartres, 1926, Text, p. 175, note 2.) While in the words of the Psalm "the queen stood at thy right side," the antiphon says that the King of kings made the Virgin sit at His right side. Could this show the influence of some lost representation of the Virgin enthroned with Christ?

15. See note 7, *supra.*

16. "Quomodo autem, vel quo tempore, aut a quibus personis sanctissimum corpus ejus inde ablatum fuerit, vel ubi transpositum, utrumne resurrexerit, nescitur; quamvis nonnulli astruere velint eam jam resuscitatam, et beata cum Christo immortalitate in coelestibus vestiri" *(P.L.,* XXX, col. 127).

17. The treatise of Pseudo-Augustine *(P.L.,* XL, cols. 1141 ff.) is tentatively ascribed to Alcuin by G. Quadrio *(Il trattato "De Assumptione beatae Mariae Virginis" dello Pseudo-Agostino e il suo influsso nella teologia assunzionistica latina* [*Analecta Gregoriana,* LII]), Rome, 1951. For the sermon of Fulbert, see *P.L.,* CXLI, col. 325.

18. John Beleth mentions the vision of Elizabeth in his *Rationale divinorum officiorum,* c. 146 *(P.L.,* CCII, col. 148), but he adds that the little book she wrote about it was not approved by the Roman Church.

19. " . . . meruit exaltari super choros angelorum." " . . . ut ultra angelorum et archangelorum dignitatem merito transcenderit" *(P.L.,* XXX, col. 132).

20. "Ascendebat autem Dei genitrix de deserto praesentis saeculi, virga de radice Jesse olim exorta" *(ibidem,* col. 134).

21. See, for instance " . . . sponsa scilicet et matre Domini Maria . . . " (Fulbert of Chartres, *Sermo VI; P.L.,* CXLI, col. 325).

22. "Sicut enim Christi mater virgo concepit, virgo peperit, virgo permansit, sic mater Ecclesia, Christi sponsa, lavacro aquae in verbo Christianos populos quotidie generat, ut virgo permaneat" *(P.L.,* CLXII, col. 570). See also St. Ambrose, *Expositio in S. Lucam* II, 7: "Bene desponsata, sed virgo, quia est Ecclesiae typus, quae est immaculata, sed nupta" *(P.L.,* XV, cols. 1635 f.). St. Augustine, *De sancta virginitate,* c. 2: "Maria corporaliter caput hujus corporis peperit: Ecclesia spiritualiter membra illius capitis parit. In utraque virginitas fecunditatem non impedit: in utraque fecunditas virginitatem non adimit" *(P.L.,* XL, col. 397).

For a thorough discussion of the concept Mary-Ecclesia, see A. Müller, *Ecclesia-Maria, Die Einheit Marias und der Kirche (Paradosis, Beiträge zur Geschichte der altchristlichen Literatur und Theologie,* V), Freiburg, Switzerland, 1951; H. Coathalem, *Le parallelisme entre la sainte Vierge et l'Eglise dans la tradition latine jusqu'à la fin du XIIᵉ siècle (Analecta Gregoriana,* LXXIV), Rome, 1954.

23. "Commemoratio beatae Mariae Virginis loco dedicationis" *(olim* Chartres, Bibl. de la Ville, MS 588 (2), fol. 370v, thirteenth century).

24. J. Beumer, "Die marianische Deutung des Hohen Liedes in der Frühscholastik," *Zeitschrift für katholische Theologie,* LXXVI (1954), pp. 411 ff.

25. "Unde cum canticum amoris, scilicet epithalamium Salomonis, specialiter et spiritualiter ad Ecclesiam referatur, tamen specialissime et spiritualissime ad gloriosam Virginem reducitur quod divino notu (prout poterimus) explicabimus" *(Elucidatio in Cantica Canticorum,* prologue; *P.L.,* CCX, col. 53).

26. See V.L. Kennedy, "The Handbook of Master Peter Chancellor of Chartres," *Mediaeval Studies,* V (1943), p. 5.

Paris, Bibl. nat., MS lat. 14435, fol. 143r: "Canticum Canticorum secundum Cancellarium Carnotensem." Fol. 144r: "Quae est ista, quae ascendit per desertum

(Cant. 3:6). Vel sic de beata Virgine loquitur Synagoga, licet Ecclesia, quae ascendit per contemptum mundi et non habet strumam peccati et ipsa habuit omnia genera virtutum in se. Omnia patent de Virgine." Fol. 145r: "Anima mea (Cant. 5:6). Istud de Ecclesia vel de beata Virgine potest legi."

27. "Cantatur hic psalmus de festo beatae Mariae Virginis, quia quae de Ecclesia generaliter hic dicuntur, ad Mariam specialiter referri possunt" *(P.L.,* CXIII, col. 911).

28. "In hoc itaque Assumptionis festo psalmi atque alia quae generatim dici consueverunt in Dedicatione ecclesiae, speciatim de B. Maria cantantur. Ut enim Ecclesia mater est omnium sanctorum, nomenque tenet virginitatis, videlicet mentis ac fidei, quae corporis praefertur virginitati, sponsa Christi dicta. Unde illud: 'Despondi vos uni viro virginem castam exhibere Christo,' sic profecto B. Maria dicta et Virgo est, et sanctissima sanctorum" (c. 146; *P.L.,* CCII, col. 150). There is a similar passage in the *Mitrale* of Siccardus (IX. 40; *P.L.,* CCXIII, col. 420).

29. See, for instance, Gregory the Great, *Liber regulae pastoralis,* II c. 11: "Quid per arcam, nisi sancta Ecclesia figuratur" *(P.L.,* LXXVII, col. 49). His interpretation was included in the *Glossa ordinaria,* Exod. XXV, 12 ff. *(P.L.,* CXIII, col. 267).

30. E. Mâle, *L'art religieux du XIIIe siècle en France,* fig. 129.

31. E. Panofsky, *Die deutsche Plastik des elften bis dreizehnten Jahrhunderts,* Munich, 1924, pl. 114; P. Vitry, *French Sculpture during the Reign of Saint Louis,* Florence-New York, 1929, pl. 66.

32. S. Abdul-Hak, *La sculpture des porches du transept de la cathédrale de Chartres,* pp. 30 ff. See also the interesting remarks of P. Kidson, *Sculpture at Chartres,* p. 35.

33. " . . . sancti ante legem, sancti sub lege, sancti sub gratia, omnes hi . . . in membris sunt Ecclesiae constituti" (Letter to Bishop John of Constantinople; *P.L.,* LXXVII, col. 740). The idea of a universal Church was expressed before by St. Augustine: "Ecclesiam autem accipite, fratres, non in his solis, qui post Domini adventum et nativitatem esse coeperunt sancti; sed omnes quotquot fuerunt sancti, ad ipsam Ecclesiam pertinent" *(Sermo IV,* 11; *P.L.,* XXXVIII, p. 39). See also J. Beumer, "Die Idee einer vorchristlichen Kirche bei Augustinus," *Münchener theologische Zeitschrift,* III (1952), pp. 161 ff.

34. "Sive igitur Abraham, sive ante illum justi, sive post eum usque ad ipsum Moysen . . . sive caeteri prophetae post eum et sancti homines Dei usque ad Joannem Baptistam, filii sunt promissionis et gratiae . . . " *(Contra duas epistolas Pelagianorum,* III, 8; *P.L.,* XLIV, col. 593).

35. "Quaerimus cur tertio desponsionis nomen repetierit. Primo enim ait: 'Sponsabo te mihi in sempiternum.' Secundo: 'Sponsabo te mihi in justitia et judicio, et in misericordia et miserationibus.' Nec hoc fine contentus jungit et tertium: 'Sponsabo te mihi in fide, et scies quia ego Dominus.' Primo despondit eam in Abraham, sive in Aegypto, ut uxorem habeat sempiternam. Secundo in monte Sinai, dans ei pro sponsalibus Legis justitiam atque judicium et junctam Legi misericordiam, ut quando peccaverit, tradatur captivitati, cum egerit poenitentiam, revocetur in patriam, et misericordiam consequatur. . . .

Ista ergo meretrix, quae primum voto sponsi in aeternos fuerat juncta complexus, ut numquam a vinculo recederet maritali, quia recessit et in Aegypto fornicata est, rursum per Legem assumitur: quam quia praeteriit, prophetis quasi sponsi sodalibus . . . interfectis, novissime venit Dei Filius, Dominus Jesus: quo crucifixo, et a mortuis resurgente, desponsatur nequaquam in Legis justitia, sed in fide et gratia Evangelii, ut cum cognoverit Unigenitum, cognoscat et Patrem" *(Commentaria in Osee,* I. 2; *P.L.,* XXV, col. 840).

36. "Christus est sponsus; sponsa Ecclesia, quam sibi desponsavit tertio, sicut per Osee ait: 'Sponsabo te mihi in sempiternum, et sponsabo te mihi in justitia et misericordia, et sponsabo te mihi in fide.' Ter dicit 'sponsabit,' qui ter eam despondit; primo in patriarchis, qui annulum suum inviolate habuerunt; et dotem legis naturalis et quorumdam coelestium praeceptorum perceperunt . . . ; secundo, tempore prophetarum, dans eis pro sponsabilibus justificationes et judicia legis Mosaicae, quibus

addidit misericordiam, monens ad poenitentiam, ut captivitatis evaderent miseriam; tertio sponsavit eam in adventu Filii, cum per Evangelium fidem declaravit Trinitatis, ubi in dotem accepit evangelica praecepta ac sacramenta; et tunc liberavit eam de manu hostium, id est daemonum, qui eam totam constupraverant, id est idolatriae reatu polluerant. Sed ipse veniens, et tertio sponsans eam, mundavit eam a peccatorum sanguine, et immaculatam exhibuit, sicut per Ezechielem ait: 'Lavi te aqua, et emundavi sanguinem tuum ex te, et unxi te oleo, et calceavi te ianthino, et cinxi te bysso, et ornavi te ornamento, et coronam dedi in capite tuo, et facta es mihi uxor.' . . . coronatur diademate aeterni decoris et ita facta est sponso amabilis" *(Sermo I in Rogationibus; P.L.,* CLXXI, cols. 568 f.).

Placidus of Nonantula quotes Hosea's prophecy in his discussion of the Church as Bride of Christ *(Liber de honore Ecclesiae; Mon. Germ. Hist., Libelli de lite,* II, p. 576).

37. "There Isaac was figuratively sacrificed by the ram, here the Son of God is sacrificed through bread and wine in the truth of His flesh and blood" (Rupert of Deutz, *Commentaria in Evangelium Joannis,* VII; for the Latin text, see *P.L.,* CLXIX, col. 491).

38. "And as Moses lifted up the serpent in the wilderness, even so must the Son of man be lifted up: That whosoever believeth in him should not perish, but have eternal life" (John 3: 14 f.).

39. "They pierced my hands and my feet" (Ps. 21:16 [22:16]).

40. See, for instance, Hugh of St. Victor, *De sacramentis,* II. 2, 1: "In sacramento autem per baptismum unimur, per corpus Christi et sanguinem vivificamur. Per baptismum efficimur membra corporis, per corpus autem Christi efficimur participes vivificationis" *(P.L.,* CLXXVI, col. 416).

41. Bamberg, Staatsbibl., MS A I. 47, fol. 4v, H. Swarzenski, *Vorgotische Miniaturen,* 2d ed., Königstein i. T., 1931, p. 30.

42. "Ipse autem per semetipsum veniens, et super cadaver humiliter sternens, et super exaequanda sibi mortui membra se collegit, quia 'cum in forma Dei esset, non rapinam arbitratus est esse se aequalem Deo, sed semet ipsum exinanivit, formam

servi accipiens, in similitudinem hominum factus' " (Hrabanus Maurus, *Commentaria in libros IV Regum,* IV, 4; *P.L.,* CIX, col. 229) .

43. "Sublevatus namque Elias Ascensionem Dominicam designavit" *(op. cit.,* II, 2; *ibidem,* col. 222).

44. "Mulier Sunamitidis sancta est Ecclesia. Jacuit mulier Sunamitidis ad pedes Elisei pro resuscitatione filii (II Kings 4:27), quia sancta Ecclesia humiliter in patribus Domino oravit pro redemptione humani generis" (Hugh of St. Victor(?), *Allegoriae in Vetus Testamentum,* VII. 25; *P.L.,* CLXXV, col. 718).

45. "Hoc ergo pallium Eliseus post transitum Eliae retinuit, quia fidem Incarnationis Christi Ecclesia post ascensionem ejus ad coelos reservavit" (Hrabanus Maurus, *op. cit.,* IV, 2; *P.L.,* CIX, col. 224).

46. J. Vanuxem, "Les portails détruits de la cathédrale de Cambrai et de Saint-Nicolas d'Amiens," *Bulletin monumental,* CIII (1945), pp. 89 ff.

At Lausanne, where Bishop Amadeus (died 1159) had left eight sermons about the Assumption of the Virgin, her Coronation was represented in about 1230 on the portal of the south porch. This representation is based on the famous passage of Psalm 44:10 [45.9]: "The queen stood at thy right side in raiments of gold." Seated in a mandorla, Christ takes a crown from an attending Angel and blesses the standing Virgin, before crowning her. The jamb and pier statues comprise personalities of the two Testaments: Simeon, John the Baptist, Moses, Jeremiah, David, and Isaiah on one side, Peter, Paul, and the four Evangelists on the other side. See J. Gantner, *Kunstgeschichte der Schweiz,* II, *Die gotische Kunst,* Frauenfeld, 1947, pp. 188 ff.

47. G. Durand, *Monographie de l'église Notre-Dame, cathédrale d'Amiens,* Amiens-Paris, 1901, I, pls. XL-XLII.

48. E. Lambert, *op. cit.,* pp. 95 ff. For the Chartres portal, see S. Abdul-Hak, *op. cit.,* pp. 62 ff.; E. Mâle, *Notre-Dame de Chartres,* pp. 56 ff.; P. Kidson, *op. cit.,* pp. 47 ff.; Abbé Bulteau, *op. cit.,* II, pp. 210 ff.

49. "Hoc quippe privilegium non naturae est, sed gratiae beatae Virginis

Mariae, de qua natus est ipse Deus et homo" *(P.L.,* XXX, col. 132). See also *Elucidatio in Canticum Canticorum,* c. 5, ascribed to Alan of Lille: "Veni ad me per ascensionem, qui veni ad te per carnis assumptionem" *(P.L.,* CCX, col. 84).

50. "Sic namque credere, honorare est matrem Domini, quae Deum nobis genuit et hominem: neque hominem sine Deo, neque sine homine Deum, sed Deum et hominem unum et verum Jesum Christum" *(P.L.,* XXX, col. 135).

51. "Unde quod concipit et parit Virgo, sicut non sine potentia Verbi est, ita non sine veritate carnis, quod pannorum fasciis jacet involutum, et in praesepio reclinatur. Porro quod stella duce a Magis adoratur, sicut deitatis est" *(ibidem,* col. 140).

52. E. Houvet, *Cathédrale de Chartres, Portail nord,* I, pls. 84–87.

53. "Sunt enim et prudentes virgines, sunt et fatuae. Et ideo, dilectissimae, imitamini, quam amatis beatam et gloriosam Virginem, cujus hodie in terris festa colitis" *(P.L.,* XXX, col. 140).

54. " . . . omnium prudentium virginum reginam" *(Sermo VI; P.L.,* CXLI, col. 328).

55. "Quam si diligentius aspicias, nihil virtutis est, nihil speciositatis, nihil candoris gloriaeque, quod ex ea non resplendeat" *(P.L.,* XXX, col. 142). "Prima ejus virtus est fundamentum omnium virtutum et custos, humilitas ipsa, de qua gloriatur: 'Quia respexit,' inquit, 'humilitatem ancillae suae: ecce enim ex hoc beatam me dicent omnes generationes' " *(ibidem,* col. 144).

In a similar manner Fulbert of Chartres says in his famous sermon on the Nativity of the Virgin that Mary did not lack any kind of virtues. He then enumerates the four cardinal virtues, and faith, charity and humility *(Sermo IV; P.L.,* CXLI, cols. 322 f.).

For detailed illustrations, see E. Houvet, *op. cit.,* pls. 84–87.

At Laon the influence of Pseudo-Jerome may be seen in yet another way. The letter states that the Virgin was foretold by the prophets, and préfigured by the patriarchs both figuratively and enigmatically *(P.L.,* XXX, col. 130). The idea of prediction and prefiguration is illustrated at Laon in the third and fourth archivolts in a compre-

hensive manner and with deliberate correspondence between the two sides. (E. Mâle [*L'art religieux du XIIIᵉ siècle,* pp. 148 ff.] has discovered that the specific figures and scenes are derived from Honorius Augustodunensis [*Speculum Ecclesiae; P.L.,* CLXXII, cols. 904 f.].) The prophecies are represented by Daniel and Ezekiel (lowest voussoirs of the third archivolt), by another Prophet and the Erythraean Sibyl (second voussoirs of the fourth archivolt).

Various symbols refer to the virgin birth of Christ: the Unicorn tamed by a virgin and the Fiery Oven that did not harm the three Hebrews (lowest voussoirs of the fourth archivolt), Habakkuk miraculously feeding Daniel in the lion's den, the Ark of the Covenant with Aaron's rod, and Ezekiel's *Porta clausa* (second and third voussoirs of the third archivolt), Gideon's Fleece, and the Burning Bush (fourth voussoirs of the third archivolt).

Still other scenes at Laon refer figuratively to Christ: Isaac sending Jacob to Mesopotamia, and Samuel anointing David, Balaam predicting that a star would rise out of Israel, and Nebuchadnezzar's Dream of the Statue (upper voussoirs of the fourth archivolt).

56. E. Mâle *(Notre-Dame de Chartres,* pp. 54 f.) interprets the statues and the archivolt figures as prototypes of Christ and Mary. He explains tympanum and lintel only literally. See also S. Abdul-Hak, *op. cit.,* pp. 88 ff.; P. Kidson, *op cit.,* pp. 49 ff.; Abbé Bulteau, *op. cit.,* II, pp. 233 ff.

57. "Sciendum quoque est quod Redemptor noster unam se personam cum sancta Ecclesia, quam assumpsit, exhibuit. De ipso enim dicitur: 'Qui est caput, Christus.' Rursumque de ejus Ecclesia scriptum est: 'Et corpus Christi, quod est Ecclesias.' Beatus igitur Job, qui Mediatoris typum eo verius tenuit quo passionem illius, non loquendo tantummodo, sed etiam patiendo prophetavit, cum in dictis factisque suis expressioni Redemptoris innititur, repente ad significationem corporis aliquando derivatur, ut quod Christum et Ecclesiam unam personam credimus, hoc etiam unius personae actibus significari videamus" *(Moralia in Job,* XXIII, 1; *P.L.,* LXXVI, col. 251).

58. "Job quippe interpretatur dolens. Quo nimirum dolore, vel Mediatoris passio, vel sanctae Ecclesiae labor exprimitur, quae multiplici praesentis vitae fatigatione cruciatur" *(op. cit.,* Praefatio, VII, 16; *P.L.,* LXXV, cols. 525 f.)

59. "A planta autem pedis usque ad verticem vulnera suscepit, quia sanctam Ecclesiam, quae corpus ejus est, non solum per extrema et ultima, sed usque ad summa membra persecutione saeviens tentator affligit" *(op. cit.,* VI, 1; *ibidem,* col. 729).

60. "Uxor vero ejus, quae eum ad maledicendum provocat, vitam carnalium designat." "Amici vero ejus, qui dum consulunt invehuntur, haereticorum figuram exprimunt, qui sub specie consulendi agunt negotium seducendi" *(op. cit.,* Praefatio, VI, 14 f.; *ibidem,* col. 525).

61. " . . . quomodo sponsus et sponsa dicuntur, sic caput et corpus. Sive ergo dicatur caput et corpus, sive sponsus et sponsa, unum intelligite. Fit enim ex duobus quasi una quaedam persona, scilicet ex capite et corpore, ex sponso et sponsa" *(Glossa ordinaria,* In Ephes. V, 32; *P.L.,* CXIV, col. 599). See also St. Augustine, *Enarratio in Psalmum CXXXVIII:* "Corpus autem ejus sancta Ecclesia, quae etiam conjux ejus" *(P.L.,* XXXVII, col. 1784).

62. "Ecclesia enim hic militat, in patria regnat: pars peregrinatur, et pars gloriatur" *(Speculum de mysteriis Ecclesiae,* I, ascribed to Hugh of Victor; *P.L.,* CLXXVII, col. 338). For the prayer of the priest, see F. Holböck, *Der eucharistische und der mystische Leib Christi,* Rome, 1941, p. 163.

63. "Et duae quidem feminae Synagoga et Ecclesia in prima facie considerationis occurunt" *(Sermo X; P.L.,* XXXVIII, col. 92). See also *Glossa ordinaria,* In I Reg. 3:21: "Duae mulieres, quarum una dilectione ardebat, in altera simulatio subrepebat Ecclesiam figurans, et Synagogam sive haereticam pravitatem. . . . Inter duas mulieres Dominus, dum id quod justum est spiritu oris sui dirimit, unicuique quod debetur restituit" *(P.L.,* CXIII, cols. 582 f.).

64. "Et tu quidem, impia Synagoga, hunc nobis filium peperisti, officio quidem matris, sed non matris affectu. Excussisti eum de sinu tuo, extra civitatem ejiciens, et elevans super terram, tanquam dicens Ec-

clesiae gentium, pariter et Ecclesiae primitivorum, quae est in coelis: 'Nec mihi, nec vobis sit, sed dividatur' " *(In vigilia nativitatis Domini sermo VI; P.L.,* CLXXXIII, cols. 115 f.).

65. See A. Weis, "Die 'Synagoge' am Münster zu Strassburg," *Das Münster,* I, (1947/48), pp. 65 ff.

66. "Samson Salvatoris nostri mortem et victoriam figuravit" (Isidore of Seville, *Allegoriae quaedam sacrae Scripturae; P.L.,* LXXXIII, col. 111). For Gideon, see note 68, *infra.*

67. "Quod ergo stetit angelus in altaris flamma, magis significasse intelligendus est illum magni consilii Angelum in forma servi, hoc est, in homine quem suscepturus erat, non accepturum sacrificium, sed ipsum sacrificium futurum" (Hrabanus Maurus, *Commentaria in librum Judicum,* II, 16; *P.L.,* CVIII, col. 1192).

68. "Iste Gedeon figuram nimirum Christi gestabat, qui sub umbra sacrae crucis, praedestinato incarnationis futurae mysterio, constitutus, rectitudine judicii, quasi per virgam, electionem sanctorum a vitiorum paleis sequestrebat" *(op. cit.,* II, 2; *P.L.,* CVIII, cols. 1157 f.).

69. "Samson . . . leonem occidit: et Christus Ecclesiam vocaturus de gentibus diabolum vicit" *(Glossa ordinaria, In Judices,* XIV, 5; *P.L.,* CXIII, col. 531).

70. "Habebat populus gentium mella, quia credidit; qui corpus feritatis erat ante, nunc Christi est" (Hrabanus Maurus, *op. cit.,* II, 19; *P.L.,* CVIII, col. 1195).

71. "Quid ergo vellus complutum et area sicca? . . . nisi quod primo una gens Hebraeorum habebat gratiae mysterium, totus orbis vacuus erat" (Hrabanus Maurus, *op. cit.,* II, 3; *P.L.,* CVIII, col. 1159).

72. "Samson vero nocte media non solum exiit, sed etiam portas civitatis tulit; quia Redemptor noster videlicet ante lucem resurgens, non solum liber de inferno exiit, sed ipsa etiam inferni claustra destruxit, portas tulit, et montis verticem subiit, quia surgendo claustra inferni abstulit, et ascendendo coelorum regna penetravit" (Hrabanus Maurus, *op. cit.,* II, 19; *P.L.,* CVIII, col. 1194).

73. "Quid per Zebee et Salmana principes Madianitarum, quos persequens Gedeon comprehendit, nisi philosophi atque

haeretici, membra diaboli, designantur?" (Hrabanus Maurus, *op cit.*, II, 8; *P.L.*, CVIII, col. 1167.)

74. "Liber Esther . . . multipliciter Christi et Ecclesiae sacramenta in mysterio continet, quia ipsa Esther in Ecclesiae typo populum de periculo liberat . . . " (Hrabanus Maurus, *Expositio in librum Esther*, Praefatio; *P.L.*, CIX, col. 635).

"Judith ergo, quod Ecclesiae typum habeat, magistrorum traditio manifestat" (Hrabanus Maurus, *Expositio in librum Judith*, c. 8; *P.L.*, CIX, col. 559). ". . . dixerim Manassem virum Judith legis decalogum sive ritum gentilitatis significare" (*ibidem,* col. 560).

75. "Septimo ergo anno Assueri, Esther accessit ad thalamum regis. Et Ecclesia ad regem Christum, in quo septiformis Spiritus gratia incommutabiliter manet, adducta atque conjuncta est. . . . In cujus capite diadema regni posuit, cum ipsam sibi consortem regni ascivit; fecitque eam regnare in loco Vasthi, hoc est Judaeorum Synagogae" (*Expositio in librum Esther*, c. 4; *P.L.*, CIX, col. 649).

76. "Et quid per Mardochaeum, nisi doctores gentium significantur? Et maxime beatus Paulus apostolus . . . " (*ibidem,* c. 3, col. 646).

77. "Potest et per Aman istum . . . Judaeorum populus sanguinolentus figurari" (*ibidem,* c. 6, col. 652). "Unde sicut Aman epistolas dirigens regis signaculo eas munire curabat . . . ita perfidia Judaeorum libros divinae legis . . . ad comprobandam haeresim suam in testimonium non recte assumens, gentium conversionem ad societatem religionis reprobare nitebatur, et Christi Evangelium quasi contrarium divinis praeceptis condemnare" (*ibidem,* c. 6, col. 653).

78. "Cum magistri Ecclesiae, audita persecutione principum terrae . . . cum jejuniis et eleemosynis, cum vigiliis et orationibus, cum lacrymis et compunctione cordis ad secreta coeli necessitates suas, in conspectu videlicet superni judicis profundere gestiunt, ut per dignitatem et preces verae reginae, hoc est sanctae Ecclesiae, quae partim adhuc peregrinatur in terris, partim autem jam cum Domino regnat in coelis, a rege omnium saeculorum exaudiri mereantur" (*ibidem,* c. 7, col. 654).

79. "Quid est ergo Esther procidere ad pedes regis eumque pro salute populi exorare, nisi sanctam Ecclesiam pro ereptione filiorum suorum quotidie Dominum omnipotentem per fidem et mysteria incarnationis Unigeniti Dei humiliter postulare, quatenus ejus gratia et hostium comprimatur audacia, et de manibus eorum fidelium liberetur innocentia" (*ibidem,* c. 11, col. 662).

80. "Cujus rei significatio in promptu est, quia Evangelii doctrina ita condita est per scriptores Novi Testamenti. . . . Ipsaque Scriptura per veredarios, hoc est, praedicatores sanctos, directa est in totum orbem terrarum" (*ibidem,* c. 11, col. 662 f.).

81. "Commendat Judith presbyteris portam, quia sacerdotibus Christi sancta Ecclesia sollicitam castrorum commendat custodiam" (Hrabanus Maurus, *Expositio in librum Judith*, c. 8; *P.L.*, CIX, col. 563).

82. "Induit se cilicio, cum poenitentiam pro peccatis agit. Cinerem super caput ponit, cum fragilitatis suae memoriam in mente recondit. Prosternens se ad Dominum clamat, dum per humilitatis affectum se a Domino exaudiri sperat" (*ibidem,* c. 9, col. 563).

83. "His ergo omnibus ornamentis se sancta Ecclesia ornat, quia omnium virtutum decore se illustrare certat" (*ibidem,* c. 10, col. 565).

84. "Quod Judith adorat Holofernem, non est perturbatio timoris, sed conservatio ordinis. Quotiens enim sancti viri terrenae potestati impendunt honorem, non ex vitio adulationis, sed ex jure dignitatis hoc faciunt" (*ibidem,* c. 13, col. 567).

85. "Quid est quod Judith ancillae suae tradidit caput Holofernis, ut mitteret illud in peram suam, nisi quod Ecclesia auditoribus suis recordationem confecti belli non vult labi a cogitatione mentis, sed sollicite servari in memoria cordis" (*ibidem,* c. 13, col. 573).

86. "Eleganter autem per lunam figuratur Ecclesia; quia, sicut luna mendicat lumen a sole, ita Ecclesia lumen justitiae a vero sole, scilicet Christo." "Per lunam Ecclesia, per stellas sancti figurantur" (Alan of Lille, *Liber in distinctionibus dictionum theologicalium; P.L.*, CCX, cols. 842, 955).

87. "Quod si est alia claritas solis, et alia claritas lunae, et alia claritas stellarum (I Cor. 15:41): una tamen claritas est,

qua illustrantur omnia" (Pseudo-Jerome, *Epistola ad Paulam et Eustochium; P.L.,* XXX, col. 143).

88. "Maxima namque Christi et Ecclesiae sacramenta, si spiritualiter intelligitur, in se continere probatur. Siquidem ipse Tobias populum Israel designat, qui, cunctis gentibus idolatriae deditis, ipse serviebat Deo fide recta et operibus justis, sicut de Tobia legitur" (Bede, *In librum beati patris Tobiae allegorica interpretatio; P.L.,* XCI, col. 923).

89. "Fatigatus est a sepultura, et caecatus, quia qui infatigabilis in bonis operibus persistit, numquam fidei luce privatur" (*ibidem,* col. 925). "Haec autem caecitas populo Israel, maxime imminente adventu Domini in carne praevaluit, cum et Romanae servitutis jugo premerentur, et legis divinae praecepta pessime vivendo violarent" (*ibidem,* col. 926).

90. "Tobias postquam factus est vir, accepit uxorem Annam ex tribu sua, etc. Et populus idem, postquam adolevit et amplificatus in Aegypto, accepit synagogam caeremoniis legalibus institutam per Moysen" (*ibidem,* col. 924).

91. "Introduxit Tobias angelum ad patrem suum. . . . Et Dominus noster per miracula quae fecit in carne, ostendit populo Judaeorum, ex quo carnem susceperat, quia ipse est Filius Dei, et angelus, id est, nuntius paternae voluntatis" (*ibidem,* col. 927).

92. "Apprehendit Dominus diabolum, et eum qui se in morte capere voluit, moriendo cepit et vicit" (*ibidem,* col. 928).

93. "Raguel indicat populum gentium, quem Dominus per praedicatores suos visitare dignatus est, ut de ejus stirpe sibi sponsam assumeret, id est, ipsam gentilitatem sibi Ecclesiam faceret" (*ibidem,* col. 929).

94. "Et Dominus accepturus Ecclesiam de gentibus, in primo dispositionis ejus initio jubet eam in singulis credentibus abrenuntiare Satanae, et omnibus operibus ejus, et omnibus pompis ejus; ac deinde confiteri fidem sanctae Trinitatis in remissionem peccatorum, quod est intima pacis viscera vivis cremare carbonibus" (*ibidem,* col. 930).

95. "Quia post abrenuntiationem diaboli, post confessionem rectae fidei, sequitur

remissio peccatorum, expulso daemonio per aquam baptismi. Ligavit autem eum, qui a fidelium laesione retinuit: quos etsi tentare aliquoties permittitur, ut probentur, superare tamen prohibetur, ne a fide deficiant" (*loc. cit.*).

96. "Et Judaeorum populus, postquam amarissimam nequissimi hostis malitiam cognoverit, amissam recipiet lucem" (*ibidem,* col. 934).

The foundation for the five archivolt cycles is provided by a Dragon (underneath the story of Gideon), a Lion (underneath the cycle of Samson), and by the heads of four Kings (underneath the stories of Esther, Judith, and Tobit). See S. Abdul-Hak, *La sculpture des porches du transept de la cathédrale de Chartres,* pp. 110 ff.

97. "Per stellam quoque ex Jacob, Ecclesia a Christo vel a populo primitivo potest significari" (Bede, *In Pentateuchum commentarii,* Numeri, XXIII, 24; *P.L.,* XCI, col. 371).

98. "Regina autem Austri, quae a finibus extremis excitata veniens, Salomonis audire sapientiam concupivit, jam tunc venturam gentibus Ecclesiam, desiderantem Christum praefigurabat" (Hrabanus Maurus, *Commentaria in libros IV Regum,* III, 10; *P.L.,* CIX, col. 192). See A. Chastel, "La rencontre de Salomon et la reine de Saba dans l'iconographie médiévale," *Gazette des Beaux-Arts,* 1949, I, pp. 99 ff.

99. "Praeterea notandum quod ille liber Salomonis, qui dicitur Ecclesiastes, et iste Jesu filii Sirach, qui Ecclesiasticus nuncupatur, ad instructionem Ecclesiae Dei, hoc est populi Christiani, sunt utilissimi. . . . Sed inter Ecclesiastem et Ecclesiasticum istam Patres posuere distantiam, quod Ecclesiastes ad Christum Dominum maxime debet referri, Ecclesiasticus vero cuicunque justo praedicatori potest absolute congruere, qui Ecclesiam Domini sanctissimis solet monitis congregare" (Hrabanus Maurus, *Commentaria in Ecclesiasticum,* Praefatio; *P.L.,* CIX, cols. 763 f.). The building of the temple during the time of Jesus Sirach is mentioned in Sir. 49:13.

100. "Et mulier injecit in eum oculos, ut adulterium committeret. Ista mulier figura erat synagogae, quae saepe, sicut scriptum est, maechata est post deos

alienos" (Bede, *op. cit.*, Genesis, XXXIX; *P.L.*, XCI, col. 264).

101. S. Abdul-Hak, *op cit.*, pp. 115 ff.; E. Mâle, *Notre-Dame de Chartres*, pp. 61 ff.; Abbé Bulteau, *Monographie de la cathédrale de Chartres*, II, pp. 204 ff., 222 ff.

102. E. Houvet, *Cathédrale de Chartres, Portail nord*, II, pls. 21-47.

103. The creation of light on the first day corresponds, according to the interpretation of the Venerable Bede, to the time from the creation of the world to the flood. The creation of heaven on the second day signifies the epoch from the flood to the tower of Babel. The separation of water and earth on the third day symbolizes the time of the patriarchs. The creation of sun and moon on the fourth day refers to the time from the reign of David and Solomon to the destruction of the Temple. The work of the fifth day, the creation of fishes and birds, denotes the epoch from the Babylonian captivity to the reign of the Romans. The creation of the animals and of Adam and Eve on the sixth day refers to the time of Christ and the birth of the Church. The seventh day, finally, denotes the time of eternal rest in the other life *(Hexaemeron; P.L.*, XCI, cols. 36 ff.).

104. " . . . Adam dormivit, quando de latere ejus Eva facta est. Adam in figura Christi, Eva in figura Ecclesiae" (St. Augustine, *Enarratio in Psalmum XL; P.L.*, XXXVI, col. 461).

105. "Mors per Evam: vita per Mariam" (St. Jerome, *Epistola XXII; P.L.*, XXII, col. 408). "Mulier a diabolo seducta mortem intulit: contra mulier ab angelo edocta salutem edidit" *(Glossa ordinaria*, In Evangelium Lucae I, 27; *P.L.*, CXIV, col. 246).

106. "Quia duo parentes nos genuerunt ad mortem, duo parentes nos genuerunt ad vitam. Parentes qui nos genuerunt ad mortem, Adam est et Eva; parentes qui nos genuerunt ad vitam, Christus est et Ecclesia" (St. Augustine, *Sermo XXII*, 10; *P.L.*, XXXVIII, col. 154).

107. E. Houvet, *op. cit.*, II, pls. 1-6, 11, 13-16.

108. *Ibidem*, pls. 1-12.

109. The story of Christ's visit to Mary and Martha forms the seventh lesson

(Chartres Breviary of the thirteenth century; *olim* Bibl. de la Ville, MS 588 II, fol. 279v). For an allegorical interpretation, see, for instance, Honorius Augustodunensis: "Per Martham activa, per Mariam contemplativa vita designatur, quam utramque perpetua virgo Maria in Christo excellentius excoluisse praedicatur" *(Speculum Ecclesiae; P.L.*, CLXXII, col. 991). See also Siccardus, *Mitrale*, IX. 40 *(P.L.*, CCXIII, col. 420),

110. The active life is symbolized by Leah or Martha, the contemplative life by Rachel or Mary (St. Gregory, *Moralia in Job*, VI, 37 *[P.L.*, LXXV, cols. 764 f.]; *Homiliae in Ezechielem* [*P.L.*, LXXVI, cols. 953 ff.]). Abbé Bulteau referred to these passages *(op. cit.*, p. 224). The active life is like the strong woman of the Scriptures. "She seeketh wool and flax and worketh willingly with her hands" (Prov. 31:13). For the various stages of the contemplative life, see Hugh of St. Victor, *De arte meditandi (P.L.*, CLXXVI, col. 993); Richard of St. Victor, *Benjamin major*, I. 6 *(P.L.*, CXCVI, cols. 70 ff.).

111. E. Houvet, *op. cit.*, II, pls. 77-90.

112. *Ibidem*, I, pl. 18.

113. *Ibidem*, I, pls. 13-17, E. Mâle sees in the statues, apart from St. Potentien and St. Modeste, kings and other personalities of the Old Testament *(Notre-Dame de Chartres*, pp. 61 ff.).

114. E. Houvet, *Cathédrale de Chartres, Architecture*, pls. 16-19. For the interpretation of the ark as a symbol of the Church, see note 29, supra. For the representation of some Liberal and Mechanical Arts, see S. Abdul-Hak, *op. cit.*, p. 144.

115. For the representation of the Church and Synagogue in French sculpture, see A. Weis, "Die 'Synagoge' am Münster zu Strassburg," *Das Münster*, I (1947/48), pp. 65 ff. Cf. also M. Schlauch, "The Allegory of Church and Synagogue," *Speculum*, XIV, 1939, pp. 448 ff.

116. Alan of Lille, *De fide catholica (P.L.*, CCX, cols. 305 ff.); Bernard Gui, *Practica officii inquisitionis heretice pravitatis*, I *(Les classiques de l'histoire de France au moyen-âge*, VIII), Paris, 1926.

117. "Item, beatam Mariam Virginem negant fuisse veram matrem Domini Jhesu Christi, nec fuisse mulierem carnalem, sed

sectam suam et ordinem suum dicunt esse Mariam Virginem" (B. Gui, *op. cit.,* p. 14).

118. "Item, duas confingunt esse ecclesias, unam benignam, quam dicunt esse sectam suam, eamque esse asserunt ecclesiam Jhesu Christi; aliam ecclesiam vocant malignam, quam dicunt esse Romanam ecclesiam, eamque impudenter appellant matrem fornicationum, Babilonem magnam, meretricem et basilicam dyaboli et Sathane synagogam" (B. Gui, *op. cit.,* p. 10).

119. *Alberici Monachi Trium-Fontium Chronicon (Recueil des historiens des Gaules et de la France,* XVIII), p. 763.

120. B. Gui, *op. cit.,* p. 12.

121. Alan of Lille, *op. cit.,* I. 37 *(P.L.,* CCX, cols. 341 f.).

122. "Ad quid Patres Veteris Testamenti descendebant ad infernum, nisi propter enorme peccatum?" (Alan of Lille, *op. cit.,* I. 37; *P.L.,* CCX, col. 342.)

123. B. Gui, *op. cit.,* p. 10.

124. *Annales Aquicinctensis Monasterii (Recueil des historiens des Gaules et de la France,* XVIII), p. 536.

125. Peter of Vaux-de-Cernay, *Historia Albigensium,* c. 41 f. *(P.L.,* CCXIII, cols. 592 ff.).

126. "Cum unus Dominus Jesus Christus unam sibi sponsam, Ecclesiam videlicet ex gentibus congregatam, elegerit . . . quae ipsi tanquam capiti suo in unitate fidei deserviret, miramur plurimum atque dolemus quod quidam . . . diversas sibi Ecclesias, imo potius Satanae Synagogas, confingunt, doctrinam evangelicam, apostolicam et propheticam depravantes" *(P.L.,* CCXIV, col. 81).

127. See the entries in various chronicles for the year 1198: *Roberti Canonici S. Mariani Autissiodorensis Chronicon (Mon. Germ. Hist., Scriptores,* XXVI, p. 258); *Chronicle of Otto of Freising (ibidem,* XX, pp. 329 ff.); *Chronicle of Roger of Hoveden, (Rerum Brit. medii aevi scriptores),* ed. W. Stubbs, London, 1871, IV, p. 76.

128. V. L. Kennedy, "The Handbook of Master Peter Chancellor of Chartres," *Mediaeval Studies,* V (1943), pp. 1 ff.

129. Avranches, Bibl. de la Ville, MS 16, fols. 64r ff.: "Job glossatus secundum Magistrum Petrum Cancellarium Carnotensem."

See, for instance, fol. 73r: "Addidit quoque Job [Job 29:1] etc. Verba sunt Job loquentis in persona Ecclesiae desiderantis statum primitivae Ecclesiae." Fol. 74v: "Si adversum me [Job 31:38] etc. Patent haec de Job in persona Ecclesiae et bonorum." Fol. 65r: "Uxor sua [Job 2:9], i.e. carnales amici et domestici." "Igitur audientes tres amici Job [Job 2:11], qui falsi amici erant et tamen ad eum consolandum venerant. Per istos intelliguntur allegorice heretici, qui dicunt se falsos amicos simplicium Christianorum." Fol. 79v: "Venerunt ad eum [Job 42:11] etc. Ad litteram patent haec. Allegorice per Job intelligitur Christus vel Ecclesia, ad quam in fine temporum venient omnes Judaei."

III THE SCULPTURES OF THE SOUTH TRANSEPT AND ITS PORCH

1. S. Abdul-Hak, *La sculpture des porches du transept de la cathédrale de Chartres,* pp. 145 ff.; E. Mâle, *Notre-Dame de Chartres,* pp. 47 ff.; P. Kidson, *Sculpture at Chartres,* pp. 37 ff.; M. Aubert, *La sculpture française au moyen-âge,* pp. 219 ff.; Abbé Bulteau, *Monographie de la cathédrale de Chartres,* II, pp. 288 ff.

The statues of the Martyrs portal represent from left to right: SS. Theodore (added after 1224), Stephen, Clement, Lawrence, Vincent, Denis, Piat, and George (added after 1224). The Confessors portal shows from left to right: SS. Laumer (added after 1224), Leo (?), Ambrose (?), Nicholas (?), Martin, Jerome, Gregory, and Avit (added after 1224).

For the role of Peter of Dreux as donor of the stained-glass windows and sculptures for the south transept, see O. von Simson, *The Gothic Cathedral,* pp. 181 f.

2. A lectionary of the Chapter of Chartres Cathedral *(olim* Bibl. de la Ville, MS 507) contains the sermon ascribed to St. Augustine *(Sermo CCX; P.L.,* XXXIX, cols. 2137 ff.).

3. "Recole quid tibi in Evangelio Veritas ipsa promiserit, et quam tibi quodam modo cautionem fecerit . . . 'Si enim,' inquit,

'dimiseritis hominibus peccata eorum, dimittet et vobis Pater vester coelestis peccata vestra. Si autem non dimiseritis, nec Pater vester dimittet debita vestra.' Videtis, fratres, quia cum Dei gratia in potestate nostra positum est, qualiter a Domino judicemur" *(ibidem,* col. 2139).

4. "Beatus ergo erit . . . qui hunc sectatus, qui hunc imitatus fuerit: et pudicitiae enim palmam, et martyrii consequetur coronam" *(ibidem,* col. 2138).

5. "Vere memor Dominus dictorum suorum (qui ante praedixerat: 'Quamdiu fecistis uni ex minimis istis, mihi fecistis') se in paupere professus est fuisse vestitum; et ad confirmandum tam boni operis testimonium, in eodem se habitu quem pauper acceperat, est dignatus ostendere" (Sulpicius Severus, *De vita beati Martini; P.L.,* XX, col. 162). The life of the saint forms part of the twelfth-century Chartres Lectionary *(olim* Bibl. de la Ville, MS 500, fols. 224r ff.).

6. The life of St. Nicholas is contained in the same lectionary (fols. 6v ff.). See "Catalogus hagiographicorum bibliothecae civitatis Carnotensis," *Analecta Bollandiana,* VIII, 1889, p. 142.

7. *Acta Sanctorum,* Sept., I, pp. 299 ff.; E. Houvet, *Cathédrale de Chartres, Portail sud,* II, pls. 32–34.

8. *Ibidem,* I, pls. 61 f.

9. "Illos qui pro Christo moriuntur vidi statim in gloriam intrare . . . Et vixerunt. Et non dico vivent et regnabunt in futuro, sed etiam in hoc praesenti, scilicet ex quo interfecti sunt vixerunt et regnaverunt cum Christo" *(Glossa ordinaria,* Apoc. XX, 4; *P.L.,* CXIV, col. 744). "Mox quippe ut a carnis colligatione exeunt, in coelesti sede requiescunt" (St. Gregory, *Moralia in Job,* IV. 29; *P.L.,* LXXV, col. 666).

10. For Saint-Denis, see S. McK. Crosby, *L'abbaye royale de Saint-Denis,* pp. 36 ff.; for Laon, E. Lambert, "Les portails sculptés de la cathédrale de Laon," *Gazette des Beaux-Arts,* 1937, I, pp. 83 ff., especially pp. 88 ff. Both tympana are heavily restored. For Chartres, see S. Abdul-Hak, *op. cit.,* pp. 167 ff. A general discussion of the Last Judgment on French church façades is given by E. Mâle, *L'art religieux du XIIe siècle en France,* pp. 176 ff.; *L'art religieux du XIIIe siècle en France,*

pp. 369 ff. See also W. H. v. d. Mülbe, *Die Darstellung des Jüngsten Gerichts an den romanischen und gotischen Kirchenportalen Frankreichs,* Leipzig, 1911.

11. "Idem enim Filius Dei filius hominis, et filius hominis Filius Dei, aliud secundum humanitatem, aliud secundum divinitatem, non tamen alius, sed unus idemque in utraque natura verus, et proprius Filius Dei" (Hrabanus Maurus, *Commentaria in Matthaeum,* VII; *P.L.,* CVII, col. 1096).

12. "Signum hic, aut crucis intelligamus, ut videant juxta Zachariam (Zech. 12:10) et Joannem (John 19:10) Judaei quem compuxerunt; aut vexillum victoriae triumphantis" (St. Jerome, *Commentarius in Evangelium secundum Matthaeum,* IV, 24; *P.L.,* XXVI, col. 187).

13. "Sicut, cum imperator ingressurus est civitatem, corona ejus, et alia insignia praeferuntur, per quae adventus ejus cognoscitur, ita Christus in ea forma, qua ascendit, cum ordinibus omnium angelorum ad judicium veniet: angeli crucem ejus ferentes praeibunt" (Honorius Augustodunensis, *Elucidarium,* III. 12; *P.L.,* CLXXII, col. 1165). E. Mâle has drawn attention to this passage *(L'art religieux du XIIIe siècle en France,* p. 374, (note 3).

According to Paschasius Radbertus, the sign of the cross signifies that He who had died humbly on the cross appears in glory for the joy of the elect, for the sorrow of the impious and of the sinners *(Expositio in Mattheaum,* XI, 24; *P.L.,* CXX, col. 818). Radulphus Ardens gives three reasons for the presentation of the cross: first, to show the transformation of the sign of ignominy and dejection into the sign of victory; second, to instill joy in those who love Him and took up His cross; third, to create confusion and fear in those who crucified Him and despised His cross *(Homilia XIX, De tempore;* for the Latin text, see *P.L.,* CLV. col. 1374).

A. Grabar has shown that the cross symbol within the Last Judgment corresponds in meaning and placement to the military trophy within imperial art *(L'empereur dans l'art byzantin,* p. 255).

14. A. K. Porter, *Romanesque Sculpture of the Pilgrimage Roads,* figs. 409–15.

15. P. Toesca, *Storia dell'arte italiana,* Turin, 1927, I, 2, fig. 651.

16. Acts of John, c. 115 (M. R. James, *The Apocryphal New Testament*, p. 270).

17. "Quod et de beato Joanne evangelista ejus ministro, cui virgini a Christo Virgo commissa est, plurimi asseverant, quia in sepulcro ejus (ut fertur) nonnisi manna invenitur" (*Epistola IX ad Paulam et Eustochium; P.L.*, XXX, col. 127).

18. "Credit itaque Christiana pietas quia Christus Deus Dei Filius Matrem suam gloriose resuscitaverit et exaltaverit super coelos, et quod beatus Joannes virgo et evangelista, qui ei ministravit in terra, gloriam ejus participare mereatur in coelo" (*Sermo V; P.L.*, CXLI, col. 325).

That the Church of Chartres was very much concerned with the close relation between the Virgin Mary and John the Disciple is also attested otherwise. A Gospel of John and an antique cameo of Jupiter and the eagle, apparently identified with John and his symbol and inscribed with a text from his Gospel, were placed in the reliquary of the Virgin's tunic. See M. Schapiro, "Two Romanesque Drawings in Auxerre and some Iconographic Problems," *Studies in Art and Literature for Belle da Costa Greene*, Princeton, 1954, p. 336, note 24.

19. M. Aubert, *La sculpture française au moyen-âge*, illus. on p. 246.

20. P. Vitry, *French Sculpture during the Reign of Saint Louis*, pls. 30, 58.

21. The Weighing of the Souls is discussed by E. Panofsky, *Early Netherlandish Painting*, pp. 270 ff.

22. "Leo aperte saevit; draco occulte insidiatur: utramque vim et potestatem habet diabolus" (St. Augustine, *Enarratio in Psalmum* XC; *P.L.*, XXXVII, col. 1168). "Sed in adventu Domini pedibus ejus, id est, a sanctis, omnia haec nocumenta prostrata sunt" (Peter Lombard, *Commentaria in Psalmos; P.L.*, CXCI, col. 853). For the iconographic history of Christ standing on the animals, see E. Baldwin Smith, *Early Christian Iconography and a School of Ivory Carvers in Provence* (*Princeton Monographs in Art and Archaeology*, VI), Princeton, 1918, pp. 146 ff.; F. Saxl, "The Ruthwell Cross," *Journal of the Warburg and Courtauld Institutes*, VI (1943), p. 12.

23. "Et ad Ecclesiam primitivorum, id est apostolorum qui primi crediderunt, quorum fidei illi adjuncti sunt. Qui apostoli conscripti sunt in coelis; a simili hoc dicit, ut olim dicebantur patres conscripti, quia eorum nomina scripta sunt in libro vitae" (Peter Lombard, *In epistolam ad Hebraeos*, XII; *P.L.*, CXCII, col. 508). It is reassuring to find that P. Kidson has quoted the same passage from the Epistle to the Hebrews (*Sculpture at Chartres*, p. 42).

24. See p. 89.

25. "Dicunt etiam haeretici quidam orationes sanctorum non prodesse vivis . . . " (*De fide catholica*, I. 72; *P.L.*, CCX, col. 373). "Nisi enim sancti qui sunt in paradiso pro nobis orent, frustratoria esset quotidiana Ecclesiae oratio, quae fit ad sanctos, ut pro nobis orent, nec locum haberent litaniae" (c. 73; *ibidem*, col. 374). "Ecclesia etiam pro schismaticis et haereticis orat, ut Deus convertat eos ad poenitentiam: quod non faceret, nisi crederet orationes posse iis prodesse . . . Stephanus pro suis lapidatoribus intercessit, quorum multi postea ad fidem sunt conversi" (*ibidem*, col. 375). See also Ermengardus, *Contra Waldenses*, c. 17; *P.L.*, CCIV, cols. 1267 f.).

26. In the left bay the statues of St. Theodore and St. George were added; in the right bay those of St. Laumer and St. Avit were added. For the archivolts, see E. Houvet, *Cathédrale de Chartres, Portail sud*, I, pls. 61–70; II, pls. 25–31, 35–38). For a discussion of the porch, see S. Abdul-Hak, *op. cit.*, pp. 244 ff.; E. Mâle, *Notre-Dame de Chartres*, pp. 59 ff.; Abbé Bulteau, *op. cit.*, II, pp. 361 ff.

27. E. Houvet, *Portail sud*, II, pls. 67–88.

28. E. Houvet, *Portail sud*, II, pls. 44–66; *Architecture*, pl. 6, See also A. Katzenellenbogen, *Allegories of the Virtues and Vices in Mediaeval Art from Early Christian Times to the Thirteenth Century*, London, 1939, pp. 75 ff.

29. E. Houvet, *Portail sud*, II, pls. 24, 89 f.

30. *Portail sud*, I, pls. 2, 4.

31. *Portail sud*, I, pl. 3.

32. "Episcopus legit primam lectionem de trinitate, secundam decanus de beata maria, tertiam cantor de angelis, alie persone legant alias. Quartam de patriarchis et prophetis et beato iohanne baptista, quintam de apostolis, sextam de martyribus,

septimam de confessoribus, octavam de virginibus, nonam de omnibus sanctis" (*olim* Bibl. de la Ville, MS 1058, fol. 305r; Y. Delaporte, *L'ordinaire chartrain du XIIIᵉ siècle publié d'après le manuscrit original*, p. 185.)

33. R. Merlet and Abbé Clerval, *Un manuscrit chartrain du XIᵉ siècle*, pp. 229 f.

34. E. Houvet, *Portail sud*, I, pl. 2.

35. *Portail sud*, I, pls. 1, 4.

36. E. Houvet, *Cathédrale de Chartres, Portail nord*, I, pls. 1–4.

37. E. Lambert, "Les portails sculptés de la cathédrale de Laon," *Gazette des Beaux-Arts*, 1937, I, pp. 83 ff.

38. M. Aubert, *La cathédrale de Notre-Dame de Paris*, pp. 116 ff.

39. M. Aubert, *La sculpture française au moyen-âge*, pp. 264 ff.

40. A. Katzenellenbogen, "The Prophets on the West Façade of the Cathedral at Amiens," *Gazette des Beaux-Arts*, 1952, II, pp. 241 ff.

IV FORM AND MEANING

1. G. Schlag gives a brief summary of various theories about attributions of the sculptures to different workshops and artists ("Die Skulpturen des Querhauses der Kathedrale von Chartres," *Westdeutsches Jahrbuch für Kunstgeschichte (Wallraf-Richartz Jahrbuch)*, XII-XIII, 1943, p. 115, note 2). See also W. Vöge, "Die Bahnbrecher des Naturstudiums um 1200," *Gesammelte Studien*, pp. 63 ff.; W. Sauer-

länder, "Beiträge zur Geschichte der 'frühgotischen' Skulptur," *Zeitschrift für Kunstgeschichte*, XIX, (1956), pp. 1 ff., especially pp. 21 ff.; J. Lipman, "A Note on the Transept Sculptures of Chartres," *Art in America*, XXVI (1938), pp. 16 ff. Dr. Sauerländer has informed me that he is preparing a study on the stylistic origins of the transept sculptures at Chartres. He is certainly right in assuming that the nonsculptural relation of some statues to subsidiary figures or objects suggests two-dimensional models ("Die Marienkrönungsportale von Senlis und Mantes," pp. 133 f.). The sculptors, however, were perfectly aware of the limitations of the three-dimensional medium by placing figures closely together (Abraham and Isaac), which in painting could be more loosely arranged.

2. "Et quia episcopi pastores gregis Dominici sunt, ut Moyses et apostoli fuerunt, ideo baculum in custodia praeferunt. Per baculum, quo infirmi sustentantur, auctoritas doctrinae designatur . . . in extremo est acutus, ut rebelles excommunicando retrudat, haereticos velut lupos ab ovili Christi potestative exterreat" (Honorius Augustodunensis, *Gemma animae*, I. 218; *P.L.*, CLXXII, col. 610). See also Hugh of St. Victor, *De sacramentis*, II. 4, 15 (*P.L.*, CLXXVI, col. 438).

3. For a detailed description of the console figures, see S. Abdul-Hak, *La sculpture des porches du transept de la cathédrale de Chartres*, pp. 30 ff., 60 ff., 91 ff., 162 ff., 193 ff., 223 ff.

4. *Ibidem*, pp. 40 .

5. *Ibidem*, pl. IX, 2.

Selected Bibliography

Abdul-Hak, Selim, *La sculpture des porches du transept de la cathédrale de Chartres*, Paris, 1942

Adams, Henry, *Mont-Saint-Michel and Chartres*, Boston–New York, 1936

Adhémar, Jean, *Influences antiques dans l'art du moyen âge français (Studies of the Warburg Institute*, VII), London, 1939

Alan of Lille, *Elucidatio in Cantica Canticorum (P.L.*, CCX)

———, *De fide catholica contra haereticos sui temporis (ibidem)*

d'Alverny, M.-Th., "La Sagesse et ses sept filles," *Mélanges F. Grat*, Paris, 1946

d'Ancona, Paolo, "Le rappresentazioni allegoriche delle arti liberali nel medio evo e nel rinascimento," *Arte*, V (1902)

Aubert, Marcel, *La cathédrale de Notre-Dame de Paris*, new ed., Paris, 1929

———, *French Sculpture at the Beginning of the Gothic Period 1140-1225*, Florence–New York, 1929

———, *Monographie de la cathédrale de Senlis*, Senlis, 1910

———, "Le portail royal et la façade occidentale de la cathédrale de Chartres, Essai sur la date de leur exécution," *Bulletin monumental*, C (1941)

———, "Le portail royal de Chartres, Essai sur la date de son exécution," *Miscellanea Leo van Puyvelde*, Brussels, 1949

———, *La sculpture française au moyen-âge*, Paris, 1946

———, "Têtes des statues-colonnes du portail occidental de Saint-Denis," *Bulletin monumental*, CIII (1945)

Augustine, St., *Enarrationes in Psalmos (P.L.*, XXXVII)

———, *Sermones (P.L.*, XXXVIII)

Bede, The Venerable, *Homiliae (P.L.*, XCIV)

———, *In librum beati patris Tobiae allegorica interpretatio (P.L.*, XCI)

———, *In Pentateuchum commentarii (ibidem)*

Beenken, Hermann, "Die Tympana von La Charité sur Loire," *Art Studies*, VI (1928)

Bernard of Clairvaux, St., *Sermones (P.L.*, CLXXXIII)

Bernard Gui, *Practica officii inquisitionis heretice pravitatis*, I (*Les classiques de l'histoire de France au moyen-âge*, VIII), Paris, 1926

Beumer, Johannes, "Die marianische Deutung des Hohen Liedes in der Frühscholastik," *Zeitschrift für katholische Theologie*, LXXVI (1954)

Boethius, *In Isagogen Porphyrii commenta (Corpus scriptorum ecclesiasticorum latinorum*, XLVIII)

———, *In librum de interpretatione (P.L.*, LXIV)

———, *Institutio arithmetica (P.L.*, LXIII)

Bulteau, Abbé, "Etude iconographique sur les calendriers figurés de la cathédrale de Chartres," *Mémoires de la Societé archéologique d'Eure-et-Loir*, VII, Chartres, 1882

———, *Monographie de la cathédrale de Chartres*, 2d ed., Chartres, 1887-92

Cartulaire de Notre-Dame de Chartres, publ. by E. de Lépinois and Lucien Merlet, Chartres, 1862-65

Chastel, André, "La rencontre de Salomon et la reine de Saba dans l'iconographie médiévale," *Gazette des Beaux-Arts*, 1949

Chenu, M.-D., *La théologie au douzième siècle (Etudes de philosophie médiévale*, XLV), Paris, 1957

Clerval, Abbé A., *Les écoles de Chartres au moyen-âge (Mémoires de la Société archéologique d'Eure-et-Loir*, XI), Chartres, 1895

———, *L'enseignement des arts libéraux à Chartres et à Paris dans la première moitié du XIIe siècle d'après l'Heptateuchon de Thierry de Chartres*, Paris, 1889

Coathalem, H., *Le parallelisme entre la sainte Vierge et l'Eglise dans la tradition latine jusqu'à la fin du XIIe siècle (Analecta Gregoriana*, LXXIV), Rome, 1954

Crosby, Sumner McK., *L'abbaye royale de Saint-Denis,* Paris, 1953

Curtius, Ernst Robert, *European Literature and the Latin Middle Ages (Bollingen Series,* XXXVI), New York, 1953

Delaporte, Abbé Yves, *Notre-Dame de Chartres,* Paris, 1957

———, *L'ordinaire chartrain du XIIIe siècle publié d'après le manuscrit original (Mémoires de la Société archéologique d'Eure-et-Loir,* XIX), Chartres, 1953

———, *Les vitraux de la cathédrale de Chartres,* Chartres, 1926

Fels, Etienne, "Die Grabung an der Fassade der Kathedrale von Chartres," *Kunst-Chronik,* VIII (1955)

Flatten, Heinrich, *Die Philosophie des Wilhelm von Conches* (Diss. Bonn), Koblenz, 1929

Focillon, Henri, *L'art des sculpteurs romans,* Paris, 1931

Frankl, Paul, "The Chronology of Chartres Cathedral," *Art Bulletin,* XXXIX (1957)

Fulbert of Chartres, *Sermones (P.L.,* CXLI)

Fulgentius of Ruspe, *Sermones (P.L.,* LXV)

Funkenstein, Joseph, *Das Alte Testament im Kampf von regnum und sacerdotium zur Zeit des Investiturstreits* (Diss. Basle), Dortmund, 1938

Gerhoh of Reichersberg, *Commentarium in Psalmos (Mon. Germ. Hist., Libelli de lite,* III)

Giesau, Hermann, "Stand der Forschung über das Figurenportal des Mittelalters," *Beiträge zur Kunst des Mittelalters,* Berlin, 1950

Gilbert de la Porrée, *Commentaria in librum de Trinitate (P.L.,* LXIV)

Gilson, Etienne, *History of Christian Philosophy in the Middle Ages,* New York, 1955

Glossa ordinaria (P.L., CXIII, CXIV)

Grabar, André, *Ampoules de Terre Sainte,* Paris, 1958

———, *L'empereur dans l'art byzantin (Publications de la faculté des lettres de l'Université de Strasbourg,* fasc. 75), Paris, 1936

Gregory the Great, St., *Homiliae (P.L.,* LXXVI)

———, *Moralia in Job (P.L.,* LXXV, LXXVI)

Grodecki, Louis, "Chronologie de la cathédrale de Chartres," *Bulletin monumental,* CXVI (1958)

———, "The Transept Portals of Chartres Cathedral: The Date of their Construction according to Archaeological Data," *Art Bulletin,* XXXIII (1951)

Hamann, Richard, *Die Abteikirche von St. Gilles und ihre künstlerische Nachfolge,* Berlin, 1955

Haring, N., "The Creation and Creator of the World according to Thierry of Chartres and Clarenbaldus of Arras," *Archives d'histoire doctrinale et littéraire du moyen âge,* XXII (1956)

Hildebert of Lavardin, *Sermones (P.L.,* CLXXI)

Holböck, Ferdinand, *Der eucharistische und der mystische Leib Christi in ihren Beziehungen zueinander nach der Lehre der Frühscholastik,* Rome, 1941

Honorius Augustodunensis, *Elucidarium (P.L.,* CLXXII)

———, *Speculum Ecclesiae (ibidem)*

———, *Summa gloria (Mon. Germ. Hist., Libelli de lite,* III)

Houvet, Etienne, *Cathédrale de Chartres,* Chelles (S. et M.), 1919

Hrabanus Maurus, *Commentaria in libros IV Regum (P.L.,* CIX)

———, *Commentaria in librum Judicum (P.L.,* CVIII)

———, *Expositio in librum Esther (P.L.,* CIX)

———, *Expositio in librum Judith (ibidem)*

Hugh of St. Victor, *Didascalion (P.L.,* CLXXVI)

———, *De sacramentis (ibidem)*

Ivo of Chartres, *Epistolae (P.L.,* CLXII)

James, Montague Rhodes, *The Apocryphal New Testament,* Oxford, 1926

Jansen, Wilhelm, *Der Kommentar des Clarenbaldus von Arras zu Boethius De Trinitate (Breslauer Studien zur historischen Theologie,* VIII), Breslau, 1926

Jeauneau, Edouard, "Le Prologus in Eptatheucon de Thierry de Chartres," *Mediaeval Studies,* XVI (1954)

Jerome, St., *Commentaria in Osee (P.L.,* XXV)

John Beleth, *Rationale divinorum officiorum (P.L.,* CCII)

John of Salisbury, *Metalogicon* (ed. C. C. J. Webb), Oxford, 1929

Jugie, Martin, *La Mort et l'assomption de la sainte Vierge* (*Studi e Testi*, CXIV), Città del Vaticano, 1944

Jusselin, Maurice, *Les traditions de l'église de Chartres* (*Mémoires de la Société archéologique d'Eure - et - Loir*, XV), Chartres, 1914

Kantorowicz, Ernst H., *Laudes regiae* (*University of California Publications in History*, XXXIII) Berkeley–Los Angeles, 1946

————, "ΣΥΝΘΡΟΝΟΣ ΔΙΚΗΙ," *American Journal of Archaeology*, LVII (1953)

Katzenellenbogen, Adolf, "The Prophets on the West Façade of the Cathedral at Amiens," *Gazette des Beaux-Arts*, 1952

Kennedy, V. L., "The Handbook of Master Peter Chancellor of Chartres," *Mediaeval Studies*, V (1943)

Kidson, Peter, *Sculpture at Chartres*, London, 1958

Kitzinger, Ernst, "The Mosaics of the Cappella Palatina in Palermo: An Essay on the Choice and Arrangement of Subjects," *Art Bulletin*, XXXI (1949)

Koehler, Wilhelm, "Byzantine Art in the West," *Dumbarton Oaks Papers*, I (1941)

Kristeller, Paul O., "The Modern System of the Arts. A Study in the History of Aesthetics (I)," *Journal of the History of Ideas*, XII (1951)

Künstle, Karl, *Ikonographie der christlichen Kunst*, Freiburg im Breisgau, 1928

Lambert, Elie, "Les portails sculptés de la cathédrale de Laon," *Gazette des Beaux-Arts*, 1937

Lanore, Maurice, "Reconstruction de la façade de la cathédrale de Chartres au XIIᵉ siècle," *Revue de l'art chrétien*, 1899, 1900

Lawrence, Marion, "Maria Regina," *Art Bulletin*, VII (1924-25)

Lefèvre-Pontalis, Eugène, "Les façades successives de la cathédrale de Chartres au XIᵉ et XIIᵉ siècles," *Congrès archéologique*, 1900

————, "Nouvelles études sur les façades et les clochers de la cathédrale de Chartres: Réponse à M. Mayeux," *Mémoires de la Société archéologique d'Eure-et-Loir*, XIII, Chartres, 1901-04

Liebeschütz, Hans, *Mediaeval Humanism in the Life and Writings of John of Salisbury* (*Studies of the Warburg Institute*, XVII), London, 1950

Lubac, Henri de, *Corpus mysticum*, 2d ed., Paris, 1949

Luchaire, M. Achille, *Histoire des institutions monarchiques de la France sous les premiers Capétiens*, 2d ed., Paris, 1891

Mâle, Emile, *L'art religieux du XIIᵉ siècle en France*, 2d ed., Paris, 1924

————, *L'art religieux du XIIIᵉ siècle en France*, 6th ed., Paris, 1925

————, *Notre-Dame de Chartres*, Paris, 1948

Mayeux, André, "Réponse à M. Eugène Lefèvre-Pontalis sur son article," *Mémoires de la Société archéologique d'Eure-et-Loir*, XIII, Chartres, 1901-04

Meier, Gabriel, *Die sieben freien Künste im Mittelalter* (*Jahresbericht über die Lehr- und Erziehungsanstalt des Benediktiner-Stiftes Maria-Einsiedeln im Studienjahre 1885/86, 1886/87*), Einsiedeln, 1886-87

Merlet, René, and Abbé Clerval, *Un manuscrit chartrain du XIᵉ siècle*, Chartres, 1893

Montfaucon, Bernard de, *Monumens de la monarchie françoise*, Paris, 1729

Müller, Alois, *Ecclesia-Maria, Die Einheit Marias und der Kirche* (*Paradosis, Beiträge zur Geschichte der altchristlichen Literatur und Theologie*, V), Freiburg, Switzerland, 1951

Oeuvres de Rigord et de Guillaume le Breton, ed. H.-F. Delaborde, Paris, 1885

Panofsky, Erwin, *Abbot Suger on the Abbey Church of St. Denis and Its Art Treasures*, Princeton, 1946

————, *Early Netherlandish Painting*, Cambridge, Mass., 1953

————, *Gothic Architecture and Scholasticism*, Latrobe, Pa., 1951

Paré, G., Brunet, A., Tremblay, P., *La renaissance du XIIᵉ siècle. Les écoles et l'enseignement* (*Publications de l'Institut d'etudes médiévales d'Ottawa*, III), Paris–Ottawa, 1933

Parent, J. M., *La doctrine de la création dans l'école de Chartres* (*ibidem*, VIII), Paris–Ottawa, 1938

Paulus Diaconus, *Homiliarius* (*P.L.*, XCV)

Peter, The Venerable, *Tractatus adversus Petrobrusianos* (*P.L.*, CLXXXIX)

Poole, Reginald L., *Illustrations of the History of Medieval Thought and Learning*, 2d ed., London, 1920

——, "The Masters of the Schools at Paris and Chartres in John of Salisbury's Time," *The English Historical Review*, XXXV (1920)

Porter, Arthur Kingsley, "Les manuscrits cisterciens et la sculpture gothique," *Saint Bernard et son temps*, Dijon, 1929

——, *Romanesque Sculpture of the Pilgrimage Roads*, Boston, 1923

——, *Spanish Romanesque Sculpture*, Florence–Paris, 1928

Priest, Alan, "The Masters of the West Façade of Chartres," *Art Studies*, I (1923)

Pseudo-Augustine, *Tractatus de assumptione B. Mariae Virginis* (*P.L.*, XL)

Pseudo-Jerome, *Epistola IX ad Paulam et Eustochium de assumptione beatae Mariae Virginis* (*P.L.*, XXX)

Ross, Marvin C., "Monumental Sculptures from St.-Denis, An Identification of Fragments from the Portal," *The Journal of the Walters Art Gallery*, III (1940)

Sauerländer, Willibald, "Beiträge zur Geschichte der 'frühgotischen' Skulptur," *Zeitschrift für Kunstgeschichte*, XIX, 1956

——, *Die Kathedrale von Chartres*, Stuttgart, 1954

——, "Die Marienportale von Senlis und Mantes," *Wallraf-Richartz Jahrbuch*, XX (1958)

——, "Zu den Westportalen von Chartres," *Kunst-Chronik*, IX (1956)

Schapiro, Meyer, "The Romanesque Sculpture of Moissac, Part I (2)," *Art Bulletin*, XIII (1931)

——, "The Sculptures of Souillac," *Medieval Studies in Memory of A. Kingsley Porter*, Cambridge, Mass., 1939

——, "Two Romanesque Drawings in Auxerre and some Iconographic Problems," *Studies in Art and Literature for Belle da Costa Greene*, Princeton, 1954

Schlag, Gottfried, "Die Skulpturen des Querhauses der Kathedrale von Chartres," *Westdeutsches Jahrbuch für Kunstgeschichte* (*Wallraf-Richartz Jahrbuch*), XII-XIII (1943)

Schramm, Percy Ernst, "Der König von Frankreich. Wahl, Krönung, Erbfolge und Königsidee vom Anfang der Kapetinger [987] bis zum Ausgang des Mittelalters," *Zeitschrift der Savigny Stiftung für Rechtsgeschichte, kanonistische Abt.*, XXV (1936)

——, "Ordines-Studien, II: Die Krönung bei den Westfranken und Angelsachsen von 878 bis um 1000," *ibidem*, XXIII (1934)

Shorr, Dorothy C., "The Iconographic Development of the Presentation in the Temple," *Art Bulletin*, XXVIII (1946)

Simson, Otto von, *The Gothic Cathedral* (*Bollingen Series*, XLVIII), New York, 1956

Stoddard, William S., *The West Portals of Saint-Denis and Chartres*, Cambridge, Mass., 1952

Suger, Abbot, *Epistolae* (*P.L.*, CLXXXVI)

Sulpicius Severus, *De vita beati Martini* (*P.L.*, XX).

Thomas, Antoine, *Les miracles de Notre-Dame de Chartres, Texte latin inédit* (*Bibliothèque de l'Ecole des Chartes*, XLII), 1881

Vanuxem, Jacques, "Les portails détruits de la cathédrale de Cambrai et de Saint-Nicolas d'Amiens," *Bulletin monumental*, CIII (1945)

——, "The Theories of Mabillon and Montfaucon on French Sculpture of the Twelfth Century," *Journal of the Warburg and Courtauld Institutes*, XX (1957)

Vernet, André, "Une épitaphe inédite de Thierry de Chartres," *Recueil de travaux offert à M. Clovis Brunel*, Paris, 1955

Vöge, Wilhelm, *Die Anfänge des monumentalen Stiles im Mittelalter*, Strasbourg, 1894

——, "Die Bahnbrecher des Naturstudiums um 1200," *Bildhauer des Mittelalters, Gesammelte Studien von Wilhelm Vöge*, Berlin, 1958

Weis, Adolf, "Die 'Synagoge' am Münster zu Strassburg," *Das Münster*, I (1947/48)

Wilhelm, Pia, *Die Marienkrönung am Westportal der Kathedrale von Senlis* (Diss. Hamburg), Hamburg, 1941

William of Conches, *De philosophia mundi* (*P.L.*, CLXXII)

William of St.-Thierry, *De sacramento altaris* (*P.L.,* CLXXX)

Wind, Edgar, "Studies in Allegorical Portraiture I," *Journal of the Warburg Institute,* I (1937-39)

Wulf, Maurice de, *Histoire de la philosophie médiévale,* 6th ed., Louvain–Paris, 1934-47

Zarnecki, George, "The Coronation of the Virgin on a Capital from Reading Abbey," *Journal of the Warburg and Courtauld Institutes,* XIII (1950)

Index

1. Chartres Cathedral, West Façade

2. Chartres Cathedral, Royal Portal

4. La Madeleine, *Vézelay, Central Portal*

3. Abbey Church, *Saint-Denis, West Façade*

6. Sainte-Marie-des-Dames, Saintes, West Façade

5. Saint-Etienne, Caen, West Façade

8. *Abbey Church, Saint-Gilles, West Façade*

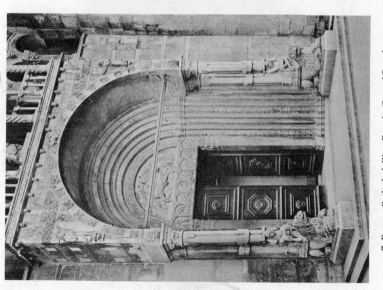

7. *Ferrara Cathedral, West Façade, Central Portal*

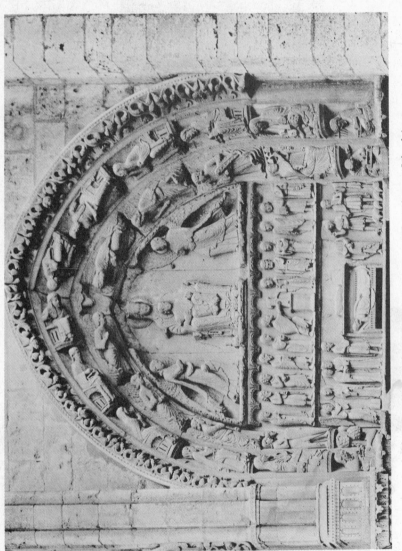

9. Chartres-West, Right Tympanum: Incarnation of Christ; the seven Liberal Arts

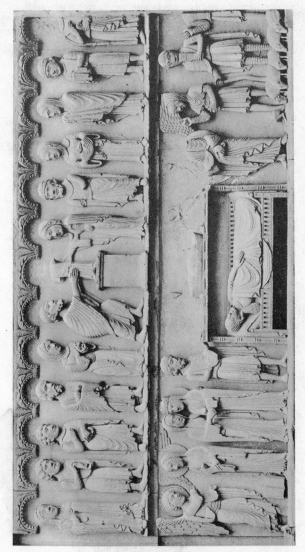

10. *Chartres-West, Right Tympanum, Detail: Incarnation of Christ*

11. La Madeleine, Vézelay, Right Tympanum: Incarnation of Christ

12. Saint-Pierre, Moissac, South Porch, Right Wall: Incarnation of Christ

13. Sainte-Croix, La Charité-sur-Loire, Tympanum: Incarnation of Christ; Christ receiving the Virgin

14. Sainte-Croix, La Charité-sur-Loire, Tympanum: Adoration of the Magi and Presentation of Christ; Transfiguration of Christ

15. *Notre-Dame, Paris, West Façade, Right Tympanum: Incarnation of Christ*

16. *La Madeleine, Vézelay, Central Tympanum: Mission of the Apostles*

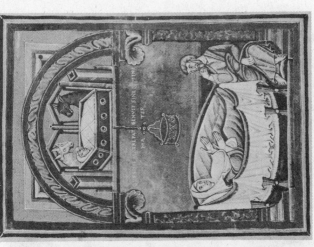

19. *Bibliothèque Royale, Brussels, MS 9428,*
fol. 7v: Nativity

18. *British Museum, London, Ivory:*
Nativity and Adoration of the Magi

17. *Monza Cathedral, Ampulla:*
Adoration of the
Magi and Shepherds

20. *Chartres-West, Capital Frieze: Scenes from the Incarnation of Christ*

21. *Chartres-West, Capital Frieze: Scenes from the Passion of Christ*

22. Saint-Julien-de-Jonzy, Tympanum: Last Supper and Christ in Heaven

23. Church of Condrieu, Tympanum: Last Supper and Christ Crucified

24. Chartres-West, Right Portal, Archivolt: Grammar teaching

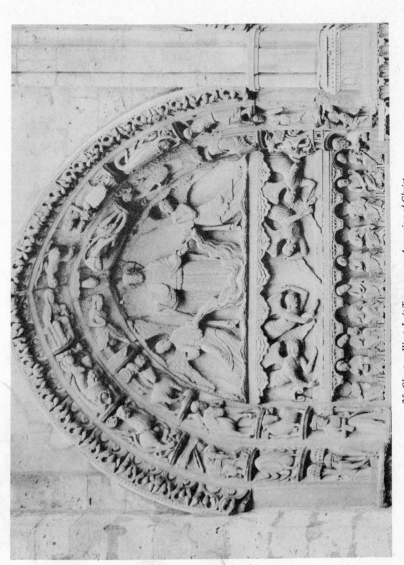

25. Chartres-West, Left Tympanum: Ascension of Christ

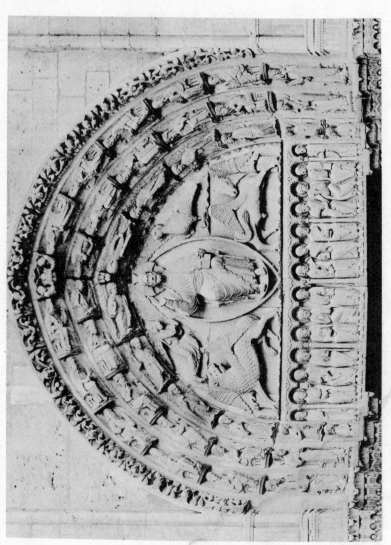

26. Chartres-West, Central Tympanum: Second Coming of Christ

27. *Chartres-West, Central Tympanum: Christ in Majesty*

28. Chartres-West, Left Portal: Old Testament figures

29. Chartres-West, Left Portal: Old Testament figures

30. *Chartres-West, Central Portal: Old Testament figures*

31. Chartres-West, Central Portal: Old Testament figures

32. Chartres-West, Right Portal: Old Testament figures

33. Chartres-West, Right Portal: Old Testament figures

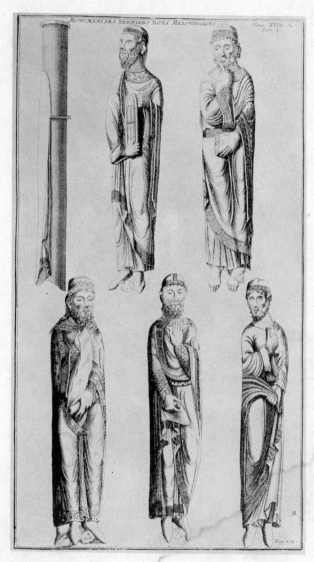

*34. Abbey Church, Saint-Denis, Right Portal: Old Testament
figures (after Montfaucon)*

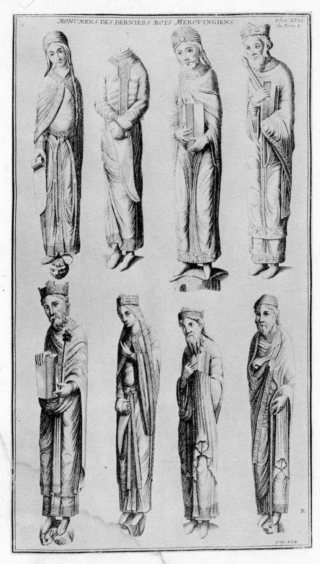

35. *Abbey Church, Saint-Denis, Central Portal: Old Testament figures (after Montfaucon)*

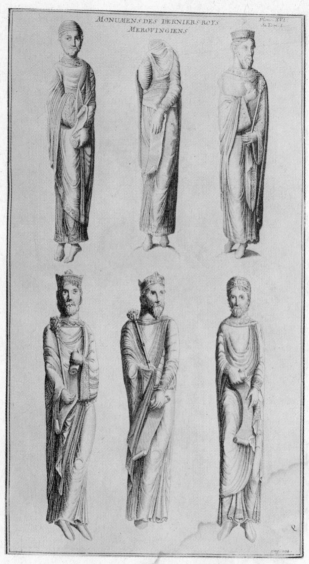

MONUMENS DES DERNIERS ROYS
MEROVINGIENS

36. *Abbey Church, Saint-Denis, Left Portal: Old Testament*
figures (after Montfaucon)

38. *Abbey Church, Saint-Gilles,*
West Façade: Apostles

37. *Saint-Pierre, Moissac, South Porch, Tympanum: Second Coming of Christ*

39. Arch of Constantine, Rome, Relief:
Hadrian sacrificing

40. Ara Pacis, Rome: Procession of vestals

41. La Madeleine, Vézelay, Central Lintel: Sacrificial scene

42. Ara Pacis, Rome: Sacrificial scene

43. Chartres-North, Façade and Porch

44. Chartres-North, Central Portal

45. Senlis Cathedral, West Façade, Tympanum: Triumph of the Virgin

46. Laon Cathedral, West Façade, Central Tympanum: Triumph of the Virgin

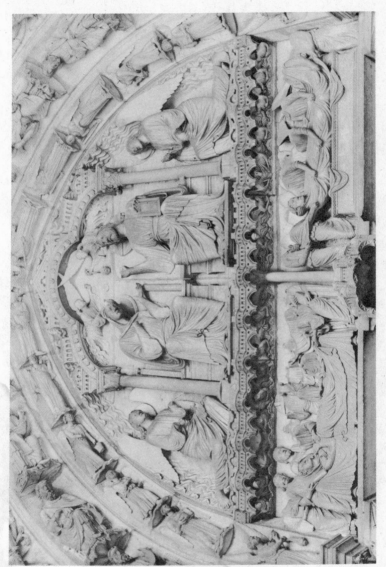

47. Chartres-North, Central Tympanum: Death, Resurrection and Triumph of the Virgin

48. Notre-Dame, Paris, West Façade, Left Tympanum: Prophets and Kings;
Resurrection and Triumph of the Virgin

49. Senlis Cathedral, West Façade, Central Portal

50. *Chartres-North, Central Portal: Elisha, Melchizedek, Abraham, Moses, Samuel, David*

51. *Chartres-North, Central Portal: Isaiah, Jeremiah, Simeon, St. John the Baptist, St. Peter, Elijah*

52. *Chartres-North, Left Portal*

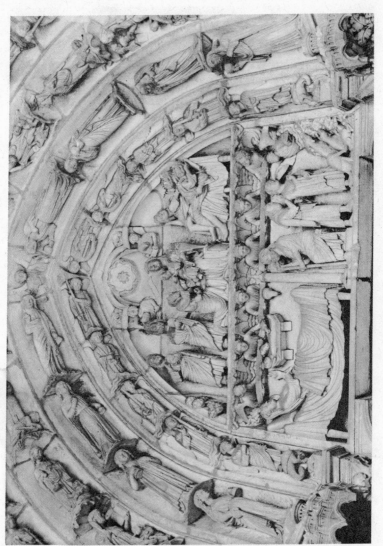

53. *Chartres-North, Left Tympanum: Incarnation of Christ*

54. *Chartres-North, Left Portal: Isaiah and Annunciation*

55. Chartres-North, Left Portal: Visitation and Daniel

56. *Laon Cathedral, West Façade, Left Tympanum (before restoration):*
Incarnation of Christ

57. *Chartres-North, Right Portal*

58. Chartres-North, Right Tympanum: Judgment of Solomon; Suffering of Job

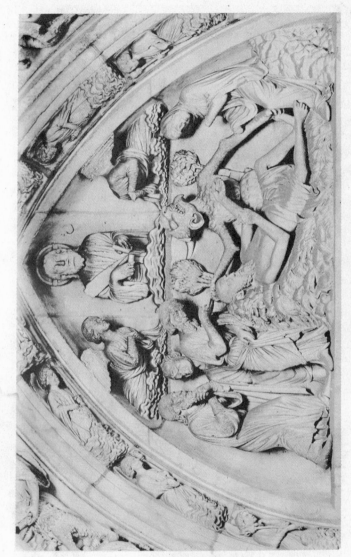

59. *Chartres-North, Right Tympanum: Suffering of Job*

60. *Chartres-North, Right Portal, Archivolts: Stories of Tobit
and Tobias, Esther and Samson*

61. Chartres-North, Right Portal, Archivolts: Stories of Gideon,
Judith, Tobit and Tobias

62. Chartres-North, Right Portal: Balaam, Queen of Sheba, Solomon

63. Chartres-North, Right Portal: Jesus Sirach, Judith, Joseph

64. Chartres-South, Façade and Porch

65. *Chartres-South, Central Portal*

66. *Chartres-South, Central Portal: SS. Simon, Matthew, Thomas, Philip, Andrew, Peter*

*67. Chartres-South, Central Portal: SS. Paul, John, James the Great,
James the Less, Bartholomew, Jude*

68. Chartres-South, Left Portal: SS. Theodore, Stephen, Clement, Lawrence

69. *Chartres-South, Left Portal: SS. Vincent, Denis, Piat, George*

70. *Chartres-South, Right Portal: SS. Laumer, Leo, Ambrose, Nicholas*

71. Chartres-South, Right Portal: SS. Martin, Jerome, Gregory, Avit

72. Chartres-South, Left Tympanum: Story of St. Stephen

73. Chartres-South, Right Tympanum: Stories of SS. Martin and Nicholas

74. *Chartres-South, Right Portal, Archivolts: Confessors*

75. *Chartres-South, Right Portal, Archivolts: Confessors*

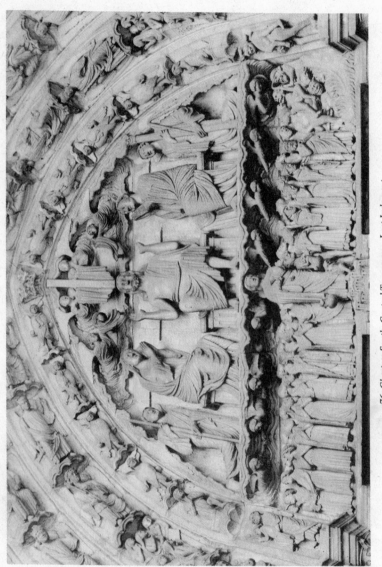

76. *Chartres-South, Central Tympanum: Last Judgment*

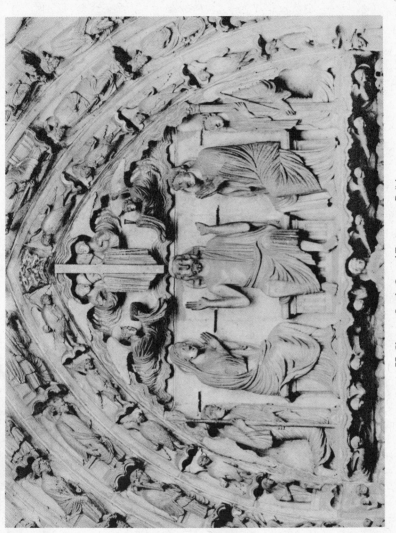

77. *Chartres-South, Central Tympanum: Deësis*

78. *Abbey Church, Saint-Denis, Central Tympanum: Last Judgment*

79. *Laon Cathedral, West Façade, Right Tympanum: Last Judgment*